D1411394

i

Printed in the United States of America

First Printing, 2020

ISBN 978-0-578-65763-9

Paradigm Shift
438 Gap View Dr.
Charleston, WV 25306

www.paradigmshiftbooks.com

fromcraigjackson@gmail.com

YOU NEED TO KNOW THIS STUFF

Craig Jackson

TABLE OF CONTENTS

INTRODUCTION - 1

THE WORLD NEEDS PEOPLE TO THINK FOR THEMSELVES - 15

LESSON ONE: GETTING TO KNOW YOUR BRAIN - 16

THE DARK NIGHT OF THE SOUL - 22

LESSON TWO: YOUR INCREDIBLE MEMORY. YES, YOUR MEMORY! - 27

THE MORNING I WOKE UP AND COULDN'T SEE - 32

LESSON THREE: YOU ARE NOT YOUR BRAIN - 36

I ALMOST DIED TWICE - 40

LESSON FOUR: YOUR SUBCONSCIOUS MIND AND BEYOND - 43

IF YOU FIGHT WITH YOUR BRAIN IT IS ALWAYS GOING TO WIN - 48

LESSON FIVE: YOUR SUBCONSCIOUS MIND AND DAYDREAMING - 53

THE IGNORANCE OF THE HUMAN RACE - 58

LESSON SIX: LET'S LEARN SOME CALCULUS - 60

YOURS IS ONE OF MANY TRUTHS - 74

LESSON SEVEN: THE HISTORY OF MOTION - 77

HOW WAS YOUR BRAIN WIRED? - 84

LESSON EIGHT: ELECTROMAGNETISM - 88

LET'S TALK ABOUT GOD - 94

LESSON NINE: THE SPECIAL THEORY OF RELATIVITY PART I - 97

STOP PLAYING THE GAME - 101

POSSESSED BY YOUR MIND - 103

LESSON TEN: THE SPECIAL THEORY OF RELATIVITY PART II - 104

STAY IN THE NOW - 107

LESSON ELEVEN: THE SPECIAL THEORY OF RELATIVITY PART III - 109

WHAT DO YOU REALLY NEED? - 113

LESSON TWELVE: YOUR REALITY - 116

YOUR EMOTIONS DETERMINE YOUR FREQUENCY - 122

IS GRATITUDE MISSING FROM YOUR LIFE? - 124

LESSON THIRTEEN: QUANTUM PHYSICS I - 126

GIN RUMMY CONTAINS THE SECRETS OF LIFE - 132

LESSON FOURTEEN: QUANTUM PHYSICS II - 137

GET PAST THE RESISTANCE – 143

HELP IS ALWAYS THERE WHEN YOU NEED IT - 144

LESSON FIFTEEN: QUANTUM PHYSICS III - 145

YOU ARE NEVER GOING TO BE SATISFIED - 150

LESSON SIXTEEN: THE HEISENBERG UNCERTAINTY PRINCIPLE - 151

UNDERSTANDING WHY PEOPLE BELIEVE THE THINGS THEY DO - 154

LESSON SEVENTEEN: THE SCHRODINGER EQUATION - 159

PROBABLE REALITIES – 162

NO ONE CAN OFFEND YOU WITHOUT YOUR PERMISSION - 163

LESSON EIGHTEEN: THE EPR EXPERIMENT - 165

DON'T MAKE THE MISTAKE OF THINKING IT CAN'T HAPPEN

    RIGHT NOW - 167

LESSON NINETEEN: CREATE YOUR REALITY - 168

LET'S DO A THOUGHT EXPERIMENT - 173

THE HEIGHT OF ARROGANCE - 175

LESSON TWENTY: RELATIVITY REVISITED – 176

A NEW WAY OF LOOKING AT MONEY - 180

STOP THINKING YOU NEED A JOB TO MAKE MONEY - 184

LESSON TWENTY-ONE: EVERYTHING IS ONE - 186

WE THINK WE ARE BEING LOGICAL AND MAKING RATIONAL

    DECISIONS - 188

LESSON TWENTY-TWO: THE LITTLE BRAIN IN THE HEART - 190

YOU HAVE TO DISAPPOINT SOME PEOPLE TO BE TRUE TO

YOURSELF – 193

THIS IS THE SECRET TO GETTING EVERYTHING YOU WANT IN LIFE - 195

LESSON TWENTY-THREE: ERASE A CLOUD WITH YOUR MIND - 199

AFTER THIS LIFE - 202

LESSON TWENTY-FOUR: DIMENSIONS - 205

BELIEF IS PERSONAL - 210

LESSON TWENTY-FIVE: FEEL THE ENERGY OF THE UNIVERSE - 213

THE THEORY OF EVOLUTION - 217

LESSON TWENTY-SIX: CONSCIOUSNESS - 223

EPIGENETICS - 226

LESSON TWENTY-SEVEN: THE GENERAL THEORY OF RELATIVITY - 231

CRISPR - 235

LESSON TWENTY-EIGHT: TIME DILATION, BLACK HOLES, AND

HOLOGRAMS - 242

YOUR HISTORY BOOKS ARE WRONG - 246

LESSON TWENTY-NINE: VIRTUAL REALITY - 250

OUR SCHOOL SYSTEM NEEDS FIXED AND HERE IS EXACTLY HOW

TO DO IT - 253

LESSON THIRTY: THE BEGINNING - 256

THIS IS A PLEA, A CALL TO BECOME ONE - 260

INTRODUCTION

I want to tell you something about yourself. You may already know it, but most don't.

You are a genius!

There is nothing, absolutely nothing in this universe which someone else understands that you cannot also understand.

If someone else can comprehend it, it can be explained to you in a way in which will become perfectly clear.

It doesn't matter what it is, math, physics, music, poetry, history, biology, psychology, philosophy, ANYTHING!

I 100% guarantee you if you want to know it, you can, and if you stick with me through this book, I will freak you out. You will learn some things which you probably thought were way out of your league.

Are you the product of an outdated and inefficient school system?

Our school system came from Prussia. In the 1840s Horace Mann went to Prussia to study what was becoming a very popular way of teaching children. He brought the system back to the United States and industry giants like Rockefeller and Carnegie fell in love with it for its ability to consistently churn out supplies of "worker bees" year after year. It produces a labor class. Not surprisingly, the school system is also called the "factory model." What is unbelievable is that nothing has changed for almost 200 years and it is robbing you of your individuality and creativity.

It is even worse. The school system told you how smart you are, and you believed it. How many incredible minds has this world lost because of the underestimation of the school system?

We are all guilty of believing we are who we think others think we are. Read that again. I didn't say who others think we are. I said who WE THINK others think we are.

No more! After reading this book you are going to develop a confidence experienced by very few.

Chances are you were never taught how to achieve your full potential. This led you to believe you were just not capable of understanding certain things. This is not true.

Chances are there were many things you should have been taught, but you were not. And that may have been on purpose.

You were never even taught how to learn.

Think about it.

Do you know what is happening with your brain when learning? Most do not. Probably most if not all the teachers you had through your school years couldn't tell you what your brain was doing either.

Does that not strike you as odd?

Should it not be essential we know what our brain is doing when learning? Doesn't it make sense that knowing what your brain is doing while it is learning will help you learn?

Were you ever taught how to learn? You were just put in a classroom and told, "Do your best."

Can you be taught how to learn?

You better believe you can!

That is why I will begin by teaching you what your brain is doing while learning and showing you simple ways to learn that will amaze you. You will be saying, "Why didn't I think to do that before?"

I will even let you know the ineffective techniques so many people believe help you learn but don't do much good.

I will provide you the solutions for the failures in the school system. We will show you your full potential.

Another benefit is you are going to drastically improve your memory.

It doesn't matter if you are 10 or 100, this book will change how you remember. You will be amazed at many things your brain can do. You will do things you thought were way beyond your abilities.

Here is my first promise to you. After finishing this book, you will have a very strong understanding of Calculus, Einstein's Theory of Special Relativity, and Quantum Physics. You will grasp these concepts so well that you can sit down with any college professor who teaches these courses and have a very intelligent conversation. And this will be fun and easy.

I chose Calculus, Relativity and Quantum Physics for a reason.

First, in the minds of most, Calculus is the math of math, incomprehensible to most mortal men and women. I will start with Calculus because once you see you can understand it your mind will be forever changed. It will be a true Paradigm Shift for you. It will instill within you a confidence you may not have experienced before. Then when we tackle Relativity and Quantum Physics you will be like, "I'm ready! Bring it on!"

Now I chose Special Relativity and Quantum Physics because...

It is an absolute necessity you understand those concepts.

Quantum Physics and Special Relativity explain the reality of the world and it is a very strange reality. Most of the world is clueless. They are unaware of some very important facts with a very big impact on their daily lives. It is sad. It is crazy these subjects are not taught in schools at an early age. Even elementary students could easily grasp the basic concepts.

You need to understand Relativity and Quantum Physics, so you can see just how strange yet wonderful this world we live in is.

$$H(t)\,|\psi(t)\rangle = i\hbar\frac{\partial}{\partial t}\,|\psi(t)\rangle$$

The strange image above is a differential equation (Calculus) known as Schrodinger's Equation. It is the essence of Quantum Physics. It tells us that everything in the universe is just a wave of probability until our consciousness brings it into reality.

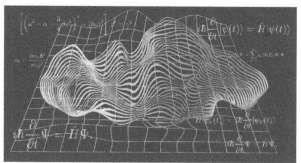

The image above is an example of a probability wave distribution produced by Schrodinger's Equation. The bigger the wave the higher the chance it will manifest into the material world. This is called the collapse of the wave function.

The question becomes how do you make sure the things you want out of life have the highest probability of collapsing the wave function and becoming your reality?

You will learn exactly how to do that in this book. Schrodinger's Equation will no longer look like a foreign language to you. You will understand it.

It is so, so, so, to your advantage to know this stuff. Please, I am begging you do not stay uninformed and in the dark anymore. Please.

Here is my second promise to you. There is a world out there which very few can see. This world is a magical place. It is a world in which you have complete control. It is a world in which you can bring all your dreams and desires into reality. After finishing this book, I guarantee you, you will see that world.

But to understand it you must understand Quantum Physics and Special Relativity. It is a necessity. There is no getting around it.

Special Relativity and Quantum Physics are strange.

Einstein's Special Theory of Relativity tells us we all experience time differently. An hour passing for you may not be the same as an hour passing for me. My hour could be longer or shorter than yours. But if we look at a clock, we will both see that an hour has passed. If your hour is passing faster than mine, you are aging faster than me. I told you this stuff was weird.

If you think that was strange, it only gets worse. Quantum Physics tells us that everything is just a wave of energy until we look, then it becomes the object we see in the material world (rocks, trees, cats, people) but only because of our observation. So, if nobody is in your kitchen is it not there? We will see.

But know this, as strange as they seem, if it were not for Special Relativity and Quantum Physics, we would not have computers, cellphones, GPS, TVs, just about every convenience we have today.

We will begin the book by learning about your brain. You will see what happens inside your brain when learning something new. Once you understand your brain you are as good as gold.

You will be taught a way to learn that you are probably not familiar with. You will literally have to get out of your mind. When you think of something, you usually see it in your head. Can you see it in your heart?

You might want to know a little about the author of this book. My name is Craig Jackson and I am the owner of Paradigm Shift (almost 300,000 likes on Facebook). Our goal is to show that life need not be the struggle everyone makes it out to be. There is a magical world out there so many cannot see. We want to show you that world. Hundreds of thousands of people weekly read what we have to say.

I am not a mathematician or scientist. I took one year of Calculus in high school and I have never taken a class in Quantum Physics or Special Relativity.

I learned by reading and a technique I will teach you which will blow your mind. With the fear of being immodest, I know Quantum Physics and Special Relativity very well. I can explain those concepts in a way that will make it easy for you to understand. Because I didn't go through the formal education route, I know the questions I had, and I know you will have them too. I know many areas you will question even before you do.

4

Often when someone knows something so well it just becomes second nature to them. They rarely do a good job of explaining to a person who has no experience. They may leave out something which to them just kind of goes without saying. But it so does not. You would be surprised how sometimes just that one left out a piece of information is often the missing key which allows everything to make perfect sense to you.

Often, repeatedly, what I thought was a hard topic was just not being explained well. And when I finally came to understand the subject, I discovered it was not hard. And so will you.

Many topics we will discuss will apply Special Relativity and Quantum Physics to spirituality and metaphysics. To many scientists, spirituality and metaphysics are taboo. They could even lose their jobs making such comparisons.

You will see you live in two universes. One universe we see and experience every day and one universe is hard for us to see and seems to make no sense, but it is there. We are in it.

These universes contradict each other, and scientists can't reconcile how they can both exist together, but they do. You and everything you see around you wouldn't exist if we didn't live in both.

The universe you cannot see may even be more real than the one you can. It is the universe in which creation occurs. Everything in the physical universe comes from the nonphysical universe. It's like your thoughts. Are your thoughts real? Yes. You will see just how big a role your thoughts play in your life.

There has been a long debate…

Where does consciousness come from? Is it a creation of the brain or is it something outside the brain? You will learn from Quantum Physics there is no doubt our consciousness comes from outside our brain. You are not your brain. You are something much more. Consciousness creates the brain, not vice versa.

My goal for this book is two-fold.

First, as I mentioned at the beginning of this introduction, most people do not realize just how smart they are and what their minds are capable of. They have very limiting beliefs about themselves and this is reflected in their lives by limiting what they accomplish.

After reading this book you will be empowered. By seeing you can understand "hard" topics you will realize so much of your potential. You will without a doubt see for yourself there is nothing, absolutely nothing, you are not capable of learning and understanding. It will change your life.

Second, we live in a fragmented world. Our world is divided in so many ways. We are divided by nation, race, religion, politics, economics… the list could go on.

5

We all see each of our fragments as the correct way of viewing the world and believe everyone else is in error. But we need to realize we are often in error because we believe our own thoughts to be the true representation of how the world is.

Look at the world today. Look at all the problems caused by fragmentation. People are killing people because of perceived differences. People are starving. We cannot be civil enough with each other to come up with solutions. What are we to do?

It is my belief this fragmentation is an illusion, keeping us from seeing we are all one, keeping us from making the changes we so desperately need. This book will help you see through the illusion.

This book is to be read a little different from most.

This book contains 30 main lessons and what I call extras which supplement what you have learned in the main lessons. Some lessons will be brief, some a little longer. Each lesson will contain what you need for that day.

Please UNDER NO CIRCUMSTANCES read more than one UNREAD lesson a day. This will ensure your brain processes the information you need before you continue to the next lesson and makes sure you don't overload your brain with too much in one day. Be sure to understand (AND YOU WILL) the contents of a lesson before you go on to a new one. Re-reading older lessons is fine and often very beneficial. Each consecutive lesson will build on what you have learned from the previous. You can read the supplements that come after the lesson, but when you come to the next lesson, please stop until the next day.

We will begin by learning about your brain. You will see what happens inside your brain when learning something new. Once you understand your brain you are as good as gold.

I'm sure by now you are very excited to start the lessons but before we go on, I think I really should make a confession first.

Not too long ago I was the biggest hypocrite on the face of the planet and that is no exaggeration. Once I tell you why I am sure you will agree. Before I can continue, I just need to get this off my chest.

Yes, I was a hypocrite. I was the hypocrite of hypocrites. I was king of the hypocrites. I was what you might even call a double hypocrite. Let me explain.

In the first half of my life, I was a devout Christian. There wasn't anything that perhaps could make me lose my faith.

I was raised in the Church of Christ. Like most denominations (although the Church of Christ claims to be non-denominational) they believe they are among the few interpreting the Bible correctly and many believe the only ones going to Heaven. I can remember thinking how lucky I was to be born into this world and revealed the truth and get to be one of the very few who get to enter The Pearly Gates. But not many members of the Church of Christ would outwardly admit that belief. Their response would be something like when non-Christians die, they will be in God's hands and God is a just god. He will do what is fair. But deep down they are thinking that person is toast.

The other claim to fame of the Church of Christ is they believe that if you play the piano, you will go to Hell.

Well, you must play the piano in a church to go to Hell.

It's not really a church thing, it's a worship thing. If you play the piano while worshiping God, you will go to Hell.

The reason for the piano phobia grew because nowhere in the New Testament do you read of Christians playing the piano while worshiping God. The "no piano" attempts to mimic closely the worship of the original early century Christians. But over the years it has gotten just a bit distorted, you think?

This is the perfect example of how almost anything can become dogma. Nowhere in the Bible does it say, "Thou shall not play the piano while singing praises to My name." Therefore, someone had to come up with that on their own and passed on their reasoning for "no piano" and it caught on. Millions could read the Bible and never have a thought like that cross their mind. But for many, it has become a truth in their life and that is scary. Imagine what that does to the psyche when you believe in a god that will punish you for all eternity for playing the piano.

I would often picture myself at judgment standing before the throne of God.

"You helped feed the poor, check. You helped clothe the naked, check. You helped shelter the homeless, check. What?! You played the piano while singing praises to my high and exalted name! Get thee behind me Satan! I know you not!"

Even during my most devout periods I never could conceive of a God that would send you to Hell for playing the piano (that was the first thing I kept to myself, but over the years I found I had to keep more and more to myself), but to say my mind had been wired for the Church of Christ would be an understatement.

My great grandfather took my maternal grandmother to the Church of Christ when she was just a little girl. My grandmother took my mother to the Church of Christ from the day she was born. My mother converted my father when he was young, so when my younger sister and I were born we were a Church of Christ family. We were all very faithful working for the church, attending services every Sunday and Wednesday. That was until my father divorced my mother when I was in high school.

I remember seeing all the divorced kids when I was going through school and foolishly thinking, "That could never be me. My parents are members of The Church. That won't happen to us."

But it did, and you might be thinking that was when my faith in Christianity faltered — actually, quite the opposite.

After high school, I attended a Christian college my first semester. But it was way too strict for my taste. Girls were not allowed in the boy's dorm. They even had a sign outside which read, "No Girls Beyond This Point."

I taught the teenage class at my church for about 20 years. At least 10 of those years, give or take, I did not believe what I was teaching. After twenty years, I am well-read and know a lot about what is written in the Bible. I have to say it is what is written in the Bible that turned me away from Christianity more than anything.

All the atrocities commanded by God. It seemed as if there wasn't anything God wouldn't command his people to do–slavery, murder, rape, genocide.

My first response was, well these are ancient barbaric people. They don't think like us. God had to deal with them harshly, so they would understand.

But they were not different from us. They had the same intellectual capacity as us. The only difference would be we have more advanced gadgets today. They had emotions like us. They had dreams and desires like us. To take a baby from a mother and brutally murder it would drive a mother back then just as insane as it would a mother today.

I know most Christians are okay with a god that ordered slavery, rape, murder, and other bad stuff but for me, it eventually became a bit of a turnoff.

Dwelling on the things in the Bible I found disgusting was the first step for me deciding I could no longer accept the Christian faith.

Christians see the world as depraved and lost. They are to live in the world but are not to be a part of the world. To Christians, the only salvation is in the world to come. This world will only get worse. If everyone believed that to be true, this world could never be made into a better place. If you have a mindset this world is evil, then that is what you will see, evil everywhere. Fortunately, although many don't see it yet, this world is changing and changing for the better. There is so much good out there. After you finish this book, you will see.

I will not go through the long process which led me to my dechristianization, just understand I went from believing every word in the Bible was the inerrant word of God to believe most of it is a myth written by a barbaric, warring, Hebrew nation.

But don't think you can't learn from myth. There are eternal truths written in the myths of every culture. It is when we stop with the absurd task of trying to make ancient stories true today and focus on the lesson behind the story the myths become remarkable and life-changing. We also find that religious traditions teach many of the same lessons.

Now here is how I became a hypocrite.

Although I believed most of the Bible (not all) about as much as I believed a Dr. Seuss book, I still attended services. I even kept teaching the teen class. Words would spew out of my mouth I just did not believe. I was just repeating the phrases I had drilled into my head all my life.

I not only continued to teach, but I still led prayers in the church. I would lead communion services, telling everyone that, "This is a time we need to clear our minds and thoughts and center on Jesus' sacrifice for each and every one of us by giving himself to die on the cross for the forgiveness of our sins and we need to realize how much he loves each and every one of us."

And while I was saying that my mind was thinking, "Well Jesus isn't so bad, but can't these people see what this says about his dad? What kind of father would demand blood and sacrifices and kill his son and call it love?"

Do you believe me now? Super-hypocrite.

But it gets worse. Let me tell you how I became a double hypocrite.

One of the first books I read that brought me to where I am today, was Dr. Wayne Dyer's *Inspiration*. It was amazing. Here was something I was completely connecting with. No crazy contradictions I had to wait until I died to understand. It made perfect sense to me right now. I could see many things he described happening in my life.

 I read other books by authors like Deepak Chopra and Eckhart Tolle. They were changing my life. I was accomplishing things in my life that before had only met with failure after failure. This was amazing. Why had I not learned of this before? I had to tell others about this.

That was when I started the Facebook Page, Paradigm Shift. A paradigm shift is a change in the way you view the world. And I had gone through a huge change.

On Paradigm Shift we would talk about the amazing things I was learning. I discovered more and more who believed as I did. I would post quotes from authors like Neale Donald Walsh, MaryAnne Williamson, Gary Zukav, on the Paradigm Shift web page which we would discuss.

Then one-day inspiration hit me. I knew I was a good writer. There wasn't any reason I couldn't write a book. I wouldn't even worry about publishing it. I would just promote it on my Facebook page. So, I did.

I wrote Theta. It was a short book. Only about 50 pages. But most everyone seemed to like what I had to say in those pages. I sold the book online and it was very successful. So, I wrote other books. I also promoted the products of those who I felt also had something worthwhile to say to the world.

Paradigm Shift became successful. The Facebook page grew to over a quarter of a million fans.

But the success of Paradigm Shift didn't keep me from driving to church in my brand-new Lexus RC-350 and teaching and praying and praying and teaching those things which I knew my business contradicted.

How in the world I hid my true business from family and church friends must have been an "act of God?" When someone from church would ask what I did for a living my go-to answer was I sold self-help books on the internet.

Do you agree I was one of the biggest hypocrites the world has ever seen? I was going to church pretending to be a Christian while I wrote and sold books and posted things online which contradicted many Christian beliefs.

I hate to say…

It gets worse.

In my books and online, a lot of the things I mentioned were how our brains were formed by society. We need to be ourselves and not let society form us. We need to stop worrying about what others say about us and live our own lives.

See the problem. I was saying it, I was profiting from it, but I was not living it.

Again, BIG hypocrite.

But I was scared (which I discovered later was not unwarranted) of the reaction of family and friends. I was hoping someone would discover my books and web pages online and confront me. Do for me what I could not do for myself. But it never happened.

But I did finally confess and "come clean". That was the best day of my life. If you are not true to yourself, you are not truly living. No more pretending to be somebody I wasn't. I could finally be myself and that felt amazing.

And that was when my life took off. The incredible things I discovered by living by my truth would not have been available had I kept living the life others expected of me.

I wanted to tell you about this part of my life because I think too often authors try to present themselves as a little above their readers like they are a guru on a higher level. I wanted to show you I am nowhere near perfect. Ask anyone who knows me. Just like everyone else I am constantly learning.

This is a book filled with a lot of proven scientific facts. This is also a book that delves into spiritual matters which may never be provable but rely on reason and experience which can be very subjective.

That is why through the course of this book I want to tell you a few things about me and my life. No, I am not some narcissistic, self-loving, conceited, vainglorious, egomaniac who thinks everyone needs to hear my story. My story is only important because I want you to get to know me, so you will better understand the reasons behind the statements I am making in this book. The reasoning behind why I believe what I believe.

I want you to understand my thoughts and see why everything you are about to read makes sense to me and hopefully, it will make sense to you.

Unlike a fundamentalist religionist (which I once was) I don't want to force you to believe what I believe. We all have our own truths. And if my truth doesn't make sense with your truth, fine. I hope that I can share something with you that will add to your truth and therefore add to your life and if I only say just one thing that adds a small light to your truth then I have done my job.

"What I really lack is to be clear in my mind what I am to do…the thing is to find a truth which is true for me, to find the idea for which I can live and die." - Soren Kierkegaard

To many of my Christian family and friends, I know parts of this book may seem like a slap in the face. But that is not my intention. This book comes from a place of love.

There are those I went to church I know have benefited from a Christian life. They have lived a wonderful, beautiful life and I would never expect them to change their belief. Christianity worked for them. They found their truth. But they are the exception, for many Christianity does not work. Check with any church and they will tell you they have a constant flux of new members joining and then leaving. Their member directory is in a constant state of change.

To Christians, I want to show you what I believe is a better way of life. An easier path with less struggle. If nothing else, if you can just remove the dogmatic belief you and family and friends can be tortured to death by fire for all eternity a huge weight will be lifted from you giving you a sense of relief, unlike anything you have ever experienced before.

I look around and I see a world struggling. Almost everyone seems unhappy. It need not be that way.

I know because I am not unhappy. I am happy. Even with its ups and downs, I enjoy my life.

As I mentioned the world is fragmented. We are all fragmented. The fragmentation is an illusion and I am working to defragment my life to see past the illusion.

I don't do the nine to five thing. I don't work. Let me say I don't consider what I do work. A lot of my income is generated online. Why work when you can have a computer do the work for you? My computer makes me a well above average income. And yes, in this book I will tell you exactly how I do that, so you can do it too if you like. But we will get to that later.

Now don't think my life hasn't been without struggles. I've had some doozies, some of which I will tell you about later. Wait until you hear about how I became an Ativan zombie.

Or you may be interested to see how I ended up on the operating table with my intestines being taken out of my body. You might think this has something to do with the zombie story, but it is a different story altogether.

I was a hypocrite. I am no longer a hypocrite. But I remember, and I know change is hard and I am very sympathetic to that. But you can make any change you want, and these lessons are going to help make that possible.

The statements which follow can be found on most of my Paradigm Shift web sites. This is my truth; I have never been presented with anything in my life which would contradict the statements below. The synchronicity still leaves me with a sense of awe. The events and circumstances of my life never fail to confirm my statements below and constantly conspire to help me attain that which I am seeking.

Without further delay…

For the most part, your brain was wired when you were a child. You may think you have come to conclusions on your own, but your brain has been conditioned to see the world in such a way to support conclusions given to you by your parents and society when you were very young. Did your childhood limit how you see the world?

Are you just a bunch of wired brain cells? Are you not more than that?

You live in a world programmed by fear. It is hard to escape because almost everyone you interact with, and you, have become a part of this world. It is hard to see a way out. From childhood on this is the only world almost everyone knows. We are so easily influenced as a child we can't even see it need not be this way. Each generation brings the next into this fearful world blinded to there being a way out. The next generation accepts this is the way it must be. It is a vicious cycle. We can put an end to the cycle and replace it with a world of kindness, gratitude, and love.

You are not just a bunch of wired brain cells.

The cool thing is because you can think of something in a different way you have the power to make it different. No matter the situation you are in if you can picture a different situation you can change.

Here is where it gets amazing. You can't just be your brain because you can reprogram your brain. Think about it. You can observe your emotions, thoughts, and feelings. That requires something separate from what is going on in your mind. That which is observed also needs an observer. You are the observer.

This is your higher self.

So, who are you?

Everything is energy. Since everything is energy, there is no distinction where energy begins and ends -- therefore we are all one.

Everything and everyone are one. But that does not mean you are not unique. You are like a wave in the ocean. You are the individual wave, but you are also the entire ocean. Everything you do affects everyone and everything.

There is a collective unconscious. If one person knows it be assured that information is available to you.

So, who are you?

You are whoever you want to be.

You are here to create. You are here to create your world in any way you want.

To create, use your imagination. Picture anything you want in your mind and add emotion. Hold that for just a minute or two each day. It is that simple.

There is nothing you cannot do, be or have.

Even after this life, you are still creating. You are creating infinite creations for all eternity.

You are so much more than your physical body. You are infinite. You are eternal.

You see a physical world around you, but it is only a spec in a forever changing and evolving incomprehensible, indescribable reality.

This is what we want the world to see.

Yet so many can't see it.

The way of thinking mentioned above is so foreign to the way their brain has been trained that they don't understand it.

What is my higher self?

What do you mean everything is energy?

I'm not a wave in an ocean. We aren't even near an ocean.

I'm creating for all eternity? What am I making?

The goal of this book is to help you understand what I mean by the statements above. To discover there are more options than just religion and atheism. To eliminate fragmentation by discovering that everything is one. To let you discover you are a genius, so you will see you live in a world where you can bring all your dreams and desires into reality.

How is that for a goal?

Please take to heart this next statement. You create your reality. Reality comes from inside you. It is not outside of you. It is not something separate from you. Look around you at the world you are experiencing right now. Everything you see, hear and touch is your creation. That bears repeating. Everything you see, hear and touch is of your creation. The world is a mirror to who you are. Don't believe me? Keep reading. You will.

Before you start the first lesson you need to find a song that represents what you want your future to be like. It needs to be an upbeat song that puts you in a good mood and inspires you. Listen to that song before you read each lesson. You will be surprised what that will do for you. Don't worry why right now. You will discover that as you go through the book. Just please do it. It is so important!

After reading each lesson there are two things you must do. Doing these two things are so important. Please do not think that it is unnecessary to do them. These two tasks will cement the new knowledge in your mind quicker than you could ever imagine.

Here are the two tasks:

1. After reading each lesson, draw a picture representing what you learned in the lesson. What do you draw? Anything you want. You need not spend a lot of time on it. It need not be a work of art. Just something that reminds you of what you just learned.

2. Teach someone else what you just learned. If no one is available pretend you are teaching someone. Get in front of a mirror and teach your reflection. Speak out loud.

Please do not skip these very important steps.

THE WORLD NEEDS PEOPLE TO THINK FOR THEMSELVES

We live in a world where the rich are getting richer and the poor are getting poorer. Those in power are telling the world how and what to think. They can get away with it because the majority do not know what to think. They don't know if what they are being told is true or false. They just don't have enough information and many times the information they are given is designed to misdirect and even deceive.

Things only get worse because most are afraid to think for themselves. They follow the crowd assuming the majority can't be wrong. But time has shown the majority is usually wrong.

The majority attach their allegiance to one they believe can guide them in the right direction. Unfortunately, their "savior" may be concerned only with personal interests and they can't see it. If too many attach themselves to one individual in the name of hope, they may be blindly led to a world of their greatest nightmare.

Sadly, in just about every area of life, most don't know what they want. They can't make their own decisions so they look to see what others are doing. You do not need others to tell you what to think and do and you do not want to follow the crowd. You can learn and discover anything your heart desires. You are a genius. You have an incredible mind.

Imagine a world where many, not the few, can discern and think for themselves. Imagine the confidence it would instill. No longer could the few control the masses. It would be impossible when the majority think for themselves.

This book will give you that confidence.

Let's start lesson one.

IMPORTANT: Before reading this lesson set the intent in your mind you will learn this material and there is absolutely no reason you can't. Determine nothing is going to stop you from mastering this lesson. It's not going to be hard.

LISTEN TO YOUR INSPIRING SONG!!! SO IMPORTANT!!!

LESSON ONE

GETTING TO KNOW YOUR BRAIN

Since you will be using your brain a lot while reading this book (don't worry it will be fun) it will be beneficial for you to learn a little bit about how your brain works.

This lesson will teach you many things you should have learned in school but don't worry it wasn't your fault. That was a failure on the part of the school system. Most teachers are not even aware of what you are about to learn. It's not their fault either. It's just the entire school system lacks in many areas.

Do you know what your brain is doing when learning something?

You are about to find out.

The main factor that will determine whether something is easy or hard for you to learn is your belief. If you think it will be hard or impossible it will be.

You are often your worst enemy when it comes to learning something. Take for example you are reading. You think you won't be able to understand what you are reading. You think it will be hard. You may feel yourself getting a little nervous. Your mind will be foggy. You will not be thinking as clearly as you normally do.

The important thing to know is you put yourself into this state mind. When you feel that happening the best thing to do is stop reading. Your mind is useless right now. Take a break and remind yourself there is nothing you can't learn. Do something else. Repeat to yourself out loud, "There is nothing I can't learn!" Say it with conviction. You will feel a confidence build in you.

Read it again. You will notice you understand it better. You may even be shocked to see you understand it and that it was quite a simple concept. You just fooled yourself into thinking it would be hard. I have done this so often.

I want to make something very clear from the beginning. If your brain can read and comprehend the concepts of addition, subtraction, multiplication, and division then there is nothing in this universe someone else understands which you cannot.

Not that it doesn't take some work and effort but if someone else knows it, know beyond a doubt you can too.

16

One of our goals is to learn some Calculus. You are just being retold what others figured out for themselves. Now, there lies the true genius.

Think about it.

Everyone says learning Calculus is hard. But now think of the mind of Isaac Newton who played a large part in inventing Calculus. He wasn't satisfied with the math of the time, so he invented a new math to help him solve problems easier. He invented Calculus! Can you say WOW! Mind-blowing! Newton did the hard part for us. Now we just have the easy task of learning what he invented

Understand when you start to learn something it may at first seem impossible. You can see no way of doing it. That is simply because your brain has not made the dendrite connections for you to understand it yet.

You can grasp the logic of anything once your brain builds the necessary dendrites.

You need to have the prerequisite dendrites. We will discuss what dendrites are later in this lesson but understand this next statement right now. **All brain processes -- knowledge, skills, talents, memories, beliefs – are dendrites in action.**

To learn Calculus, you need to already have the dendrite connections for basic math, or it will do you no good to try and understand Calculus. It is a building process.

If you don't know how to do something it does not mean you can't learn how. All it means is you have not yet made the necessary dendrite connections.

The prerequisite for building dendrites is a belief in yourself. The greater your belief the faster you will make dendrite connections and the stronger they will become.

The more you see yourself learning the stronger your belief will become that you can learn more.

Your inability to grasp a subject in school was not a reflection of your intelligence. It was a reflection of the way you were taught which affected your belief to learn the subject. Do not blame your teachers because they were taught the same way you were.

We need our brains to learn. Duh! Therefore, to take full advantage of our brain we need to know just what our brain is doing when learning. This step alone will make a huge difference in how fast you can acquire new skills. Once you see how the brain works, you will be more able to visualize the steps in later lessons and know exactly what your brain is doing to process the information. We can't overemphasize the importance of knowing how your brain works. It will boost your confidence.

Did you know the brain is the only organ in the body that sculpts itself from outside experience? Every time you learn something new your brain changes. Your experience becomes biology. This is called neuroplasticity. Your brain is constantly renewing itself.

We highly suggest reading any book by Dr. Joe Dispenza.

Brain cells are called neurons. You have around 100 billion. They can each perform over 100,000 functions per second. Yes, that means your brain too. There is no way you can make the excuse you cannot understand what I will teach you in this book.

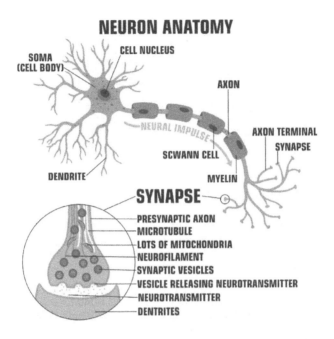

Picture 1 - A brain cell aka neuron.

Dendrites are fibers that grow out of the neurons when you learn.
Learning = Growth of Dendrites

Look at the picture of the neuron above. Find the **dendrites** on the left of the neuron. Now find the **axon terminals** on the right of the neuron. Neurons form contact points from their axon terminals to the dendrites of other cells. The contact point between the dendrites and axon terminals is called a **synapse.**

The contact point may be misleading when describing a synapse. Look at the enlarged synapse in the photo above. It is a small gap. Chemicals called neurotransmitters carry electrical signals across the synapse. This is known as the cell firing. As you learn something, as you practice something, neurons make more connections with other neurons and fire faster and faster.

One neuron can make up to 100,000 connections.

WHAT THIS MEANS IS YOU CAN TRANSFORM YOUR BRAIN INTO THE POWERHOUSE IT WAS MEANT TO BE BY INCREASING AND GROWING

YOUR NEURON'S DENDRITES AND MAKING MANY CONNECTIONS WITH OTHER NEURONS.

The neurons cluster together, and this is called a neural network. In this book, we will use the words neuron cluster and neural network interchangeably. You have a separate neural network (neuron cluster) for everything you know.

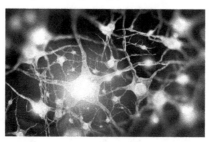

Picture 2 - A Neural Network

The bigger the cluster (neural network) the better you understand a subject or the better you able to perform certain tasks. As the cluster gets bigger, the connections between each dendrite will get faster and faster. They call it firing. Technology is good enough now we can see neurons firing. The chemical electric neurotransmitters are zipping across the neural network at incredible speeds. It looks like an electrical storm in your brain.

A person with a Ph.D. in math has a larger cluster in the brain for math than a student. The Ph.D. is firing neurons way faster than the student. A pro golfer has a larger cluster in the brain allowing him to play golf better than an amateur. Consider Tiger Woods. In his prime, his neural network for golf was way bigger than any professional golfer and his neurons were firing at amazing rates. But as of this writing, he has not been performing as well. His neuron cluster has gotten smaller and is not firing as fast. Although this last year he has improved his neural network. He is getting better again.

There are 3 ways to make your brain grow dendrites and make neuron clusters.

a. Through the experience of doing something.
b. Through imagination.
c. Through Infinite Intelligence.

We will talk about each of these more in later lessons.

When you think the same thought over again, the neurons keep firing in the same way and it strengthens the relationship between neurons. This strengthening of neuron relationships is your brain learning. After a while the learning becomes automatic. You don't even have to think, you just do it. It just happens.

It is like riding a bike. At first, it is very hard because your brain has no neurons developed for riding a bike. But you practice and then neurons develop, you develop a neural network for riding a bike and you get better. More neurons develop and cluster together and then it gets easier. Finally, so many neurons cluster together it becomes automatic. You don't even have to think about it, your body just does it.

Now here is where there is often a problem. You want to make sure the neural networks you are creating, and strengthening are beneficial. So often networks are created with false information, but they are so ingrained in the person's brain they cannot see it is false. Consider a person is saying something negative about themselves daily. They will strengthen that conviction in their brain and nothing you can say to them will convince them otherwise until the connection is weakened. This is also how we form bad habits. Any bad habit you have was created by your brain strengthening its neural connections for that habit. You need to weaken the connection.

I will show you how to take advantage of the fact that you have an incredible amount of influence over how your neuron clusters are created.

Here is something very interesting. Your brain can prune itself. It takes neurons away from clusters you are not using and adds to clusters you are using. For example, I had not ridden a bike since I was sixteen. After I got my car, I had no use for a bike. A few weeks ago, I tried to ride my nephew's electric bike. It was clear my brain had taken away neurons from the cluster in my brain in which I had learned to ride a bike. The bike riding did not go well.

Pruning can also be done just by thinking. Think about good things to add to a helpful cluster. Stop thinking about bad things to take away from the cluster of a habit you do not want. You can form your brain with your thoughts. Think of the power you have.

The main thing I want you to remember is when you learn something new at first it may not make sense to you and you may see no possible way it ever could. But as you take in new information, new neurons will be made, and new connections will form. You will notice when that happens because one of the many new facts you have put in your brain will suddenly make sense to you. If you go over the information again, you will see a connection you didn't see before. Neurons will continue to cluster, and more connections will be made. Something else will make sense. You are understanding. Just keep the neurons firing by thinking about what you are trying to learn. You will eventually understand it completely.

If you stick with it and do not give up, you will grow new neuron clusters. However, it is unnecessary to constantly concentrate on what you are trying to learn to keep the neurons firing. Constantly concentrating on something new can be very counterproductive.

When reading this book never spend more than half an hour at a time going over the material. And if you spend a half-hour going over the material at least spend half an hour not thinking about it. Not thinking about it will not stop your neurons from clustering.
Taking your mind off things for a while can be very beneficial. You need only to make

sure you set an intention in your mind to learn. You will be surprised how often you will be doing something unrelated to this book and something in your mind will just click. Something you may not have understood before, you will suddenly understand. You won't know exactly why you now understand it, but there it is, making perfect sense. You will be amazed at how much your subconscious will do to your brain without you being aware. This will be a subject in a later lesson.

The most important thing you need to do is believe that you can understand it. It will come. It must.

This is the end of lesson 1. In lesson 2 we will learn ways to grow dendrites faster which will make you learn faster.

As I mentioned in the intro, you now have two tasks.

Draw a picture that represents what you have just learned and teach someone else. Please do this. It is very important. You will understand why as we get into later lessons.

THE DARK NIGHT OF THE SOUL

There was a time when I thought I was in complete control of my thoughts. I knew I was the observer of my thoughts. I was not my thoughts. (More on that later.) As far as I was concerned no matter what life threw at me, I could handle it.

As is so often the case, I was wrong. My life became a horror movie. My thoughts came at me with a vengeance. Try as I might, I could no longer be the observer. I was trapped in the movie of my mind. This was really happening to me and I could find no way to escape.

This was after I started Paradigm Shift. As I said before, I still had so much to learn.

They say if you are a spiritual seeker to truly understand you must experience the Dark Night of the Soul.

Many don't even know the factors that bring on their dark night. I knew mine all too well. In a very short time, my father died, I almost died, a good friend was jailed for selling drugs, I discovered I was diabetic and I thought I was going blind.

As the name implies, the Dark Night of the Soul is a very dark place. I withdrew into a state of chronic depression and anxiety. You feel alone. You feel trapped. You feel as if you will never see any kind of light again.

Your emotions are your body's reaction to your mind. When your mind completely takes over all the negative emotions you have suppressed your entire life ravish you in a flood. If you have never experienced it, you can't understand the complete and utter despair that has found its way into you. You lose all hope. You care about nothing and I mean absolutely nothing. All you want is for the pain and anguish, both mental and physical, to end. You are suffering. You are suffering at a level you did not know was possible.

This is hard to write about.

I guess a part of me is afraid it will bring back the emotions in their full intensity.

I do not want to go through that again.

I would never wish that on anyone.

It is around 3:00 AM and I am in my bed. It is still dark outside. Thank goodness. I have more time. I am fine. Just a little nervous. I am in control. Maybe, just maybe it won't happen again.

My cat is laying at the foot of my bed. I can hear her purring. Everything is fine. I can get more sleep. But if I sleep, it will come sooner. But I need to sleep.

I do sleep.

It is a little after 5:00 AM. I open my eyes and can see the first rays of the day's sun spilling through the window. I can hear the morning birds chirping.

Oh no, I think. It's time again. I can't do this again.

I tell myself to be calm. Stay calm. There is nothing to worry about. It's not happening yet.

Concentrate on your breathing. Just breathe slowly in and slowly out. Long deep breaths in through your nose. Hold it. Release out through your mouth. Repeat. Repeat. Repeat.

Okay, I still feel a little calm. Maybe I can fall back asleep and get another hour's sleep.

I roll over on my side, still aware of my breathing.

A few minutes pass. And then…

It's back!

I can feel it again. It's not that strong yet. But I can feel it.

No, please I can't do this again. Breathe slowly.

I try but my breathing becomes quick and shallow.

I can feel it getting stronger. It is growing in me. No! Please No! Stop!

I begin to sweat. My heart is racing. Soon my hair is soaked.

Not again! Not again! Not again!

It happens so fast. I am in a state of sheer terror. Something bad is going to happen. But I don't know what it is.

My body hurts. I can't think. I am trembling. I can't breathe.

This can't go on.

Am I losing my mind?

Am I dying?

Perhaps that would be best. This can't go on. I can't live like this.

No! Never think like that!

But what do I do?

I don't know what to do.

I find myself in a fetal position in the corner of my bed crying. I don't know what to do! I don't know what to do. Repeating over and over, I don't know what to do.

I must face the day and I can't. I can't go through another day like I did yesterday. It is sheer terror. But if I stay in bed, it is sheer terror too.

There is no escape.

What is going to happen? It's not going to be good. It is going to be bad. My life as I have known it is over.

It is going to be terrible. Just let it happen. Just get it over with.

No, don't let it happen. I won't be able to handle it.

I don't know what to do. I don't know what to do.

Somebody, please help me. Please. I need help.

Nothing is helping. No one is helping.

There is nothing anyone can do to help me.

But then the feeling would start to subside. I could feel myself breathing a little better. I could feel myself gaining a little more control.

The fear was still there. I could still feel the nervousness in every cell in my body. I still didn't know why. But at least I didn't feel like I was losing my mind or about to die.

At least enjoy the little tiny release you have been given while it lasts.

I get up and walk into the kitchen and get a glass of water. My hair is still soaked with sweat.

I sit down at the kitchen table and take a few sips of the water. It tastes good. My breathing is still very shallow. I lower my head and rest it in my arms on my table. I am tired. Very tired. But oh, so nervous and afraid.

And then…

Oh no! No!

It's building again.

My breathing and heart are racing again.

It's getting stronger again. It is growing in me again. No! Please No! Stop!

I am sweating again. I can feel it rolling down the side of my cheek.

Not again! Not again! Not again!

It's never going to end.

It's never going to end.

It's never going to end.

It's never going to end.

It's never going to end.

It does end.

It is a huge detox. My ego was dying, and it was making a strong final attempt to hold on to life. Dying maybe a strong word, for in this life you never truly lose your ego, nor would you want to.

For a while, it did possess me and separate me from my true self. There was a division in my life. A bridge I once crossed was now a chasm. I was at the mercy of my mind. It had me trapped and would not allow me to return to a place where I could access my higher self. I was not able to detach myself from my mind and see I was not my mind but the observer of my mind. I could remember the incredible benefits of disconnecting from my mind, but I was beginning to doubt if that would ever happen again. Day after day, week after week, I kept feeling myself fading away and soon I was sure the person I once was would no longer exist.

It is as your life has taken a detour and you find yourself on a path you never expected. A path you falsely assumed you would never find yourself on and you are convinced that you are never going to get off.

It was completely debilitating. The incapacitating emotion was unlike anything I had ever felt before. I could only sit and stare into space and let my mind ravish me. I would leave the house and drive not even knowing where I was going. I thought maybe by leaving the house I would find a little relief. But I didn't. I usually ended up pulling into a parking lot and sitting for hours constantly bombarded by emotions draining the life out of me.

But I did get my life back and I do still exist and after it is over you are blessed. You find a place within you where you can go anytime to find a peace you never knew existed. You know a comfort that very few know. What you thought was the end of your life was just the beginning. You begin to see the world in a different light.

You look back on the experience with a sense of peace. That does not mean you want to remember the despair and pain, as I said earlier that is hard to think about. but you now see the whole picture. You see it as a triumph. You see it as your greatest accomplishment. You see it as the greatest thing that has ever happened to you in your life. You have a strength you didn't have before. You now know there is nothing you can't overcome.

It is incredible.

One goal of this book is to give you that peace of mind and strength without you having to go through the complete torture I did. I will tell you how I regained my peace of mind. First, it is important to go back so I can show you what caused all the insanity.

But before we do that you need to read lesson two.

IMPORTANT: Before reading this lesson set the intent in your mind you will learn this material and there is absolutely no reason whatsoever you can't. Determine nothing will stop you from mastering this lesson. It's not even going to be hard.

LISTEN TO YOUR INSPIRING SONG!!! SO IMPORTANT!!!

LESSON TWO
YOUR INCREDIBLE MEMORY. YES, YOUR MEMORY!

As we mentioned in the last chapter learning is neurons in your brain clustering to make a neural network related to what you are trying to learn. The larger the neural cluster the more you are a master of the topic, activity, skill.

One of the best ways to learn (make those neurons cluster) is to connect something you are trying to learn to something you already know. Make those neural networks grow faster by connecting new neurons to old neurons you already know something about.

Find some way to connect this book to something you are interested in. How can you use the information in this book to complement or aide you in something you like? Do you have a hobby? Is there some way the information in this class can help you add to the enjoyment of your hobby? Think about it. You probably won't have to think too hard.

I like to paint. I like to paint abstract art related to the concepts of Special Relativity and Quantum Physics because as you will see those concepts can be way out there. In just a few lessons you will discover this for yourself.

We will tell you other ways to connect this book to things you already know, but you must do some things first.

First, understand that a powerful, learning brain that can take in and remember information with ease is not a gift. Those who do incredible things with their mind, such as perform what seems impossible feats of memory, had to develop and practice that memory skill. Convince yourself that you can do that too. In this lesson, you will do that.

Second, clear all that clutter in your mind. You know what I'm talking about. Your mind can have over 50,000 thoughts a day. Most thoughts are repetitive. A lot are useless. A lot very strange. So strange you would never tell another soul. They would think you were insane even though they have similar thoughts. Crazy isn't it?

Think about it, how can you retain new information in your mind if it needs to compete with 50,000 crazy thoughts a day? You can't!

Learn to quiet your mind.

Before reading the rest of this lesson find a comfortable place to sit. Now just pay attention to your breathing. Have no doubt thoughts will pop back into your head.

When that happens just return your attention to your breathing. Try to do this for about ten minutes. After ten minutes you will notice you are in a much calmer state. You will now be more receptive to the information in this book. Do this exercise before each new lesson in the book. Do not skip it. The benefit will be incredible.

Now we will show you an incredible way to boost your memory to a level you never thought possible. This is very fun.

Your mind is very creative. You need to use your imagination.

When trying to learn something, you need to see a picture in your mind that relates to what you are learning.

What is easier to remember a picture or a page with hundreds of words? Obviously, the picture.

Let's make it even easier to remember a picture. We can do it in two ways. Make the picture ridiculous. Add action to the picture.

It's time to prove it to you.

In less than a minute, you will have the 10 words below memorized and you will know them forward and backward.

House, Pig, Airplane, Monkey, Violin, Spaceship, Grandmother, Chair, Gold, Sun

Vividly picture the story I am about to tell you in your mind.

Picture your house. A giant pink pig sits on and smashes your house. Suddenly, an airplane crashes into the pig and explodes. A monkey runs out of the burning plane into your yard and grabs a violin and plays it. A spaceship zooms over the monkey's head. The spaceship is being driven by your grandmother. She is sitting in a chair way too big for her. The chair turns into solid gold. The spaceship continues zooming towards a bright orange sun.

You now have those 10 words memorized. Not only that, you know the exact order they were listed. Test yourself and see.

Let's try another similar memory technique.

Remember how we said the best way to learn is to connect something you are trying to learn to something you are already very familiar with?

Let's see how to do that and stick with creating a crazy image.

What is one thing in this world you are very familiar with?

How about your house?

Now I want you to picture Albert Einstein with his wild crazy hair changing a light bulb in some room in your house. If you don't know what Einstein looks like look him up on the internet. See a vivid picture of Einstein changing that light bulb in your house.

Why that image? The main concept of The Theory of Special Relativity deals with the strange nature of light.

Trust me when I say you have now cemented that picture in your brain, and it is going to be almost impossible for you to forget and so is the information you have connected to the picture. You now know Special Relativity and light are related.

But we can go even farther. Take a moment, just a minute or two, and doodle that picture on a piece of paper. You don't have to be an artist. It can suck. Just as long as you know what it is.

Now put that piece of paper in a conspicuous place where you will see it often. Every time you see the paper you will be reminded what it means. This will strengthen your neural connections every single time.

You have already started learning The Theory of Relativity.

This is why I will have you draw a picture of each lesson in the class.

This process may seem kind of weird at first, and it is weird, but that is why it works. Our brain easily remembers weird things.

You can't talk about improving your memory without discussing mind mapping.

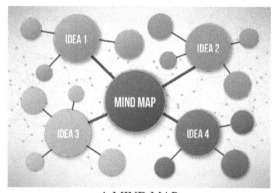

A MIND MAP

Mind mapping was originally used as a replacement for taking notes, but it can also be used for planning, organizing, and problem-solving.

Before we discuss mind mapping, I have to say note taking SUCKS! It has been scientifically proven to be a terrible way to remember something. After taking the notes you will remember little of what you wrote down. Plus, you will often miss key information because you are concentrating on writing.

Note-taking is linear and as we have shown memory is associative. You associate what you are learning with images and things you already know.

Mind mapping is easy. On a piece of paper, write your main topic in the center and circle it.

As you cover subtopics draw branches extending from the center circle and label them. Then as you learn something more about the subtopic make branches off from your subtopic branch and label them. You can branch off as often as you need. Try and label each branch with just one word or very short phrase.

Here are three tips to make your mind maps even better.

1. Use images often.
2. Use different colors for each topic.
3. Develop your own style. There is no wrong way to do a mind map. If it works for you then you are doing it right.

Below is an example of a mind map for health. Notice you don't have to use just words. You can use pictures, symbols anything you want to help you make the connection in your mind.

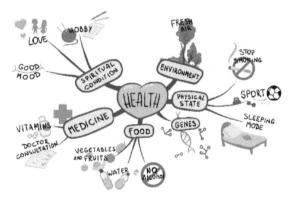

Make a mind map for each lesson. When we start talking about Special Relativity and Quantum Physics mind maps will be so helpful.

One last thing before we end this lesson and this is very important.

Every night when you go to sleep review the day's lesson in your mind. Let it be one of your last thoughts before you fall asleep. This will pass it on to your subconscious mind. That is when magic is created. We will discuss the power of your subconscious mind in an upcoming lesson.

Okay, now it is time to draw a picture that represents what you have just learned and teach someone else. Again, please do this. It is very important. You will understand why as we get into later lessons.

These first lessons we have been learning about your brain and mind. In the next lesson, you will see that you are not your brain nor your mind.

THE MORNING I WOKE UP AND COULDN'T SEE

It was perhaps one of the most frightening times in my life. This was the event that led to my ultimate breakdown I described to you earlier in this book. Yes, other events led to the breakdown of my mind, which I will also relate to you, but this was the catalyst.

I went to bed and everything was fine. I slept great that night but when I woke up in the morning I could barely see.

Everything was extremely blurry. I could still make out what things were, but they were a complete distortion of the original shape I knew it to be.

Last night my vision had been fine. I didn't understand it. I had never even needed glasses, and this was so bad I was scared that even glasses wouldn't help.

I had just recently been diagnosed with diabetes. I knew diabetes could cause damage to your vision. But did it happen that fast?

I had heard that anxiety could cause vision problems. I had been going through a lot lately perhaps that was the reason.

That thought gave me a little, very little, but a little comfort. If it was anxiety, then perhaps it was more my mind causing the eye problems. I had heard that what we see is 10% eyesight and 90% brain.

I hated going to doctors. I decided I would just try and relax and perhaps my eyesight would get better. So that became my plan. Just relax today and if you don't see some improvement you will call the doctor tomorrow.

Yeah right. Relax?

I spent the day constantly checking my eyesight. I couldn't stop. Every minute I had to confirm to myself whether my eyesight was getting worse, better or staying the same.

I would look at an object. Did it look blurrier than it did a few minutes before?

Maybe not.

Maybe.

Who knows?

All right, I knew this wasn't helping the goal for today was to relax.

But how could I relax?

I couldn't read. I couldn't make out the words.

I could do nothing on the computer. Everything was unrecognizable.

I couldn't watch tv. All I saw were images of melding colors I couldn't make out.

Anything I tried to do was aggravating and more distressing.

What was I to do?

I sit down in a chair.

What do I do?

Just close my eyes and see the blackness.

But that is what I am trying to avoid.

Please tell me I'm not going blind. Please I don't want to be blind. Please.

How can I relax?

My fear is everywhere around me.

At least with most fears, you can find a place of solitude, a way to escape for a while.

My fear was my sight. Something I was constantly aware of.

For me, there was no escape.

I begin the cycle of examining my sight over and over.

I would look at an object. Did it look blurrier than it did a few minutes before?

Maybe not.

Maybe.

Who knows?

That was how I would spend every waking minute of the day.

I would look at an object. Did it look blurrier than it did a few minutes before?

Maybe not.

Maybe.

Who knows?

I would look at an object. Did it look blurrier than it did a few minutes before?

Maybe not.

Maybe.

Who knows?

I would look at an object. Did it look blurrier than it did a few minutes before?

Maybe not.

Maybe.

Who knows?

I went to bed early that night. At least when I fell asleep, I would be free from the anxiety and being in a dark room I could not constantly examine my vision. Going to bed brought a little relief.

Don't think I was oblivious to the irony. I saw it all too clearly. At least I saw something clearly. My fear was losing my eyesight, but I was calmer now that I was in a dark room and unable to see. How about that?

But at that point, I didn't care. And who knows perhaps tomorrow I would wake up and my sight would be better.

Surprisingly I had a good night's sleep. It didn't take me long to fall asleep.

I just woke up once during the night. It was still dark out and I couldn't tell how my vision was. I fell back to sleep quickly.

The next morning, I was awoken by birds chirping. I could see the morning light spilling through my bedroom windows. The sun had not completely risen yet, but it was bright enough for me to look around the room and discover...

My vision had gotten worse.

Like I said that was the catalyst to my ultimate breakdown. But there were other events which lead to the breakdown. They were the events that led to my brain being a garbled mess of entangled neurons, a conglomeration of weeds that strangled and killed all that was beautiful and good in my brain. I am sure if not for these events already screwing up my brain, I would have dealt with the sight issue much better. As I mentioned in the introduction I have almost died twice. I will tell you how that happened and let you know the present state of my sight but first, you need to read lesson three.

IMPORTANT: Before reading this lesson set the intent in your mind you will learn this material and there is absolutely no reason whatsoever you can't. Determine nothing is going to stop you from mastering this lesson. It's not even going to be that hard.

LISTEN TO YOUR INSPIRING SONG!!! SO IMPORTANT!!!

LESSON 3
YOU ARE NOT YOUR BRAIN

We've spent a lot of time talking about the brain.

But now you need to know something very important…

You are not your brain.

You are not your mind.

You are not that which answers to your name. You are not your job. You are not your beliefs. You are not those things that have happened to you in your life.

You are so much more.

You know that voice you hear in your head? It's crazy isn't it and it never seems to shut up does it?

It is constantly saying this, then that, and then back to this and then something completely different. It just won't quit. If you listen to it the voice is describing your world for you be it true or false. And most of what it is saying is negative isn't it?

It is telling you why you are not satisfied with your life.

It is telling you about something potentially bad that could happen to you in the near future.

You can hear it say all this stuff you aren't controlling. You don't know what it will say next. It just pops in your mind seemingly out of nowhere. But you can take control of the voice. Make it say something. Make it say, "apple." Now make it shout, "amazing." Now make it whisper, "strange."

It is strange. You can take control of this voice and make it say anything you want but if you leave it alone it doesn't go away, and it takes control of your mind and says whatever it wants.

Sometimes it says good things and sometimes it says bad things.

So, is this voice you?

Is it you when it says the good things?

Is it you when it says the bad things?

Get ready for this next statement it is huge.

You are not the voice in your head. You are not the voice of your mind. You are not your mind. You are the one who is observing the voice.

Think about this. The observer cannot be that which is being observed. If you see an apple on a table, you cannot be the apple or the table. The same with the voice in your head. You can pay attention to what it is doing. You can even make judgments about what it is doing. Therefore, it can't be you.

So, who are you?

What is the part of you doing the observing?

Your consciousness. Your soul. Your higher self. All three of these are separate but be assured they are all YOU.

Consciousness is awareness. Without consciousness there is nothing. You do not exist. But if there is consciousness there can be absolutely nothing and you will notice the nothingness. Can you see the difference?

You are the consciousness. You are the awareness. You are therefore unlimited.

We will talk a lot more about consciousness later. Right now, let's learn more about this voice in your head and what we can do with it.

If you pay attention to the voice you will notice that a lot of what it says is useless. It even takes on both sides of arguments in your head. You have about 50,000 thoughts a day. Do you even remember what most were yesterday? Of course not.

I will bet they were negative thoughts. I bet you are sure of that.

Your inner voice can be downright mean. It is constantly telling you bad things about yourself. It is constantly making you upset, nervous, and angry.

Would you say the things your mind says to you to another person? No way.

So why in the world do you keep saying those things to yourself? Stop it.

Can you stop the voice?

Not entirely.

You need to understand the voice will never be content. It will present you with problem after problem. If you solve one problem another will immediately be there to take its place.

Your voice is like a little child. Treat it as such. It is throwing a tantrum.

Don't get caught up in the tantrum. Don't give in to the child. Don't give in to your mind.

Feel empathy for the mind/child. It doesn't know how to make sense of the world. All it wants is to feel safe and secure, but it doesn't know how. It is scared.

Step outside your mind. Do this by just observing your mind. You are the observer so observe your thoughts and emotions. If you are experiencing a strong negative emotion don't fight it. Don't judge it. Just experience it. Just let it flow.

It may be hard and uncomfortable at first but soon you will notice the negative feeling weakening a little. Continue to observe it and it will get even weaker. The strong negative feeling will eventually subside.

It may come back, but it will not be as strong as before. When it comes back just detach and observe it again. Soon it will no longer have a hold on you.

You can take control of how the voice makes you feel. You can take control of how you react to the voice and once you let the voice stop getting to you it can be beneficial. You can learn from what it is saying.

For the next ten minutes try this experiment. Try and keep your mind as quiet as possible. Concentrate on your breathing. Take long deep breaths. Do your best to keep your awareness on your breath.

You will notice it won't take long, and you will forget about your breath and thoughts will pop back into your head. That is fine just return your attention to your breathing. Again, the thoughts will return. Again, center on your breathing.

After ten minutes think back to the thoughts that came into your mind. What were they about? Do they tell you anything about yourself? You better believe they do.

Now think about this. We usually think our brain determines how smart we are. But if we are consciously observing our brain does there not have to be an intelligence in our consciousness? So, what is smarter our brain or our consciousness?

Later we will show you ways to use the part of you who is observing your thoughts to access intelligence way beyond what you ever thought possible. I first wanted to introduce you to the observer and let it sink in that the observer is you. You are not your thoughts.

Okay, now it is time to draw a picture that represents what you have just learned and teach someone else. Again, please do this. It is very important. You will understand why as we get into later lessons.

In the next lesson we will talk about your subconscious mind and beyond but first I want to tell you how I almost died twice.

I ALMOST DIED TWICE

It was a strange feeling.

My stomach felt weird. It was unlike any feeling I had felt before.

My stomach wasn't upset. There was no nausea. There were no aches and pains.

There was this uncomfortable tingling. Like when you sit or sleep in an awkward position and a body part "falls asleep" and you get that tingling, prickly sensation.

I also found myself going in and out of consciousness.

To make a long story short...

WARNING: This may get a little gross.

It turns out my appendix had rotted. The hard sharp edge of my rotted appendix had punctured my colon and the waste (you know I could have used a few more common terms) was leaking into my body.

I told you it was gross and it gets worse.

They had to cut me open to clean me out. My intestines were actually taken out of my body to be "hosed down" and then stuffed back in me.

The doctor said if I had waited one more day before coming in there would have been nothing they could have done. My entire body would have been filled with you know what.

I am very glad to say everything was a success and everything is working as it should.

That was just the first time I almost died, a few years later I almost died again from ketoacidosis (you can look it up if you want to know the details). I became diabetic. My father, who was my best friend and my rock, passed with cancer. My vision was drastically blurred for over two months. One of my closest friends was put in drug rehab. It just all hit me in a short time. Was it any wonder I developed an anxiety disorder and had daily panic attacks for nine months?

But I came through it.

After it is over you are blessed. You find a place within you where you can go anytime to find a peace you never knew existed. You know a comfort that very few know. What you thought was the end of your life was just the beginning. You have a strength you didn't have before. You now know there is nothing you can't overcome.

I mentioned earlier I would tell you how my eyesight turned out. The blurriness came because I was put on insulin for my diabetes. My blood sugar levels were high and lowering my blood sugar was causing my eyes to become very watery and blur my vision. This process took almost two months before my watery eyes became normal.

Even then another problem arose because I didn't know what normal was for my sight. Before all this started, I was becoming a little farsighted. I had to push a book a little away from my face to read. When you are constantly examining your vision, you discover things you didn't know before. I want to tell you one thing I discovered, and this applies to your sight as well. If you haven't heard this before it may shock you a little.

Donald Hoffman explains it best in his book – *The Case Against Reality*.

"Although our visual field extends two hundred degrees horizontally and one hundred fifty degrees vertically, we enjoy high resolution in only the two degrees that surround the center of gaze. The visible width of your thumb when you see it extended at arm's length is one degree. Staring at your thumb on your outstretched arm brings home how tiny your window of detail really is: its area is ten thousand times smaller than your field of vision. Why is it, then, that most of us never notice this limit of vision, and mistakenly believe that we see the whole field of vision in high resolution? The answer lies in the incessant movement of our eyes. They look and jump, look and jump, about three times a second—more when you read, less when you stare. The looks are called fixations and the jumps are known as saccades. Each time you look at something, you view it through a tiny window replete with detail. Normally you don't look and see a blur. So we find it natural to assume that we see everything, at once, in great detail."

Look at a photo with more than one person in it. You can only see one face clearly, depending on which face you concentrate on.

Look at your pet. You really can't see the face and the tail without one or the other being a little blurry. This is how I first noticed how little we view in detail. I would look at my cat's face and I could see the tail was a little blurry. As I looked around most of what I was seeing was blurry. This was normal but I didn't know that. It's weird how you can live your entire life and not realize how little focus the eye has.

This, of course, brought back the fear.

Was my vision closing in on me?

Would everything eventually be a blur?

Would it get even worse?

41

Could I go blind?

And here we are back at this stage again?

Not fun. Not fun at all!

When you are in that state of mind, common sense just walks out the door and takes a super long vacation. I will show you that anytime you try and fight with your brain it will win. But first, you need to read lesson four.

LESSON 4

YOUR SUBCONSCIOUS MIND AND BEYOND

When I sit down to play the piano my subconscious takes over. It must.

There is no way you could consciously think, put this finger here and that finger there and that finger there with this hand. Now with your other hand put that finger there and that finger there and hold them there for half a beat with this hand and two full beats with that hand. Now after the first half beat put this finger here and that finger there and that finger there... As the saying goes you just do it.

You can't let your conscience come into play. When you consciously try to think about what you are doing you start making mistakes. Your fingers just won't go where they are supposed to. Your conscious mind is not capable of playing the piano.

I have been able to play the piano since I was a child. I took no lessons. I was given no instruction. So why was I able to play the piano?

You hear the phrase, "Playing by ear." But what causes you to play by ear? At that young point in my life, I had no musical experience. I couldn't even tell you what the notes on the piano were. I could hear a song in my head, sit down at the piano and my fingers would find the correct keys to play the song I was hearing in my head. I didn't know how my fingers were doing that. How did I know this key and this key and this key were the right ones to play with this hand? And how did I know that key and that key were the correct ones to play with that hand?

I've already answered part of the question. I was playing the piano with my subconscious mind. But still, if I had never taken any kind of music lessons in my life then how did I, even subconsciously, play the piano?

The answer... Somehow my subconscious mind already knew how to play the piano.

Now skip forward a few years. I was twelve years old and I just got my first computer, a Commodore 64. To me, the computer was the most powerful thing in the world. With a computer, there wasn't anything you couldn't do. I was determined to learn to program this computer and gain this incredible power.

I began reading the little book that came with the computer entitled, *BASIC Programming on the Commodore 64*. I might as well have been reading a book written in a foreign language (I guess part of it was). I read through the entire book and when finished I was no closer to learning to program a computer than when I began. So, I read the book repeatedly, over and over. I remember going back and reading single paragraphs, again and again, trying to understand what I was being told, but I just didn't get it.

But then something clicked! I still remember it vividly. I was reading the chapter on variables and it was making sense. This led to the other sections in the book making sense and within the next few months, I had created this little sword fighting game which I thought I would sell and make millions.

Okay, I didn't make millions. I didn't even make a $1. Give me a break I was only twelve. But getting back to the point the question is what in me clicked? What was it that suddenly led me to understand what I was reading in that book? Let's take it even farther. Without someone instructing me or telling me how to do it, what led me to not only understand the information in the pages of that book but also take that information and transfer it to the logical flow needed to make a computer program come to life and do what you want it to do? My subconscious was playing a part. But how did my subconscious know what to do?

The answer...

My subconscious mind already knew how to program a computer, play the piano and other skills. Was I just born with the skills?

Yes, I was. But so is everyone else. The only way to explain it is we all have the potential to know how to do everything. There is an infinite mind which we are all a part. If one person has done it then be assured one person has paved the way for the rest of us.

But that doesn't mean you can automatically do everything. Your brain still must be wired as we discussed in the first lesson. You still need the neuron connections and clusters.

Now here is probably one of the most important statements in this entire book.

The infinite mind which we are all a part of can program your brain for you. It can be automatic, and you may not even know it. It is a quantum leap. The neuron cluster is not there then it suddenly is. You suddenly know how to do something you previously did not.

I never took the necessary steps to wire my brain for piano playing. Yet I can play the piano. Obviously, my brain is wired for piano playing. How? My infinite mind did it.

The problem is the majority do not know how to access this infinite knowledge. This is where playing the piano and programming a computer helped me. You wouldn't think there were similarities in playing the piano and programming a computer. There are, especially where the mind is concerned. When playing the piano, often I would go into an almost trance-like state bypassing my conscience. What I found interesting is when working on a computer program I would fall into an identical trance-like state. When writing a program, you need to figure out the logical steps to make the program do what you want it to do. Sometimes that doesn't always come easy. Every time I struggled to find a solution the answer always came after slipping into and back out of a trance-like state.

This is when I became interested in states of brain activity. Our brain operates at different frequencies. When we are wide awake and alert, we are in a beta frequency which falls between 14-30 Hz. When relaxed we are in an alpha frequency between 8-13 Hz. When we are in a trance-like daydreaming state, we are in a theta frequency between 4-7 Hz. When we are asleep, we are in a Delta frequency between 0.5-4 Hz.

Five women were hooked up to an EEG while playing the piano. It was found that all five of their brain frequencies ranged between 5 and 7 Hz. They were in theta. This is important because theta is also the state of mind we need to be in to influence our subconscious and discover our infinite mind.

I can play the piano, never having had a lesson, not because I was born with some special gift of music. Or when I create a new computer program it isn't because I was born with great analytical and logical skills. All I am doing is putting my brain into a theta state and accessing Infinite Intelligence through my subconscious mind. This is something we ALL do every day, whether we know it or not. It is so important to learn how to put our minds into a theta state. It lets us become creators of our own universe by putting us into direct contact with Infinite Intelligence.

But that is only half the story. The other half involves the heart. This may come as a shock, but the heart is also a feeling and thinking organ like the brain. Separate from the brain it has its own neural networks. The brain is more rational while the heart is more intuitive. Your brain opens the doorway to Infinite Intelligence while your heart does the actual communicating.

How does it communicate?

Through your emotions. Concentrate on your heart and you produce a field of electromagnetic energy. Concentrate on the emotions of your heart's desire and that field of electromagnetic energy will align with the energy of the universe, which we can also call the Quantum Universe. This will bring your intentions into reality. Learn how to use your brain to open the doorway to the Quantum Universe. Learn how to use your heart to speak with Infinite Intelligence. Learn to easily create your world into anything you want it to be. See why I said it is very important to understand Quantum Physics? Once you understand Quantum Physics we will teach you very specific ways to access the Quantum Universe and Infinite Intelligence.

Let's briefly go over this again. It is important.

I have been able to play the piano and guitar and other instruments with no instruction. I could play the instruments, but for the longest time, I didn't know why I could play them. It was a mystery. I would sit down at the piano and play a song I might have heard earlier on the radio. But no one had taught me how to do that.

Even more of a mystery, I didn't seem to have any conscious control over what I was playing. I wasn't sitting there thinking put this finger here and that finger there and that finger there and this finger here. I was just playing. It remained a mystery until I discovered Carl Jung suggested there is a collective unconscious. A database full of all human experience, we are unconscious of, but anyone can pull from if they know how. This explained why I could play the piano or the guitar or other instruments or program a computer. This collective unconscious is also known as the Quantum Universe or Infinite Intelligence. We will use the words interchangeably in this book. I was accessing this collective unconscious/Quantum Universe/Infinite Intelligence and pulling from information from its database.

Do you want to know how?

Our mind is often compared to an iceberg. The small percentage of the iceberg that rises above the surface of the water is our conscious mind. The larger percentage of the iceberg below the surface of the water is our subconscious mind and the collective unconscious. At the level just below the water, we find our subconscious mind. Compared to our conscious mind the size of the subconscious mind is enormous. Below the subconscious mind, we have an even larger part of the "iceberg" which is the collective unconscious or the Quantum Universe. Our subconscious mind links our conscious mind to the Quantum Universe. Accessing the collective unconscious is the process of passing information from the Quantum Universe by your subconscious mind to your conscious mind to make neural networks in your brain.

You have access to Infinite Intelligence. There is an infinite mind which we are all a part. There is nothing you can't do. If one person has done it then be assured that one person has paved the way for the rest of us to do it too. All you need do is access the Quantum Universe.

Foremost, accept that what I have just stated is at least a possibility. Many simply don't believe a Collective Unconscious/Quantum Universe/Infinite Intelligence exists, and that is why we will spend a lot of time in this book learning about Quantum Physics.

Belief is the first step. You must proceed with an open mind. You don't have to be 100% convinced. The stronger your belief in your ability to access the Quantum Universe, the better your results.

Here lies a very important fact. No one was born smarter or more skilled than you. They just have more experience accessing the Quantum Universe in areas you don't. Be assured any knowledge, any skill you want to obtain is yours for the taking from the collective unconscious.

I have always said I am glad I was introduced to the piano at an early age. The openness of a child led me to first access the collective unconscious. I had no preconceived notions of what I could and couldn't do. Had I first sat down at a piano as an adult, my mind would have already been conditioned to believe as everyone else that it would take years of training and practice to become proficient at playing the piano. Perhaps the biggest blessing in my life was that my grandparents had a piano I could play with when I was very young. You must believe you can access Infinite Intelligence.

After belief, your ego is your biggest block to accessing collective intelligence. You know it, you can do it, but your ego makes you think you can't or afraid you can't. Your ego lies to you and tells you that your value as a person depends on what you can and can't do and how smart you are.

I want you to get the idea of an IQ out of your head right now. Think about it. No one knows for sure what intelligence is. There is verbal-linguistic intelligence. There is logical-mathematical intelligence. There is spatial intelligence. There is musical intelligence. There is kinesthetic intelligence. There is social interpersonal intelligence. We can't even define intelligence so how can we measure it.

I have taken many IQ tests and each time my score gets higher. I kept retaking the tests and scoring higher and higher passing the genius mark of 130 and still going higher and higher. So, am I a genius now and wasn't when I took the first test? Or did I become very familiar with the questions asked on the test and how to solve them?

In the next lesson, we are going to discuss ways to look into your subconscious mind and see if we can start influencing it. I am going to show how to have a conversation with your subconscious. Your subconscious is the mediator between your conscious and Infinite Intelligence. We are going to see how to consciously pass things on to our subconscious mind so it can pass them on to Infinite Intelligence.

IF YOU FIGHT WITH YOUR BRAIN IT IS ALWAYS GOING TO WIN

You have little control over your thoughts.

Try this. The next thing you read, do not picture it in your mind.

Pink Elephant.

You just saw a pink elephant in your mind.

Red Apple.

You just saw a red apple in your mind. You can't stop yourself from picturing in your mind what I have written.

Blue Couch.

See I just did it to you again. I am controlling your mind.

Your mind is usually on automatic. You have over 50,000 thoughts a day. Where are those thoughts coming from? Are you creating each and every thought? Most of our thoughts are going on subconsciously. Only a thought or two will pop into our conscious mind at a time. The content of our thoughts is largely determined by the culture we were born into. Those thoughts can range from anything that has happened to us in our lifetime to thoughts coming from the collective conscious we discussed in the last lesson. Recent events in our life determine much of our thoughts.

You need to learn to take control of your mind.

Think of someone you know. Picture them in your mind. Decide what they are wearing. Now have them perform some kind of action. You decide. Now have them say something. You decide what they say. Now have them scream it out loud. Now have them whisper it. Now change to a new person wearing the same clothes as the first.

See you can take some control of your mind. But there is also a part of your mind you have no control over. When a thought just pops into your head where did it come from? Were you in control of that thought? Did you will that thought to pop into your head? Did you know it was coming? Could you have done anything to prevent that thought from entering your consciousness?

There is absolutely nothing you could have done at that moment to prevent that thought. I know that all too well. When I struggled with anxiety my thoughts were coming at me with a vengeance and bringing with them the appropriate emotional response and for almost nine months there seemed no way to escape my constant nightmare.

Common sense goes right out the door. You can try to talk to yourself rationally. Even tell yourself that your thoughts are foolish. Trust me, all such attempts are a huge waste of time.

We all struggle during our lives. One thing is constant. It doesn't matter who you are or what you are going through, time will help. Time will ease the pain. I went from being worried about losing a limb, or going blind, or dying at an early age because of my diabetes too, "You bought French Silk Chocolate Pie? Okay, let me crank my insulin shot up a unit or two." (That is the only piece of bad advice in this book.)

For anyone going through any ordeal my main piece of advice is to give it time. Time will help. We talked about neuron clusters. When anxiety attacks it is because you have created a huge monster of a neuron cluster in your brain.

I about died from a rotted appendix. Negative neuron clusters were created.

My father, my rock, the person I turned to when I needed help getting through this life died. Perhaps there is no worse pain than grief over the death of a loved one. You are reaching out for someone who has always been there for you, knowing they can never be there again. The emotion is suffocating. The neuron cluster got a lot bigger.

My close friend became messed up on drugs. The neuron cluster gets even bigger.

I almost died a second time from ketoacidosis, and I discovered I was diabetic. This neuron cluster is now a monster in my brain.

I woke up and could barely see. Are you kidding me? So many things in so little a time. It was like my entire brain was a negative cluster beating me relentlessly with undesirable thought after undesirable thought.

Billions of brain cells were firing, chemicals were being released, to make me feel the anxiety and fear. It feels hopeless. You see no way out. You feel as if this will continue forever. There is no way you can make this neuron cluster suddenly stop and leave you alone. You feel lost.

You are not lost. You can reduce the size of the cluster. Time will help. In time the neuron cluster will reduce in size and as it does, so will your anxiety and fear, but it doesn't just happen in a single moment.

You may think, "I don't have time. If I don't make it through this now, I'm just not going to make it." You do have time. There is absolutely nothing you can go through that you do not have the power within you to overcome. Absolutely nothing. Nada. Zilch.

I was in a dreadful place in which I believed I would never escape. I thought I was losing my mind. I thought my mind was going insane.

But now think of that last sentence. I thought my mind was going insane. Who was observing my mind going insane? That which is doing the observing can't be that being observed. If I was observing my mind going insane, I couldn't be my mind.

That was my turning point. You can't describe the relief you feel when you discover you are not your mind. You are that which observes your mind. The peace that comes by spending more and more time as the observer is indescribable.

It may not feel like it when going through it. At first, you will see no way out and you will think I am an idiot and this book is stupid, but once you overcome it, and you will if you just give it time, you will look back and see you had more than enough power within you to see yourself through.

Here is the good part. You can do things to help speed the reduction of the neuron cluster.

How? It is very anti-intuitive, but you must not struggle and stop trying to mentally stop the negative emotion. You just can't do it. It was like when you read "pink elephant" earlier. You can't not think about it. Your brain automatically does.

Big Furry Black Spider.

See?

If you try and mentally struggle against any negative emotion it will only make it worse. You have no choice but to surrender. Trust me I have had panic attack after panic attack prove that. Take my word for it you do not want to go through that.

So, what do you do?

Accept your emotional state.

What?

That may seem to be a crazy thing to do but you can do it.

Don't fight with your emotions just let them come. Observe them. Experience them. Learn from them.

Again, this may sound crazy, but you will discover many things about yourself and who you really are.

Ask yourself questions.

What exactly am I feeling right now?

Can I describe the sensation?

Do I feel it in certain parts of my body?

What thoughts are going through my mind?

What am I saying to myself?

Are there any dominant words I keep repeating?

Am I seeing images in my mind's eye?

What are they?

Remember as I have said, YOU ARE NOT YOUR MIND. You are the conscious observer. Remove yourself from your thoughts and emotions. Observe them as if you were watching a movie.

Try to separate yourself from the anxiety as long as possible. At first, you probably can't do this long. Your emotions will take over and put you back in the state of mind you dread.

Keep trying. Every time the negative emotion appears, try to be an impartial observer for as long as you can. This is bringing you back into the present moment. This is keeping you in the NOW. The more you can stay in the NOW the faster your negative emotions will diminish.

You will soon discover each time you do this you can do it longer and longer. You will soon discover you can do it long enough to make the negative emotion lessen. Eventually, you will get to where you can observe until the emotion fades away.

It will come back. But it won't be as strong.

It will come back again. But it will be even weaker.

It will come back again. It will be even weaker still.

The neuron cluster in your brain is getting smaller and smaller. You are ridding yourself of your negative emotions. Soon it will be just an annoying little passing thought.

It's like watching a scary movie. The first time you watch it, you may not even be able to finish the movie. The second time you watch it, you may get through the movie, but it will leave you with an uneasy feeling for the rest of the day. The third time you watch it you will get through it, but it doesn't bother you after you finish watching it. The more you watch it the less impact the movie will have on you. Eventually, you will get to where you think there is that boring old movie. You could easily sit down and watch the movie and not have any huge emotional reaction like you had the first time you watched it.

The exact same thing happens when you "watch" your negative emotions. The neuron cluster becomes small and insignificant. The emotions lose their control over you. You are free!

Even more, than being free you now have a newfound strength. You have overcome what you once thought was an insurmountable obstacle. You realize this was a learning process, one which you desperately needed. You are going through a needed change. That is empowering.

It gets even better. You experienced what it was like to take a negative brain cluster and disintegrate it down to nothing. But now you know beyond a doubt you can do the opposite. You can start from nothing and create a positive brain cluster. What can you create the brain cluster to do? Make you and your world into anything your heart desires. You are limited only by your imagination.

The more you face your emotions the better you will get at it, the faster you can shut unwanted emotions down. When your imagination takes over and you begin to worry about an imagined future, you can stop the worry. Instead of tossing and turning in bed at night you will see you don't have to indulge your mind. That is a blessing.

Later we will discuss how society has a huge influence over that crazy mind of yours but for now, time to go to lesson five.

LESSON FIVE

YOUR SUBCONSCIOUS MIND AND DAYDREAMING

The human brain learns both consciously and unconsciously. This means you have different kinds of memories. You have explicit memories which are conscious memories you can recall. You also have implicit memories which are unconscious memories you cannot bring to mind but they still influence your behavior.

Amnesia studies have taught us a lot about how we learn.

There are two types of amnesia, retrograde amnesia where old memories are forgotten and anterograde where the person with amnesia remembers nothing new. They can be introduced to a person, the person can leave the room and come back, and they must be introduced again.

I want you to do an experiment.

Draw a large star on a sheet of paper. Now go to a mirror. Lay the paper flat in front of you. Look at the star through the mirror. Now, only looking at the star in the mirror try and trace the star with your finger on the sheet of paper. Important, we are not tracing the reflection. You are trying to trace the actual star on the actual sheet of paper but use the reflection.

It will be a lot harder than you think. You will get better if you practice.

Many anterograde amnesia patients can also get better and better at something the more they practice. They can't remember names and faces but they can learn to become better at something by daily practice. The learning is unconscious.

The amnesia patient will have no recall of practicing. They will need a task explained to them daily, yet they will be improving even though they don't know they are practicing.

What does this mean for you?

This finite, conscious mind you have will only play a minor role in your learning. You can put any insecurities aside, because the part of your mind that may be making you apprehensive, or insecure, is of little consequence. It may feel insecure and question what it doesn't understand, but trust us your subconscious mind knows nothing of insecurity or doubt.

Remember the iceberg analogy?

The mind is like an iceberg. Only a small portion of the iceberg is visible above the water. This is the conscious mind. Most of the iceberg (sometimes well over 90%) is submerged below the water. This is our subconscious mind. The subconscious mind has so much more responsibility than our conscious mind. It controls our heart rate, our breathing, and just about every bodily function needed to keep us alive. The subconscious mind holds our memories and emotions. It never forgets a thing.

Imagine the waterline of an iceberg. This is the spot at which the conscious and subconscious meet and communicate. This is where we imagine and dream. Imagination is one of the best ways to communicate with our subconscious mind. We tell our subconscious mind what we want through what we imagine. The stronger our imagination, the more vividly we see the images in our mind and the stronger the emotions we feel, the more contact we have with our subconscious.

IMPORTANT: Don't forget communication between the conscious and subconscious is two way. Our subconscious sends information to our conscious, most of the time we just aren't aware of it. We need to learn to listen to our subconscious. Our conscious mind has its best contact with the subconscious mind when dreaming.

Intend to remember your dreams. Replay your dreams in your mind and ask yourself what your subconscious is trying to tell you. Fortunately, we can access and listen to our subconscious while we aren't asleep.

Daydreaming!

And they used to tell you daydreaming is bad. Hardly!

Did you know Post-It notes were invented because of a daydream? Did you know Einstein constantly attributed daydreaming to his discoveries? Everyone knows what it is like to daydream. You enter a trance-like state, and you become oblivious to everything going on around you. You are submerged in your thoughts. The good thing about daydreaming (unlike MOST dreaming) is you can consciously choose the topic of communication between your conscious and subconscious mind. You initiate the process by imagining with your conscious mind then your subconscious mind will take over.

Like sleep, daydreaming cannot be forced. The harder you try to make yourself daydream the less the chance you will enter the daydreaming state. You just let it happen. And it will. You have done it so often in the past. So how do you just let it happen?

First, let's go back and talk a little more about the brain. Your brain operates on different frequencies.

When you are awake your brain operates on a frequency between 14-30 Hz. This is known as the Beta state.

When you are asleep your brainwaves are around 1-3 Hz. This is known as the Delta State.

When you are daydreaming you are in the Alpha State (9-13 Hz) or the Theta State (4-8 Hz). The deeper you can go, the slower you can make your brain waves without drifting into the Delta (sleep) state, the more conscious contact you can have with your subconscious.

You have experienced different levels of daydreaming. Sometimes you may be slightly aware of your surroundings (Alpha) while other times you are so lost in thought (Theta) that a little tap on the back startles you back into full consciousness. You can't concentrate on entering a daydreaming state. Concentration will only increase your brain activity, increase your brain waves and keep you in a Beta state of alertness. To get into a daydreaming state start with these steps:

Decide beforehand what your topic of conversation will be with your subconscious. What do you want to daydream about? What images are you already seeing in your mind? Get in a state of homeostasis (balance). Make sure you aren't hungry, go to the bathroom and drink a glass of water.

Find a place where you will not be interrupted. Relax your mind. Take a few deep breaths. Now just concentrate on your breathing, in and out, in and out, in and out. Next concentrate on slowing your breathing. Don't hold your breath. Just take longer inhales and exhales, in... and out..., in... and out..., in... and out...

Now act out, in your mind, the topic of conversation you want to have with your subconscious. For example, let's say you have been wanting to learn to play the piano. To find out what your subconscious has to say about you playing the piano, you might picture yourself playing a song on the piano in front of some of your friends. View it in your mind just like you would a movie. At first, you consciously decide what will happen. What song are you playing? What is the reaction of your friends? What are your friends saying to you and each other? Use your imagination vividly. Put feeling into it. How does playing this song make you feel? The more you use your imagination the easier it will be for you to slip into the daydreaming state (Alpha-Theta, 13 to 4 Hz).

Eventually, your subconscious will take over. It will become like you are watching a movie in your head you have no control over. This is when your subconscious is talking to you. Eventually, you will snap out of the daydreaming state. The reasons could be numerous. Something external distracted you, a thought may have found its way in and disrupted your daydream. Perhaps your conscious mind has said all it wanted to at this time. This is the point where you absolutely MUST, stop and review your daydream. It is fresh in your mind. If you don't review your daydream NOW, you will forget important details later. It may even be helpful to write down a detailed description of your daydream when you come out of the daydreaming state. After reviewing your daydream ask yourself what your subconscious was trying to tell you. Did anything change from when you consciously had control to when your subconscious took over? Were you playing a different song? Was the reaction of your friends still the same? Did the daydream switch to something completely different than what you initially intended? Did the daydream end with you still playing the piano with your friends or something not even remotely related?

Understand that no one is more qualified to interpret your daydreams than you. Your subconscious mind is telling you something and it has told it to you in a way you are meant to understand. Nobody knows you better than your subconscious. Often, during the day you will slip in and out of a daydream state. When you find yourself coming out of a daydream be sure to take advantage, RIGHT THEN, of the opportunity to learn from your subconscious.

If you find you are having trouble daydreaming the following may help.

This technique can help you get into an alpha/theta state of mind.

Look straight ahead and pick out an object directly in front of you. Make sure it is close enough to you not to be blurry. While you continue to look at the object in front of you also notice another object in your peripheral vision to your left. Staying aware of the two objects notice an object in your peripheral vision to your right. Next, notice an object between you and the first object directly in front of you. You should now be aware of four objects. Finally, notice one last object anywhere in your peripheral vision. You should now be aware of five objects.

You will find the sensation pleasurable. Your eyes will probably glaze over. This is fine. The main point to remember is to stay aware of all five objects. This technique will help you get into a relaxed, calming alpha/theta state. It will help clear all the clutter of your conscious mind and help you communicate with your subconscious mind.

You might also want to consider brainwave entrainment. It is quite simple AND SAFE. Entrainment is the syncing of two vibrating systems. Here we are referring to your brain and an audio recording that simulates the waves your brain produces. Once your brain enters an alpha/theta stage, all the unwanted, crazy noise of your conscious mind fades making it easier for you to communicate with your subconscious mind. Entrainment is most often accomplished by one of two methods - binaural beats or isochronic tones. Binaural beats require the listener to wear headphones. A different tone is heard in each ear. The brain interprets the difference as a pulse or beat. For example, one ear may hear a 200-hertz frequency and the other ear a 210-hertz frequency. The brain interprets this as the difference and hears just a 10-hertz frequency. Isochronic tones turn a tone on and off to simulate the desired frequency.

When contacting your subconscious through daydreaming you need to decide on a goal. Something you have been wanting to accomplish but haven't.

1. Set a specific, measurable goal. For example, let's use learning to play the piano again.

2. Write down your goal. On a sheet of paper, write down your goal. Use the word "WILL". Don't write something like, "I want to learn to play the piano." Want does not have the same conviction as WILL. Put the paper where you will see it multiple times daily.

3. Announce your goal. Tell friends and family you will learn to play the piano this year. This will make you accountable. You will be amazed at what this will do for your

mindset.

4. IMPORTANT: Always remember what you need to know to accomplish your goal is out there and it will come to you sometimes in startling ways. Ways that will make you just have to pause for a minute and just kind of say "WOW!"

5. Every day declare your intention to achieve your goal. Say it out loud.

6. Get excited! You are about to discover incredible things about yourself!

"It's not that I'm so smart, it's just that I stay with problems longer."
–Albert Einstein

This whole lesson can be summed up in three words…

Relax
Imagine
Believe

You will soon see learning how to communicate with your subconscious is so important because it is your subconscious that communicates with Infinite Intelligence.

We have learned a lot about our minds. We have learned how our mind learns and techniques to make our mind more efficient.

In the next lesson, we will start putting what we have learned to use. We will tell you when and how to use the techniques. In the next lesson, we will start learning Calculus. It will be fun.

You need to draw your picture and teach this to someone else but before you do, we need to talk about how ignorant I am. But so are you. Everybody is ignorant.

THE IGNORANCE OF THE HUMAN RACE

Don't be insulted by the word, "ignorant." It just means you don't know something. I am ignorant of many things. You are ignorant of many things. This world would be a much better place if we could all see we are ignorant about so many more things than we think we are.

It is straight forward but very few see it.

We were all taught what to believe and what we were taught is determined by the area in which we were born and raised.

Almost everyone believes what they were taught is correct and any cultural view which goes against what they believe is incorrect.

Cultural traditions, family values, religious beliefs are mostly determined by where you live.

Here is where it gets almost funny. Everyone can look around and see that each culture has its own set of beliefs and values, but most individuals believe they have determined their own beliefs by themselves. They believe they have gained enough information and have done the necessary evaluation. They think the beliefs they hold are because of their choosing, even though they can clearly see they are very similar to the beliefs of the culture they grew up in.

There is the ignorance.

Everyone can see that each culture has its own set of beliefs.

Everyone can see that each culture thinks its beliefs are correct.

Even seeing that, almost everyone still thinks when it comes to conflicting beliefs their culture is correct and the other culture is wrong.

Whether we want to believe it or not we are all by-products of the society we grew up in. There is so much going on in us subconsciously we can never fully break free from our cultural prejudices. If this were not the case, then our neighborhoods would mimic the entire world. Our neighborhoods would be as diverse as the entire world. Visiting a neighbor would be like visiting another country. But we can look around and see that is not the case. Our neighbors are very much like ourselves.

But then some will argue there may be differing beliefs, but someone must be right.

There is no single culture that is the "right" culture. Just like there is no one shoe size. What fits one person will not fit another. What works for one person will not work for another.

This is where we need to learn tolerance. We should all be learning from each other. All cultures have so much they can teach others. It is when the individual thinks their culture is the one "true" way that problems start. We can see the devastating effects of this happening all around us.

We have many cultural biases very good for us.

We have many cultural biases very bad for us.

Our goal should be to keep an open mind and allow ourselves to experience the rich diverseness this world offers.

You need to start paying attention to your internal dialogue. Pay attention to what you are saying to yourself. Then learn to quiet the voices.

QUESTION EVERYTHING!

Look at things from different perspectives. You will soon discover that you have been wrong about so many things. Things you thought were true are not and things you thought were not true are. You will open yourself up to an incredible, magical world you never knew existed. You will open yourself up to a world of unlimited opportunity for YOU.

This is where you can choose a purpose. Something you want to accomplish. Something that excites you and makes you happy. And when you set out to achieve that purpose you will know you have the diversity of the world backing you. You will not be hindered by holding on to a very limited set of beliefs.

You will be amazed by what you accomplish.

We need to discuss how everyone needs to have and live their truth but right now you need to learn some Calculus.

LESSON SIX

LET'S LEARN SOME CALCULUS

Okay. Get ready. We will start with a bang.

I am going to teach you Calculus.

You can do this. You will be amazed. You will probably freak yourself out.

I will teach you how to use things like rats and bunnies and slicky slides to learn Calculus.

The first thing to do is answer the question, "Just what is Calculus?"

The funny thing is if you ask most high school or college students taking Calculus that question, they won't know the answer. I know I didn't. They can tell you how to do the problems, but they don't know the significance of what they are doing.

There are two main ideas in Calculus. The first is differentiation and the second is integration.

We will deal with differentiation.

Differentiation is finding a derivative and a derivative is a rate.

Consider driving in your car. How fast are you driving? The miles per hour is the rate at which you are driving. The rate you are driving is the derivative. Not too complicated a concept is it?

Here is another. When you were a kid and you slid down a slicky slide. The derivative will tell you how fast you were going down the slide.

Okay, repeat this out loud...

Finding a derivative is deriving a rate.

Now picture a huge rat wearing a bright red toboggan with the letter "E" on it driving your car down a road. Why? Because "rate" is "rat" with an "e". And when you take a derivative you are deriving (sounds almost like driving) a rate.

So, the obvious next question is...

Just what does this derivative thing look like and how do you use it to find a rate?

To understand you that first need to know what a function is.

60

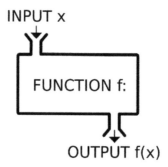

INPUT x

FUNCTION f:

OUTPUT f(x)

Consider a function an input/output machine. You put a number into the function, replace x with a number, and you get an output.

A function looks like this mathematically.

$f(x) = x+1$

You replace x in the function with a number to solve the function.

For example, if you replace x with the number 1 then

$f(1) = 1+1$

$f(1) = 2$

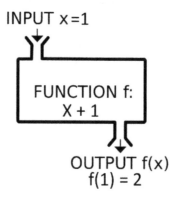

INPUT x =1

FUNCTION f:
X + 1

OUTPUT f(x)
f(1) = 2

Get it? Basic math isn't it?

So what is the answer if you replace x with 2 in the function $f(x) = x+1$?

$f(2) = 2+1$

f(2) = 3

Let's try this function.

f(x) = 2x + 3

Let's get bold and place 4 in this function. Replace the x with 4.

f(4) = 2(4) + 3

This function has a two in front of the x so you multiply whatever you put into x by two. So, 2 times 4 is 8 and then add 3 to get 11 as your answer.

f(4) = 8 + 3

f(4) = 11

Functions can get more difficult but now you know what one is and now I will show you how to use functions.

But before we go on let's remind ourselves we are learning about functions, so we can find a derivative and we know a derivative is a rate of change like driving in a car at a certain mile per hour or sliding down a slicky slide at so many feet per second.

Don't make this hard. Just picture yourself in your car driving down the road or sliding down that slide. If you can picture that then you are doing fine.

Okay, repeat this out loud…

Taking a derivative is finding a rate.

Now let's see how to put functions to use.

To do that you need a Cartesian Coordinate System.

Don't freak out that is just a piece of graph paper with a big plus sign on it.

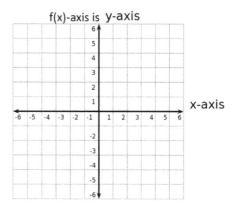

x-axis

The horizontal line is called the x-axis. The vertical line is the y or f(x) axis.

Does the f(x) look familiar?

The cartesian coordinate system is used for plotting points using a function.

Let's do that with the function f(x) = x+2

Let's start with a 1 for x so...

f(1) = 1+2

f(1) = 3

So now we look on the graph on the x line at 1 since we put in a one for x and we see that f(1) or y = 3 so we go to the point where x is 1 and y is 3 which also can be written as (x,y) or in this case (1,3) and we put a point on the graph.

f(x)-axis is y-axis

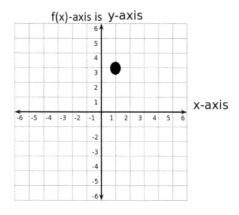

x-axis

Let's do it again with x = 2 for f(x) = x + 2

$f(2) = 2 + 2$

$f(2) = 4$

So x is equal to 2 and y or $f(2) = 4$ also written as (2,4), we add a second point.

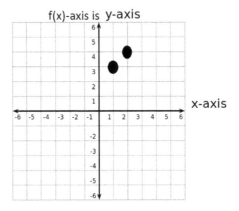

One more time with x = 3.

$f(3) = 3 + 2$

$f(3) = 5$

So x =3 and y or $f(3) = 5$ also written as (3,5), we add a third point.

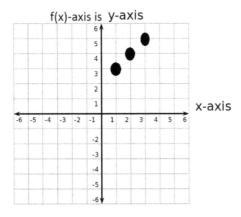

Notice how you can draw a line through the points. This is a graph of the function $f(x) = x+1$

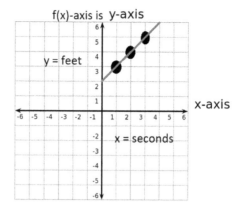

f(x)-axis is y-axis

What does it mean? It could mean a lot of things, but this time let's let x = seconds and y or f(x) = feet.

So now let's say you have a pet rabbit and this graph is showing how your rabbit is hopping.

At 1 second your rabbit is 3 feet away from you. After 2 seconds your rabbit is 4 feet away from you. After 3 seconds your rabbit is 5 feet away from you.

It is easy to see from the graph that after each second passes the rabbit is another foot away from you, so the rabbit is hopping at a rate of 1 foot per second.

What is a derivative?

Taking a derivative is finding a rate.

So did you just find a derivative?

Yes. A derivative is just finding a rate. You haven't had to do Calculus yet, but we are getting there.

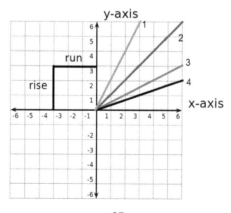

Notice the lines in the figure above have a slope. The slope is how steep the line is.

It is easy to see that line 1 is a lot steeper than the other lines.

Consider a roller coaster. Some roller coasters have very steep slopes. The steeper the slope the faster the coaster goes. Which roller coaster would be scarier to ride, 1,2,3, or 4?

Obviously 1.

Slope can also be defined as rise (going up and down) over run (going left and right) which is a change in y over change in x.

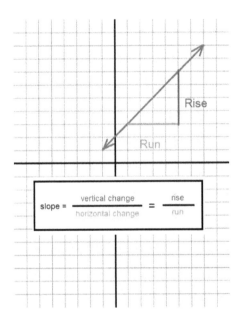

Look back at the picture with the 4 numbered lines.

Line 4 rises 1 y for every 3 x. Its slope is 1/3.

Line 3 rises 1 y for every 2 x. Its slope is 1/2.

Line 2 rises 1 y for every 1 x. Its slope is 1/1 which is 1.

Line 1 rises 2 y for every 1 x. Its slope is 2/1 which is 2.

Line 1 has the largest slope of 2 and line 4 has the smallest slope of 1/3.

Look at the graph and see all the lines are straight.

Now, look at the graph below. How is it different from the rabbit graph we just made?

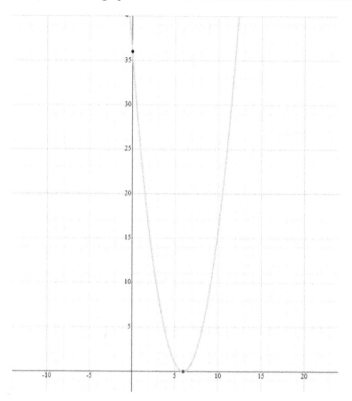

The graph is curved. It is not a straight line.

So what is the slope of the curved line?

You can't tell because it is constantly changing. The rise over run is different on different parts of the curve. Notice the straight-line rabbit graph, the change is the same from every point to point. The 4 line is always up 1 over 3. The 1 line is always up 2 over 1. You can't just have one rise and run with a curve. There are many and it depends on what part of the curve you are talking about.

This is where we use Calculus, specifically differentiation. With straight lines, we use Algebra, but when graphs curve, we use Calculus. Algebra just isn't good enough anymore. Algebra can't handle curves.

How do we start?

Since the curve is always changing you decide what point on the curve you want to find the slope -- how fast the curve is changing. After you pick that point, we are now in full-

67

blown Calculus mode.

Let's start.

Do this. Pick a point on the curve then shrink yourself down so you are so small that the curve looks like a straight line to you or flat. Think of it as the earth. We all know the earth is curved but it looks relatively flat to us because we are so small compared to the earth.

Go ahead and shrink yourself down so small that the curve you are looking at is as big as the earth is to you right now. That way the curve will look flat and you can use Algebra to find the slope or rate of change of the curve.

Okay. Well, since you can't do that we have to do the next best thing and use Calculus to find the derivative of the function of the curve at a point we choose and then determine the slope/rate of change at that point.

Look at the graph below and let's pretend the left side of the curve is a graph of some crazy slicky slide. As you can see it is over 36 feet high and very steep. We will start down the slide at 36 feet in the air. That is like three stories. Picture yourself standing at the top of this slide getting ready to go down it. Can you feel yourself getting nervous? The strong wind blowing your hair. Are you even going to go down the slide? Let's learn a little more about the slide to help you decide.

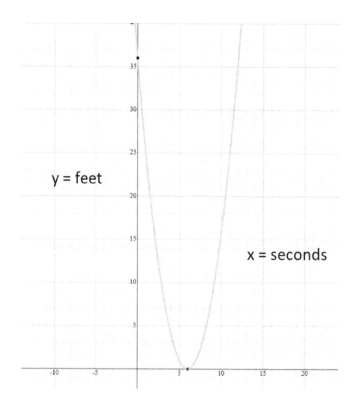

y = feet

x = seconds

The function of the slide is f(x)= x²– 12x + 36.

We want to pick out a spot on that slide at a certain time (x) and see how high we are (y) and how fast we are going. To discover how fast we are going we will take the derivative of the function.

That is a little more complicated than the ones we did earlier, but this is Calculus. You still got this. This is easy.

First, let's make sure you know what an exponent is.

Look back at the function of the slide above. The exponent is the little 2 above the first x in the function. When you see an exponent, it tells you how many times to multiply the number by itself. An exponent is also known as a power. Keep that word in mind you will see it again in a few minutes.

Let's do the following example.

2^3 is 2 x 2 x 2 = 8 - Multiply 3 twos.

3^2 is 3 x 3 = 9 - Multiply 2 threes.

Ok. Let's look at the slicky slide at let's see where we are on the slide after sliding for 2 seconds.

Let's put 2 in the function above.

Don't worry about how we came up with the function. That is a little beyond the scope of this book. But trust me when I say it's not that hard.

Here we go. The function below tells us where we are on the slide at a certain time. So let's see where we are at 2 seconds by plugging a two into the function.

$f(x) = x^2 - 12x + 36$

$f(2) = (2)^2 - 12(2) + 36$

$f(2) = 4 - 24 + 36$

$f(2) = 16$ also the same as $y = 16$

After 2 seconds we are 16 feet high on the slide. Remember we started at about 36 feet.

Now we want to see how fast we are going at that point and to do that we finally take the derivative.

All the notations below tell you a derivative has been taken. All the solutions below are the derivative for $x^2 - 12x + 36$. In a minute you will see how we got the answer $2x - 12$.

derivative of $y = 2x - 12$

y prime $= y' = 2x - 12$

$f'(x) = 2x - 12$

$\frac{dy}{dx} = 2x - 12$

$\frac{d}{dx}(y) = 2x - 12$

$\lim_{\Delta x \to 0} \frac{f(x + \Delta x) - f(x)}{\Delta(x)} = 2x - 12$

You can see many notations tell you to take a derivative. We will use a few of them interchangeably in this class. Just understand they all mean the same thing.

The symbol dy/dx is one of the symbols for taking a derivative so let's take the derivative of our function.

$f(x) = x^2 - 12x + 36$

70

dy/dx =

This says "take the derivative of y with respect to x." To take this derivative we will use the **power rule**. I said you would see the word power again. This is so simple. Remember my ten-year-old niece did this.

$$f(x) = \overset{\text{move}}{x}\,\underset{\substack{\text{decrease} \\ \text{by 1}}}{^n} = nx^{n-1}$$

The Power Rule

$f(x) = x^2 - 12x + 36$

$f'(x) =$

Notice the new notation. This tells you to find "f prime of x." Which also means taking the derivative.

To take the derivative start with the x^2. You take the exponent which is two and multiply it by the number in front of the x.

But wait a minute there is no number in front of the x.

Yes, there is. If you don't see a number, it means the number 1 is there. You could write 1x.

We take the 1 and multiply it by the number 2 (the exponent) then decrease the exponent 2 by 1. Now the exponent is 1. The first part of the derivative is now $2x^1$ which is 2x. Don't forget you don't have to write ones.

Now, look at the -12x. Numbers with just an x after them just lose the x. The second part of the derivative is just -12.

Finally, look at 36. Numbers by themselves with no letter just disappear. So, 36 is gone.

We finally did it.

$f(x) = x^2 - 12x + 36$

dy/dx = 2x - 12

The derivative of the function x^2 -12x +36 is 2x -12.

So now let's see how fast we are going on the slide after 3 seconds. To find this out we replace x with 3 into the derivative.

f'(x) = 2x - 12
f'(3) = 2(3) - 12
f'(3) = 6 - 12
f'(3) = -6

After 3 seconds you are going down the slide at a rate of -6 feet per second.

What? How can you slide negative feet?

All that means in Calculus is you are going down or backward. If the number is positive it means you are going up or forwards. You are going down the slide, so the number is negative.

Okay, let's do one more real quick.

This time let's see how high and fast we are going at 5 seconds on the slide.

First, discover how high you are by going back to the original function and inputting 5.

$f(x) = x^2 - 12x + 36$

$f(5) = (5)^2 - 12(5) + 36$

$f(5) = 25 - 60 + 36$

$f(5) = 1$

At 5 seconds you are now only 1 foot high on the slide.

How fast are you going?

We already took the derivative. So now we plug 5 into it.

Remember the derivative is 2x -12.

f'(x) = 2x - 12
f'(5) = 2(5) - 12
f'(5) = 10 - 12
f'(5) = -2

Remember the answer is negative because you are going down.

At 5 seconds you have slowed down to -2 feet per second.

You can see that makes sense because the slope is getting smaller.

So now that you have all your information do you want to go down the slide? What do you think?

You just did Calculus. You get it don't you? Wasn't too hard, was it?

You just took on the math of math. Calculus! Calculus makes Algebra look like a wimp.

Most things are so much easier than you think they are. Many things which many think are hard are easy if you will just take a little time.

Congratulations you now know more Calculus than probably 90% if not more of the people on the planet. That has to make you feel good about yourself.

Okay. Yes, we did do some very easy Calculus. The math in Calculus can get so hard that only computers can do it. But be assured you now know enough Calculus for this book. You will use your newfound skill for taking derivatives in future classes. It will come in handy when we discuss Quantum Theory.

Okay, now it is time to draw a picture that represents what you have just learned and teach someone else. Again, please do this. It is very important. You will understand why as we get into later lessons.

Next lesson we need to discuss motion and light, but first, let's discuss your truth.

YOURS IS ONE OF MANY TRUTHS

We are all immersed in the culture we grew up in. So much in fact that we are never going to be able to escape its influence.

If you were born in America, you will never really understand Chinese culture. Your brain was just not wired to do so.

The problem comes when we believe our culture is better than another culture or our culture is the correct way of doing things and others are wrong.

We should only look at our way as different. Difference is necessary for this world to thrive. The uniqueness of each culture makes our world a diverse and incredible place to live.

In no area do we see more struggle and conflict because of the differences in culture play out than through religion.

It is the pattern (and there are exceptions) to believe the religion of your culture to be correct.

No one is correct, and everyone is correct. It's a paradox. Sometimes something can be both true and false. We will discuss that more when we learn about Quantum Physics.

It is easy to see why many become lost in believing their religion is "the one and only truth".

Religion immerses them even deeper into their culture.

Consider a church service.

You may go to an incredible structure dedicated to your religion. The building is truly impressive. The intricate, architectural design of the building, the stained-glass windows, the total atmosphere can be awe-inspiring. Surely this is real.

There is artwork in the building. Art created by men and women who threw unbridled passion, commitment and feeling into their work. You see skilled masterpieces created by men and women with incredible talents and perhaps know more than you about what your religion means to the world and how to express that meaning. Surely this is real.

You sing hymns that stir your heart to feelings of indescribable bliss. Those who wrote those lyrics that speak to your heart and brought about those euphoric melodies had to be inspired by something outside themselves. Surely this is real.

You listen to a person speak with passion and power about your religion. You see real emotion. You sometimes experience joy. You sometimes experience sadness. You see the laughter and the tears. Surely this is real.

You are surrounded by a group that believes what you do. You can see you are all feeling the emotion. You are sharing in other's joy. You are sharing in other's sadness. Surely this is real.

It is real.

It is very real.

But it is also real for other cultures experiencing the same thing but in a different way.

Yours is not "the truth". Yours is one of many truths.

We all have access to our higher selves, and we all have the right to interpret our higher selves in any way we want. Just like I have my own unique personality compared to you. My personality reflects my higher self.

We feel and experience our higher self every day, but we limit our higher self when we think this experience can only come through our world view. This is when we see our higher self as separate and not a part of us and as something which chooses one individual over another. But that is impossible. As we will see later in this book, we are all connected. We are all one.

It is a hard concept for many to understand. But when you finally grasp it your world truly does become unlimited.

Think about this for a minute. When surrounded by those of like faith, such as in a church service, this is when your faith is the strongest. Your faith is reinforced by being around many who's beliefs "seem" to match yours. When you are no longer around many who share your beliefs, such as when you are at work your faith is not as strong. If you believe it is, you are fooling yourself. There is strength in numbers.

Now let's go from your work to the mall. Look at all the people with different beliefs than you. No one there believes exactly as you do.

Next, we go to a big sporting event with thousands and thousands of people. Most don't believe what you believe. Most will think what you believe is wrong because it contradicts what they believe and of course we all believe we are correct.

After the game, we fly to a foreign country where a completely different religion than yours dominates the culture. Most don't know what you believe because they haven't taken the time to learn about any other religions besides their own. Because of the culture, they grew up in, your beliefs are very strange to them. Because of the language barrier, they really can't even understand you and your beliefs. You are now a far cry away from the group of like individuals you meet within your small space on planet Earth.

But let's not stop at planet Earth. Our galaxy, The Milky Way, has over a billion suns with planets orbiting them. To say that life could not exist on another one of those billions of planets is to be very closed-minded. Especially when you go out farther into the universe and realize there are billions of galaxies with billions of planets.

We can even go farther. There may also be billions of universes, with billions of galaxies, with billions of planets.

Let's not stop there. There may even be infinite realities that our brains are not aware of on each of the billions of universes with billions of galaxies with billions of planets. Our finite minds can't grasp the concept of infinity.

Does it make sense that an infinite creator would choose one small planet, and on that planet, pick one small nation and say, "These are my chosen people"?

Doesn't it make more sense you are reading the interpretation of Infinite Intelligence by an ancient race that existed thousands of years ago?

To me, these are humbling thoughts. Please just give that some thought.

When you hold to your truth as the one and only truth you are limiting yourself, creating huge blind spots in your ability to perceive. You are keeping yourself from experiencing so many wonders this world offers. Imagine putting yourself in a little box and only allowing yourself to experience the box. You may not be limiting yourself to that degree but compared to the infinite universe you are close. You are living in a black and white universe and have no idea what a rainbow is.

We want to discuss more about truth and how your brain was wired and how that affects what you see as truth but first, you need to read the lesson on the History of Motion.

LESSON 7

THE HISTORY OF MOTION

What is physics?

Physics is the science of matter and energy. Matter is any physical substance you can touch. Energy in physics is the capacity for doing work.

Physics sprung from the desire to understand our world and the universe we live in. Physics tries to help us make sense of things. This is also the purpose of this book, to help you make sense of your life by understanding how this universe you live in works.

Today there are two branches of physics, classical and modern.

Classical physics includes everything physicists discovered before the 1900s also known as Newtonian Physics named after Isaac Newton. Modern physics came about because scientists saw things that Classical Physics said should not be happening.

Modern physics refers to the Theories of Special Relativity developed by Albert Einstein and Quantum Physics developed by many scientists including Einstein and is still being developed today.

Relativity says it doesn't matter where you are the laws of physics are the same for you as for everyone else. If you are on another planet and I am on Earth, physics is the same for both of us. If you are in a rocket ship zooming to the moon and I am sitting in a chair in my house on earth, physics is the same for both of us.

Quantum physics deals with the universe at microscopic levels and it says everything is chunky. The universe consists of bundles of matter and energy. The universe comes in chunks.

This tells us the universe is not deterministic. Deterministic means everything can be determined before it happens. The universe went from being deterministic to statistical. This will not happen, it has a 0% chance, this may happen with a 58% chance, this is happening, 100% chance.

Again, relativity means the laws of physics are the same for everyone no matter where they are. Picture yourself and two friends. Picture yourself standing on the ground. Picture one friend driving past very fast in a car. Picture your other friend zooming even faster over your head in an airplane. Now picture all three of you throwing a ball straight up directly over your heads and catching it as it falls back down into your hand. You all three get the same result. The ball, if thrown directly above your head falls straight back down into your hand.

If some of what we have said seems a little vague right now that is okay. It will make a lot more sense as we go through more lessons.

We will change pace for a minute and talk about motion.

What is moving?

Motion is going from one location to another in time. You drive from home to work or school in a certain amount of time.

Here is a question to think about.

Is it normal for something to be motionless, not moving, at a state of rest or is it normal for something to be constantly moving until something affects it?

Let's answer this question by going over some physics history.

To begin we must start in ancient Greece with three great philosophers. You have probably heard their names – Socrates, Plato, and Aristotle.

Socrates implored us to question everything. He told us, "The wise man is the man who knows that he doesn't know."

Plato, the pupil of Socrates, gave us the Allegory of the Cave. He tells us a story about slaves chained inside a cave and can only see the back wall of the cave. A fire glows behind them and casts shadows on the wall created from the world outside the cave. All the slaves know are the shadows. They have never seen the outside world. To them, the outside world is only dark and shadowy. They do not know its true beauty. This Plato said was the state of most.

Sadly, today almost everyone is still a slave and only sees a world of shadows. Most of the world are chained by their own mind and see no way of escaping the chains even though the key is dangling right in front of their face. This book will help them see the key.

Aristotle, who was a student of Plato, came next. He is considered by many to be one of the first scientists.

He believed the earth and heavens obeyed different laws of physics. (Of course, he wouldn't have used the word physics because the science hadn't been invented yet.)

He believed that the earth was the center of the universe and everything was drawn to the center of the universe. That is why when you drop something it falls to the ground, he reasoned.

He thought everything in the heavens moved in perfect circles. Everything continued in motion and did not come to a state of rest. The sun and planets revolved around the earth in perfect circles.

This was the belief for a thousand years until we entered the age of the Renaissance and Nicholas Copernicus in 1543 said the sun was the center of the universe, not the earth. The earth and planets revolved around the sun. This showed the earth was not special. You can understand why this was not very popular with the church at the time (the church believed the earth to be God's special creation located at the center of the universe) and if found yourself at odds with the church you could find yourself in a dangerous situation.

In the Dark Ages before the Renaissance, the church told everyone what to think and what to believe. Often the church was even more powerful than kings, giving them the power to go to war in the name of the church. Thus, started the Crusades. Millions were tortured and killed because they refused to accept the god of the Christian Bible.

Galileo Galilei was next on the physics scene and unfortunately, he did not escape the wrath of the Church as did Copernicus.

Galileo loved astronomy and he developed the first telescope. Through his telescope, he saw the planet Jupiter and its revolving moons. Here was another "little" universe.

Again, he showed the earth was not special.

It was said Galileo dropped objects off the Leaning Tower of Pisa to show objects fall to earth with the same acceleration, speeding up at the same rate.

Galileo believed an object moving in a straight line at a constant speed without friction will never stop. The natural state of motion is to move in a straight line at a constant speed. It doesn't take a push to get something moving. It takes no force to keep something moving.

This is known as the Law of Inertia. A natural tendency to keep moving at a constant speed. It doesn't seem true to us or is hard to see because of friction. Friction is the resistance that one surface or object encounters when moving over another. For example, you will have more friction trying to move something across a rough concrete floor as opposed to sliding it across ice. A change in motion means a push or pull has occurred.

Galileo believed Copernicus was correct and the planets revolved around the sun. Galileo thought the Bible should not be interpreted literally. He published his book, *Dialogue on the Two Chief World Systems*, and it got him arrested and brought to trial before the Roman Church.

After being told to recant the statements in his book, he was given a tour of the church torture chamber. And his response…

I recant.

You can't blame him. I researched those medieval inquisition torture devices. Warning the next seven paragraphs will get graphic. You can skip them if you like. Just know you would have read some horrendous horror movie stuff.

Okay don't read the next six paragraphs unless you want to, it's bad.

You're still reading. You were warned. This is the first paragraph. So now don't read the next five.

One of the favored torture devices of the Catholic Inquisition was the Judas Cradle, which would literally rip you a new butt hole.

It was a stool with a razor-sharp, pointed pyramid as a seat. The individual was stripped naked and was forced to sit on the seat and the razor, the sharp point of the pyramid would be inserted into their anus or vagina, ripping apart the flesh, blood pouring out of the body.

I told you and it gets worse.

They would also tie ropes to the arms and legs of the victim and slowly pull so the point would creep deeper and deeper inside the person's body resulting in agonizing pain and screams, as flesh and blood fell out of the rectum or vagina to the ground.

They would continue until the pyramid went deep inside the person's body, many times going all the way through, resulting in death by impalement.

After seeing that thing I would have been doing the cross thing over my chest (and I wasn't even Catholic). Forgive me, father, I have sinned. The earth is the center of the universe. The sun and the planets revolve around the earth being pushed by Heaven's angels themselves. Yes, the common belief at one time was all the stars and planets moved because angels were pushing them. Just keep that stool away from my butt. Stool is supposed to come out not go in.

Believe it or not, it wasn't until 1992 under Pope John Paul II that the Catholic Church officially admitted they were wrong.

The next person to take on the physics state was Isaac Newton. He is considered by most to be the greatest physicist who ever lived, even better than Einstein.

Isaac Newton developed the three laws of motion.

1. The Law of Inertia – An object moves in a straight line and constant speed unless acted upon by an outside force.

2. F=ma – Force equals mass times acceleration. This says the bigger the object the harder you need to push it to get it moving.

3. Every action has an equal and opposite reaction. If you push on a wall with a force the wall pushes back with the same force.

This led to the belief in a clockwork universe which as we discussed earlier means everything is deterministic. If it were possible to view everything in the universe you could predict every future event. It was like something wound up the universe and set it off in a very predictable way. Everything that happens is predictable. There is no free will. A higher power became laughable.

We were insignificant. Nothing more than molecules bouncing around for no apparent reason. We were separate from the world we lived in. It was a dog eat dog world and everyone was out for themselves.

Luckily, we have Quantum Physics to save us from that bleak existence. Remember Quantum Physics said everything has a probability of happening. Probability by its very name is not deterministic. You have only a 20% probability of this happening or an 80% probability of that happening. Even if you have a .0001% probability of something happening you can never know for sure until it does or doesn't happen. Although it is likely not to happen.

But we are getting a little ahead of ourselves. Before we discuss Quantum Physics let's learn a little more about Isaac Newton.

You have probably (again with the probability) heard the story Newton sat under an apple tree and an apple fell and hit him on the head and he discovered gravity. There was probably more to it than a falling apple, but Newton discovered the Law of Gravitation.

Most of the time when someone describes gravity, they say what goes up must come down. This is not exactly true. What is happening is every object attracts every other object. The more mass an object has the more the attraction. The closer you are to an object the more the attraction. The force of gravitational attraction depends directly upon the masses of both objects and is inversely proportional to the square of the distance between their centers. To put it in numbers if you double the distance between two objects the gravitational attraction is one-fourth of what it was. At five times the distance the gravitational attraction is only one twenty-fifth the original attraction.

Newton invented Calculus, so he could use the Law of Gravitation to describe the motion of planets. Remember you need Calculus to determine rates of curves.

It is usually the belief that Einstein came up with relativity. Relativity was already known before Einstein came on the scene. Einstein discovered what was to become known as Special Relativity, but it was Newton's Laws of Motion and Gravitation which showed the laws of physics apply everywhere in the universe. There is no special place where the laws will ever differ.

The laws of physics work the same for everyone in uniform motion. Uniform motion is moving at a constant speed in one direction -- no accelerating.

Pretend you are driving in your car holding steady at 80 miles per hour. You have a heavy foot. You have the steering wheel in one hand and your favorite beverage in the other. I know that's not exactly ten and two but who drives that way anyway? My favorite way to drive is resting my left arm on the car door and drive one-handed with my right hand around four. If I am drinking a nice cold Coke Zero my right hand holds the Coke and my left is around eight. But that's beside the point. You are driving and drinking, no alcohol, yet you still hit a huge pothole. Your car is now gyrating and bumping, moving up and down in an uncontrolled manner, jarring you, and your favorite beverage is now all over you, your clothes, and the car. You are no longer in uniform motion. You are no longer moving in a straight line at a constant speed.

I am moving is a meaningless statement. If you are driving a car and see someone standing next to the road it is just as accurate to say the person on the road is moving and you are still. Look as you drive down the road does it not appear as if the road signs and lights and trees and people are moving past you?

Picture yourself on a school bus. Now cover all the windows (hope you have a really good bus driver). As long as the bus moves straight ahead and does not change direction or speed there is no experiment you can do to prove you are moving if you can't see out the windows. Everything you do will be exactly the same as if you were doing it in your house.

To repeat what we said earlier, relativity says it doesn't matter where you are, physics looks the same to you as it does for everyone else. It makes us all equal. There is no special place or state of motion. It doesn't matter where you are. If you are on another planet physics is the same for you as it is for me on Earth. It doesn't matter how you are moving. If you are in a rocket ship zooming to the moon physics is the same for you as it is for me on Earth. Relativity says no place in the entire universe is special.

In the next lesson, we will learn about another part of classical physics called electromagnetism. It was because of a very unique property of electromagnetism that Einstein developed his Special Theory of Relativity.

Once again, draw that picture and teach this to someone else. You might also want to read about how your brain was wired.

HOW WAS YOUR BRAIN WIRED?

I left Christianity, but I am not an atheist. So many in the world today think there are only two choices -- religion or atheism. That is so far from the truth. That is a fact you will see by the time you finish this book.

I am more spiritual now than I have ever been my entire life. I freed myself from the dogma of religion. I finally found something that to me rang true.

I found my truth and I wish that for everyone. For when you find and express your truth you are no longer concerned about the opinions of others. You understand they are seeing you as a reflection of their world. What they think and say about you is not a reflection of you. It reflects them. They see you through the eyes of their past experiences. They are seeing you through who they are.

It may seem in this book I am singling out Christians. This is a book with a lot of science so let's bring scientists into our discussion.

Most scientists are a byproduct of the education system. They attend classes and are told what to think. Then they memorize what they are told to think and regurgitate it back on to an exam paper. It's a process they repeat over and over again for years and years.

There has always been a struggle between science and religion. But if you think about it, scientists have a lot in common with a Christian, Jew, Muslim, etc.

They all have a building they go to and learn what they believe -- a church, a temple, a classroom at a university, etc.

They all have their sacred books -- Bible, Koran, approved textbooks, etc.

They are told what to think by a higher power -- God, Pastor, Professor, Older Peers, etc.

Think about it. A young mind attending college is just like a young mind going to church. They are both told what they need to think. It one case it is to achieve eternal salvation, in another case it is to achieve a passing grade.

Professors have a lot of influence over their students. Most students would never question a professor just like most Christians won't question the Bible. Students often come to revere their professors to such a high degree to at least in the students' minds the professor is infallible when it comes to his or her branch of study. When many students graduate with a degree, they become not a free-thinking, individual mind but a carbon copy of their professor's thoughts and beliefs. After all, that is what they had to do to pass their class, regurgitate back what their professor told them was true. To question something the professor said was true and not answer like the professor wanted could result in failure.

We usually link fundamentalism with religion, but schools, colleges, universities also create fundamentalists. Strict adherence to one's beliefs with an unwillingness to even consider alternatives can be seen on both sides. As you will see later in the book many scientists adhere to Darwin's Origin of Species as Christians do to the Bible. The Origin of Species is the infallible word of Darwin and to contradict it is blasphemy. I'm not joking. Wait and see.

We must be constantly willing to question everything for that is a necessity for change and change is a necessity for growth. Failure to question who we are and what we believe can only lead to stagnation and that is a very dangerous road to travel.

We discussed in the first lesson that your belief helps determine how well you can learn something new. The stronger your belief the faster your brain makes dendrite connections and forms neural clusters.

But remember back to the beginning of lesson one we said brain processes -- knowledge, skills, talents, memories, beliefs – are dendrites in action. Our beliefs are determined by our brain's neural connections made from past experiences. We have past neural connections determining future neural connections. Can you see a problem with that? Your future is nothing more than a repeat of your past.

To make it even worst, as we have mentioned, many of our beliefs are not our own. Most of our beliefs were given to us by our family and culture. Until we are about seven our minds soak up so much information without using a filter to determine what is right and wrong. Our brain is programmed by our environment.

We trusted our parents. We saw our parents as the protectors they were. We, therefore, believed everything our parents told us was true. Most of the time our parents believed what they were telling us was true. They were not purposely passing along misinformation. They were also taught it to be true. But that doesn't mean it wasn't in error and a deterrent which keeps us from living the life we want to live.

We did not get to choose the environment we were born into, but our values and beliefs are almost completely determined by the society we grew up in.

The world which came before us has determined what we believe today.

We are also programming ourselves with beliefs (many of which are harmful) and don't even know it.

How do we do this? Here come some very important statements, never forget them.

We all engage in self-talk. We are constantly talking to ourselves all day long. Self-talk is one of the fastest ways we grow neural connections.

For most self-talk is very negative. You need to understand for every negative statement you say to yourself you are increasing a negative neural connection in your brain.

When you tell yourself you can't do something you are increasing a neuron cluster in your brain. As long as that cluster is present you really can't see any way to do it, and you won't until you decrease the cluster and develop a neural connection which tells your brain you can. After developing the "you can" cluster your brain will show you many things you were once blind to.

How do you make the change from negative to positive?

When you find yourself saying negative things in your head, STOP IT. Immediately think of something positive to say. You will be surprised at how fast the negative cluster shrinks and the positive cluster grows.

We need to examine ourselves. We need to ask questions.

I'm going to ask you a couple of questions and I want you to be very honest with yourself. Do your beliefs come from contemplating the same information over and over among those who believe as you do? Do you ever put yourself in situations where your beliefs are put to the test?

Do you ever just think about and question your beliefs? Have you ever considered even if for the briefest of moments if you may be wrong or mistaken?

We need to see that many of the "truths" we hold are false. This can be a very painful process. Especially if we have held those "truths" for a long time. Those "truths" have become a part of us.

Did you know your senses bombard your brain with so much data at any one time (about 10 million bits of information per second), to maintain your sanity, you only process a very small fraction of the incoming data (about 40 bits per second)? What your brain accesses is dictated by filters that are combinations of your values and beliefs and your memories.

To take it a step farther your memories are so influenced by your values and beliefs that many memories you hold in your head are inaccurate. Yes, you heard me right. Consider those memories you have zipping around on those neural connections in your head of past events, you are not "seeing" a lot as they happened.

If you compared your memories to actual videos of the real events, you would find yourself in a state of shock. We don't see things the way they are, we see things the way WE are.

Memories are also changing. Not only do memories fade in time but your brain can completely re-write memories to be very different not only from the actual event but your original memory of the event. For example, think of a special event that happened a year ago, the memory you have now may not be the same as what happened and you may remember the event different five years from now than you remember it today. A memory is not just stored in just one section of your brain. When you relive a memory in your mind your brain is pulling from many areas to reprocess the memory.

We all respond to the world we have created with our brains. Therefore, other's worlds rarely make sense to us. We need to be careful when criticizing the beliefs of others.

Defining ourselves and not letting ourselves be defined by others is one of the most difficult challenges we face. Until we are true to ourselves, we are never living. Too often we remain in a comfort zone and deny ourselves and the world our full potential.

Humanity is still a newborn baby in the universe. To think we are even close to knowing "it all" is beyond arrogance... beyond foolishness.

We cannot grow unless we begin a journey of self-discovery. Once you begin that journey you will be amazed. Things you thought were impossible will become possible. Things you thought did not exist will appear right in front of your very eyes.

SIMPLE CHANGE: Write down 5 things you once believed you now know are not true. Now here is where you need to be very honest with yourself. Write down 5 things you are not sure whether they are true or not. Now try and discover for sure.

We need to talk about God but first, read the lesson on electromagnetism. That may get us closer to God than many ever realize.

LESSON EIGHT

ELECTROMAGNETISM

What is electromagnetism?

Electromagnetism is the interaction of electric currents or fields and magnetic fields.

Don't worry if you don't quite understand that yet. You will after this lesson.

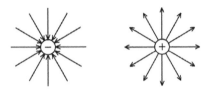

What do you think of when you hear the word "electricity"?

Is it that stuff that flows through the wires in our house to keep our lights on and electronics running? Is it that stuff that if you touch might shock you and kill you?

Yes, but there is more to it than that.

Electricity comes in two charges positive and negative.

Like charges repel. Opposite charges attract. Two positive or two negative charges will repel. A positive and negative charge will attract.

Magnetism is like electricity. Magnets have two poles a north pole and a south pole. The same poles will repel each other, and opposite poles attract.

What we have said so far may be a little bit miss leading. There is a magnetic field that surrounds magnetic objects. It is the field doing the attracting or repelling. The stronger the field the stronger the attraction or repulsion. Many factors can affect the field strength of a magnet including the size of the magnet, heat, radiation and electric current to name a few.

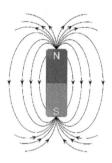

The magnetic field lines of a simple magnet are shown in the picture above. They point from the north pole to the south pole. However, the magnetic field lines do not just end at the tip of the magnet. They go right through it so that inside the magnet the magnetic field points from the south pole to the north.

You can place iron filings around a magnet and as you see in the picture above, they will take the shape of the magnetic field. Get a magnet and try it. It is pretty cool.

Look at the picture above. The Earth itself is a magnet and has a magnetic field. The Earth's magnetic field is believed to be generated by electric currents in its core created by heat escaping from the core. The Earth's north pole is its magnetic south pole and vice versa.

The Earth's magnetic field should not be confused with its gravitational field. There is also a gravitational field of force that surrounds the Earth. A gravitational field is the region of space surrounding a body in which another body experiences a force of gravitational attraction. The gravitational field pulls objects like the moon to the Earth. It is not the Earth itself that does the pulling.

There is a relationship between electricity and magnetism. When you hold a magnet, it is the electric charges moving in the atoms that make it magnetic. You can make electricity by moving a magnet. If you shake a magnet it changes its magnetic field and that creates an electric field.

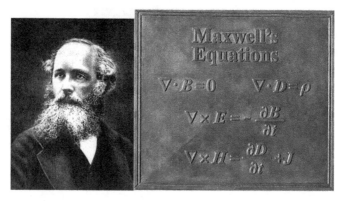

It is now time to introduce James Clerk Maxwell. He developed four equations that cover everything needed to know about magnetism and electricity. We will not go into detail on the equations.

In 1860 Maxwell introduced the world to electromagnetism. His basic thought was if changing magnetic fields creates electric fields then we should be able to change electric fields and make magnetic fields. He was correct and that led to the discovery of electromagnetic waves.

Electromagnetic waves are waves of electricity changing to magnetism, then magnetism changing to electricity, then electricity changing to magnetism, then magnetism changing to electricity and so on and so on...

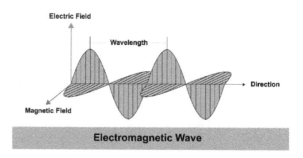

This changing of magnetism and electricity moves on its own through space as a wave of electromagnetic energy. It is self-propagating meaning it doesn't need a medium to move through like a water wave needs water or a sound wave needs air. It's out there on its own.

Maxwell not only predicted electromagnetic waves but also predicted how fast they move through space. Maxwell used his equations we mentioned earlier to show an electromagnetic wave's speed is 299,792,458 meters per second (it can go around the earth 7.5 times in one second) which is 670,616,629 miles per hour. That was the speed of light. Light is an electromagnetic wave.

This bears repeating. Maxwell determined that electromagnetic waves moved at the speed of light therefore light was an electromagnetic wave. That was huge. Do whatever you have to do to never forget that light is an electromagnetic wave! Light being an electromagnetic wave is the foundation of our universe. Paint "light = electromagnetic wave" on a wall in your house (not really, unless you really want to.) Just never, never, never forget that. Not only is that important in this book, but it is also so very important in your life.

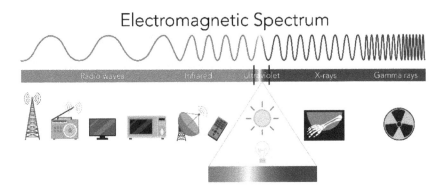

Maxwell's equations also showed there are other forms of electromagnetic waves besides light. There are radio waves, microwaves, infrared waves, ultraviolet rays, x-rays, and gamma rays. The waves differ by their frequency which is how rapidly they vibrate. We will talk A LOT more about waves in later lessons.

Remember in lesson four when we said your heart produces electromagnetic waves created by your emotions. How much better now can you visualize that?

It's kind of strange when you think about it, isn't it? Your heart is sending out alternating magnetic and electric waves and so is your brain. Soon you will learn how to create the electromagnetic waves necessary to create your world.

We will stop here. This lesson is a little short but so important. I want you to grasp everything we have just said. We want those dendrites to be clustering. The information in this lesson is life-changing.

Draw your picture and teach someone else. Make sure you see your picture many times a day.

Get ready! Next lesson we cover Einstein's Theory of Relativity but first let's talk about God.

LET'S TALK ABOUT GOD

When I left Christianity, everyone thought I was an atheist. Hardly!

I now have an understanding of God that enriches my life way better than God described in the Bible.

I say understanding but the paradox is God is unknowable. God is not describable. Our finite mind is not capable of grasping the infinity that is God. I don't like to use the word "God" because it brings up pictures of an actual being separate from us. God is not some old man in the sky looking down upon us and judging us.

In the Bible, God chose one little warring, barbaric nation to be His chosen people. But that is impossible since we are all God; God is in all of us.

Infinite Intelligence, Our Source, The Universe, Love, Pure Energy, All That Is, may be better words to use than God.

God is not just a god of Earth.

God has created infinite worlds. God has created infinite universes. God has created infinite realities. Through God, there are infinite possibilities.

Everything is energy and energy can take any form it wants. Think of your smartphone. It is transforming energy into images you view on the screen. If someone can think of it they can put an image of anything they want on your screen by simply manipulating what you see on your phone through various programs.

What many can't conceive or do not want to believe is there are infinite realities. Don't believe that the reality we live in is the only possibility. If you can think of it, it exists, perhaps not in our reality, but be sure it does in probably many others.

There is nothing Infinite Intelligence can't create. Do you think Infinite Intelligence has limited its creations to just what is possible in our reality? What an ultimate waste that would be. How sad would that be?

Consider computer games. There is nothing we can't create in a computer game. We can create worlds vastly different from our own. If we can conceive it then we can make it happen in a computer game.

94

Infinite Intelligence also creates whatever it wants and that is way more than just our one, minuscule, finite reality we live in.

It's amazing so many scientists are only willing to accept our reality as the only reality. Especially since they know electromagnetic waves are infinite and we can only see a very small finite part of those waves. Why in the world would they think infinity can be explained only by what we experience?

We only "experience" about 5% of our universe. The other 95% is made of dark matter and dark energy of which scientists are clueless. We know the three particles which make everything in our known universe. They are the electron, up quark, and down quark. However, there are many more particles, as for what they do, again scientists are clueless. When we discuss Special Relativity, we will see time my be an illusion. When we discuss Quantum Physics we will see that once something gets so small, we can't know everything about it.

There has been a long debate between science and religion over how our universe was created. It appears as if both sides are lacking.

Would an all-powerful God even limit itself to one creation? Then come up with just one, single plan and reveal that plan to one, single race to be passed down through a book which is the end all be all of everything. As I said earlier what a waste and how sad would that be?

In many ways, the Bible trivializes God. God is given all our human emotions and deals with them as we would good or bad. God does not become angry or vengeful. God does not become jealous or demand justice. God doesn't order the death of babies and children or the genocide of nations. God is so beyond anything that we can experience in our reality. God doesn't have senses like us. To see, hear, touch, taste, and smell are just an infinitesimally weak way of knowing reality compared to God. Even love. Love, as we can just barely grasp and understand it as humans, is just a four-letter meaningless word on a page compared to "love" as God would experience it. And even experience is an improper word. Can you see how we can't describe or even understand God?

Man cannot be created in the image of God. Man creates God in his image. In the west, we have a culture that has predominately been monarchial. Kings and emperors have ruled through the centuries. Therefore, it makes perfect sense we would create the god of the Bible to be the King of Kings and Lord of Lords to rule over and judge everything just like an earthly king. To be the ultimate authority.

Think about it. Every religion's concept of God is a god that reflects the values of the culture in which the religion began. This is why you see two Gods in the Bible. The vengeful god of the Old Testaments reflects a warring Hebrew nation while the god of the New Testament reflects a more peaceful loving god during more peaceful times. God can only expand the mind, values, and beliefs of a culture. God could never lower itself to the level of finite minds.

One little moment can never reveal God. We can only see a speck or a grain of God.

God will never cast you aside and punish or torture you for a mistake that is only a blip in eternity. One of the best days of my life was the day I realized I didn't have to wait until I died to discover if I was a good person or not.

God will love you and grow with you as you expand into endless realities for all eternity.

Speaking of eternity. It's time to learn about Einstein's Special Theory of Relativity. It may have a few things to show us about eternity.

THE SPECIAL THEORY OF RELATIVITY I

In 1905 Albert Einstein published four papers while working in a Swiss Patent office. He was only 26 years old. *On the Electrodynamics of Moving Bodies* was the name of his paper on Special Relativity. Electrodynamics refers to electromagnetism we discussed in the last lesson.

Einstein asked, "In what frame of reference is electromagnetism valid?" We learned in lesson 7 that motion is valid in any frame of reference but what about electromagnetism? Are the electromagnetic waves the same no matter where you are?

The answer is yes and that is Special Relativity.

Relativity says all laws of physics are the same for all observers in uniform motion. As we discussed in lesson 7 uniform motion is moving in one direction at a constant speed. You can do physics anywhere you want and get the same results including electrodynamics.

This led to some very strange consequences, especially for space and time.

Knowing that electromagnetism was valid for any observer moving in a uniform frame of reference and that the speed of light was 670,616,529 mph, Einstein, forever changed our concept of space and time.

For future reference, the speed of light is also known as c.

Therefore, if electromagnetism is valid for any uniformly moving frame of reference then c must be measured at 670,616,529 mph by everyone. Can you see where this is going? You will.

The speed of light is measured the same for everyone even if they are moving relative to each other.

What does it mean to be moving relative to each other? If I am driving my car and I pass you standing on the road we are moving relative to each other. Remember, driving in my car I can just as easily say you are moving relative to me as I am moving relative to you. If I drive by you at 60 mph it is just as correct for me to say I saw you moving at 60 mph as it is for you to say you saw me moving at 60 mph.

Let's say after driving past you I continue in my car heading north at 60 mph and another car driving south passes me also driving 60 mph. I will see that car moving at 120 mph (60mph + 60 mph). We add our speeds. When the other car passes you since you are standing on the road (0 mph) you will see it pass at 60 mph (60 mph + 0 mph).

Now here is where it gets strange. If instead of a car I pass a beam of light coming towards me and measure the light, I will measure the light moving at 670,616,529 mph. Unlike when a car comes towards me, I don't get a measurement of our speeds added together 670,616,529 mph + 60 mph.

Then when the speed of light passes you, you also measure 670,616,529 mph.

What?!?

It doesn't matter your speed you will always measure the speed of light moving at 670,616,529 mph.

Let's make it even more dramatic.

If you are standing on the road and measure a beam of light coming towards you the light will be coming at you at 670,616,529 mph. If I am in a spaceship zooming away at half the speed of light it is still coming at me at 670,616,529 mph. The light is catching up with me zooming away from it in the spaceship just as fast as it is catching up with you standing still.

Think about how crazy that is?

Here is another example. If you are playing tag you will obviously catch someone standing still before you catch someone running. But light doesn't work that way. Light will catch them both equally.

Woah!

No matter what we are doing we all get the same value for the speed of light.

Now let's see what all this crazy light stuff means for space and time.

First, you need to know what an event is. An event needs to have a time and a location. For example, your birth is an event. You were born at a specific location and time. Just a date, for example, October 18, 1972, is not an event. You need a location to go along with it.

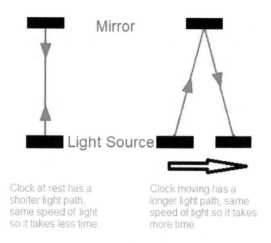

Mirror

Light Source

Clock at rest has a
shorter light path,
same speed of light
so it takes less time.

Clock moving has a
longer light path, same
speed of light so it takes
more time.

Look at the image above. It represents a light clock. A light clock is a box with a light source at one end and a mirror at the other. Light leaves the source and reflects off the mirror and returns to the source. This gives us two events, the light leaving and the light returning to the source. This makes a clock. We want to know how long the time is between the two events. How long it takes the light to go up and reflect down to the source.

We will start in a frame of reference where the light clock is at rest, not moving. We know the light goes up and back. So, we know the distance the light travels is twice the length of the box.

But not let's say you are in a car with the light clock and you are driving down the road. You see the light clocking moving straight up and down. You drive past your friend and your friend sees your car and the light clock moving to the right. Now because the light clock is moving to the right your friend sees light is moving diagonally when it hits the top and diagonally when it returns to the bottom. Because the path is diagonal this makes the light path longer. But remember light always moves at the same speed. So, if light is moving at the same speed it must take more time to take a longer path than a shorter path. Just like if you are driving 60 miles an hour it will take you longer to drive 60 miles than 30 miles.

This means the time in the two events is different. Time is moving slower for the person driving in the car. Let's say the light moves up and down in one second. This means for the person in the car a second lasts longer than for the person standing still. The person in the car is aging slower. Understand this has nothing to do with the clock. The clock is keeping perfect time. It is just being seen from two perspectives.

This is called time dilation. Time was slower or faster depending on your frame of reference. The clock's time depends on your point of view.

Impossible? Nope!

What causes time to dilate?

The speed you are moving.

The faster you move the slower time moves relative to another person. This does not mean you feel yourself moving slower. For you everything is normal. It is as it should be. It is all relative.

The reason we don't experience time dilation is that we move too slow. You have to move at speeds close to the speed of light to notice any effect. Since the speed of light is 670,616,529 mph and the fastest most of us move in a day may be 60 to 70 mph in our car (some of us a little faster) we are nowhere moving close to the speed of light and experiencing minuscule unnoticeable time dilation.

Okay. Have we blown your mind enough today? Are your dendrites firing like crazy? What you learned today is nothing compared to our next lesson. What if we told you time travel is possible?

We know this lesson can get confusing.

Before tomorrow draw your picture and teach someone this lesson but first, you need to stop playing the game. What does that mean? Read on and see.

STOP PLAYING THE GAME

You are playing a game with the entire world. Sometimes it can be enjoyable and fun, but most of the time it's hard and complicated. Sometimes it can just be sadistic and cruel.

Your ego loves playing the game. It loves comparing itself to others to see who is winning. To see who has the most money. To see who has the most power. To see who is the best. To see who is happier. To see who is making the most out of their life.

Every person you meet your ego is sizing them up. Deciding who is ahead in the game. But here is the catch. We may make the comparisons, but we constantly feel we are losing. We know there is something out there we don't have. We may not even know what it is. We just have that empty feeling that tells us it is missing.

Guess what? That empty feeling will not go away. If we look out into the world to fill the void, the empty space may get bigger and bigger. We are chasing something we can never catch. We are playing a game in which there can be no winner.

Yet we keep playing the game and sometimes the game flies completely out of our control. Your mind has over 50,000 thoughts a day. Are you going to tell me you are in control of all those thoughts? Do you even know what those thoughts are? Most are repetitive and useless. The same thoughts you have over and over every day but accomplish nothing. Most just bring worry and misery.

Even though you aren't consciously aware of all the thoughts you know they are there. You can feel them. That underlying current of unease is in all of us. Sometimes we feel it more intensely. Sometimes in moments of intense anger or grief, it can overwhelm us. But even in moments of relative peace, we can still feel it lurking in the background.

The game keeps us searching, comparing and fighting for relief but there is none. Perhaps brief flashes of liberation, but they are always fleeting.

So, is there anything we can do? Yes! Quit playing the game. Surrender. Just give up. Decide you will not play the game anymore.

Don't get me wrong. I am not saying give up on life. I am saying end the game. Now watch what happens in your life. Turn your life over to your higher self. Trust in the part of you that is infinite. A part of you that, believe it or not, is omnipotent - all-knowing.

101

Why in the world would you want to limit yourself to your finite mind? A mind so cluttered and full of lies and deceit it really can't even see the world for what it truly is. Accept that you are more than this jumbled mess of thoughts and emotions, walking sometimes aimlessly in a trap of flesh and bone. Realize that you can access infinite possibilities. Understand there is no need for competition because everyone has this ability. Everyone is pure unlimited potential. You can coordinate the universe so precise anything you desire is possible.

How? Embrace the unknown and uncertainty. Know that everything you could ever want is yours for the taking. Just don't get caught up in the "how" and "why" anymore. Find the joy in yourself. What makes you feel good? Let that feeling guide you. If you are having fun in what you are doing, everything else will take care of itself. But most won't believe it. Most will just continue playing the game. For them, the struggle will never end. Sad. Stop playing the game.

We will show you how to stop playing the game. But our discussion must first go to a dark place to get to a lighter place.

Did you know you are possessed? We are all possessed. No, we are not talking about demons and exorcisms, but the consequences may be just as bad.

POSSESSED BY YOUR MIND

If you asked someone in today's day and age if they believed in demon possession, they would think you were out of your mind. But in a sense, we are all possessed, and it is by our mind.

Did you know you have over 50,000 thoughts a day? Do you have conscience control of all those thoughts? Then what does? Can you observe your thoughts? Doesn't the act of observation imply two, an observer and that being observed?

Our mind feeds on worry and misery. Our mind feeds on the past and an imagined future. Our mind loves conflict and turmoil. It wants to be at odds, fighting against everything going on in its world. It is like we are adrift in a little boat in the middle of the ocean and our mind is a hurricane, a raging storm that just won't stop.

But we can stop the mind. We can learn to silence our minds. We can learn to calm the raging storm and still the ocean and that is when we learn who we really are and all that we are capable of.

Sadly, so many are so possessed by their mind they cannot calm the storm. They have never discovered the peace of silencing the mind. Their days are spent in constant conflict and constant struggle with their mind.

The worry and fear eat at them minute after minute. They think there is no relief. Sleepless nights and agonizing days are their prisons.

We can free ourselves from the prison. We can free ourselves from the mind, even if only temporarily.

Perhaps in this life, we can't fully exorcise that "mind demon" that is in all of us. But we can take away a lot of its strength and power. We can escape from it and enter a place of peace of mind, a place where we just know that everything will be okay. It's almost unexplainable unless you have been there.

Unfortunately, many have never been there. Their mind has them trapped. All they can do is worry, fret, and complain. To them, the world is a place of fear, a place where everyone and everything is conspiring against them. Their life is a constant nightmare and there is no waking.

They are truly possessed.

I have shown you ways to free yourself from your mind and I am going to show you many more. Until then continue your discovery of Special Relativity.

LESSON TEN

LESSON TEN

THE SPECIAL THEORY OF RELATIVITY II

You can no longer say one event happens before or after another.

The laws of physics are the same for everyone no matter where they are and as long as they are in uniform motion. The speed of light is c in all reference frames. Everyone will measure time as c if they are moving in a straight line at a constant speed. As we showed this changes how we experience time in different frames of reference. This is time dilation.

You can no longer say one event happens before or after another. Time does not move in one linear direction. If I am experiencing one time and you are experiencing another, and we are both correct then there can be no set past or future. Only this moment. Only events. Only NOW. Have you ever experienced any other moment than Now? No, you have not.

We talked about events having a time and a place. Events can be experienced in a different order by different individuals. We will discuss this later. Think of the NOW as a library. Think of each book in the library as an event. If you are in the library (NOW) you can go to any book you want. It doesn't matter when the event of the book takes place. But we can go farther. Each book will also have its own events. You don't have to read the book linearly from front to back. You can skip to any page you want. Read the end before you even know what happens at the beginning. We are going to come back to this library analogy many times in this book.

As we discussed in the last lesson the faster you move the slower time elapses for you, but you need to be traveling at very fast speeds, like the speed of light (670,616,529 mph) to notice anything.

Time dilation has been proven to be a fact and one of the first experiments to prove it involved Muons.

Muons are unstable subatomic particles of the same class as an electron, but with a mass around 200 times greater. Muons make up much of the cosmic radiation reaching the earth's surface.

These particles are radioactive and have a rate at which they decay. Therefore, they can be considered to be a clock. It has been proven because muons move at speeds close to the speed of light, they decay more slowly than at slower speeds. Everything fits perfectly with Einstein's relativity calculations. The muons survive longer (age slower) because they move at fast, crazy speeds close to the speed of light.

Experiments have also been done by using atomic clocks which can measure very short periods. They kept one clock on the ground and flew one around in a very fast airplane. The clock in the plane slowed down when compared to the clock on the ground. Less time passed on the clock on the plane.

Did you know because of relativity time travel is possible?

To understand you first need to know what a light-year is. A light-year is the distance light travels in one year which is about 6 trillion miles. Remember a light-year is a unit of distance, not time. If a star is 10 light-years away from earth it would take us 10 years to get to that star if we were traveling in a spaceship going the speed of light (670,616,529 mph).

Now let's say on Earth we develop the technology to travel at half the speed of light and we travel to that star 10 light-years away. How long will the trip take?

We can figure this out with very simple elementary school math.

Time = Distance/Speed.

We take the distance of 10 light-years (remember a light-year is a unit of distance) and divide it by the speed of .5 the speed of light since we are moving at half (.5) the speed of light. Our calculation gives us a time of 20 years. Which makes perfect sense.

So, you get in the spaceship and fly to a star 10 light-years away at a speed half the speed of light, it will take double the time to get to the star which is 20 years. You make a round trip and that will bring you back to earth in 40 years.

Here is where it gets wild. The forty-year trip is from the view of the people on Earth. However, since you are moving very fast at half the speed of light you will experience time dilation. We won't do the calculations but from Einstein's Special Relativity equations we can determine the time to reach the star from your perspective will be only 17 years, so your round trip will be 34 years. Everyone on Earth will have aged 40 years while you will only have aged 34.

This is often called the twin paradox. Find two twins. Leave one on Earth and send the second twin on the trip into space we just discussed. When the second twin returns to Earth, he will find he is now 6 years younger than his twin. It is like he has traveled 6 years into the future.

But haven't we been saying everything is relative? Couldn't we say the Earth was moving away from the ship at half the speed of light? Yes, we can. So why can't we say the twin on Earth is younger?

This takes us back to motion. Relativity only applies to things in uniform motion. So, if you speed up, slow down, change directions you are no longer in uniform motion and this is exactly what the twin in the spaceship did when returning home.

The twin on Earth stayed in uniform motion the entire trip the twin in the spaceship did not. Therefore, the twins' age at different rates.

But make it even wilder. Let's say the twin goes to a star 100 light-years away this time traveling at the speed of light. Traveling at the speed of light the trip to the star and back will seem almost instantaneous. When the twin returns to Earth 200 years will have passed on Earth, but he will not have aged. He will get to see what the Earth is like 200 years from the time he left but everyone on Earth he knows will be dead.

Think about this. What if he goes to a star 1000 light-years or 10,000 light-years or even 1,000,000 light-years away? There is no limit to how far he could go into the future. However, he could never go back to the past. Time travel is a one-way trip.

Okay I know we've blown your mind this time and we will keep doing that repeatedly in this book.

Next lesson we will continue discussing Special Relativity. Do you think you can handle it?

Draw that picture. Teach someone. But first, we have mentioned the NOW many times let's take the time to see just what the NOW is.

In the third lesson, you learned you are not your mind or your brain or your thoughts or anything in this physical world. You are the consciousness aware of the thoughts creating your physical world. But your consciousness, while concentrating on this physical world, knows only an infinitesimal spec of reality and the role you play in it.

We can't grasp who we really are, but we will see if we can push the limits in this book. It's going to be crazy fun and super beneficially life-changing. Maybe you will be the one to take the insights in this book to the next level. It might be your experience that is the connecting piece to allow us to see that which we have never seen before.

Before I continue, I must mention the information in this section and a couple of others were highly influenced by Eckhart Tolle and his books, *The Power of Now* and *A New Earth.* Anyone who has read his books will see that to be true. And if you have not read his books, I highly suggest you read them, after you finish this book of course.

We have mentioned your thoughts were given to you by your family, friends, and society. You need to make sure you do not create your identity based on those thoughts. You can learn to go beyond your thoughts. As Eckhart Tolle said, "At the heart of new consciousness lies the transcendence of thought, of realizing a dimension within yourself that is infinitely more vast than thought." No longer limit yourself by your thoughts. Once you learn to do that you will discover a peace unlike any you have felt before. It feels good!

Many times a day we connect with our higher self. Often we don't even notice it. Often we are distracted by the endless chatter of our mind and the connection becomes very brief. When you do become aware of the connection you are overcome with a feeling of complete peace. All other thoughts and emotions vanish. It is incredible. This is the Now!

When I was diagnosed with severe anxiety disorder the contrast was so huge I noticed the connection to my higher self every time. It was such a relief to feel the connection. Unfortunately, the feeling didn't last long. When the mind starts to take back over the peaceful feeling fades quickly.

When you discover the peace within you and then feel it fading, this is when you need to remember you are not your mind. You are not your thoughts. Observe your thoughts and try not to judge them. Try to just experience them as an impartial observer. You will soon recognize you are not the thought. You are the observer of the thought. That puts you on a higher level of experience. If you can be diligent you will notice your thoughts and the associated negative emotions your thoughts created within you are losing their control over you, they fade away. The more you observe your thoughts and emotions the longer you will stay connected to your higher self and the longer you will be at peace.

You are bringing yourself into the Now, the present moment which is the place of all your source and power. This is the only place where you can feel the connection with your higher self. When your mind is running wild obsessing and worrying over its repetitive 50,000 plus thoughts about the past and future you are not in the Now. When regretting the past or worrying about an unknown future you are not in the Now. You are relinquishing all control you have over your life. Your goal should be to stay in the Now as long as possible. The longer you stay the greater the benefit. You will notice things just work out for you in your life.

When you are in the Now you cannot experience negative emotions. You can only experience negative emotions when your mind is focusing on the past or the future. Neither of which exist. Einstein's Relativity taught us that. We seem to see a lot of evidence around us for the past and future. But have you ever been to either? Think about it. The only place you have ever been is Now. The only place you will ever find yourself is Now. This is your reality. This is your place of power. This is where you create your Now to be anything you want it to be.

The best thing you can do every day is to start with the thought you are pure energy. The physical world you see around you is an illusion. (We will discuss that more when we get into Quantum Physics.) It is secondary, it is not the real you. Become aware of your breath. When you notice your breath you instantly bring yourself into the present moment, the Now. For a brief moment, your mind stops. Just notice two or three breaths and you are good. The key is to do it often during the day. Notice your breath and bring yourself into the Now.

While in the Now observe your thoughts. Don't try and force yourself to feel a particular emotion. Don't try and force yourself to be happy. Don't try and resist being sad. Just accept the moment as it is. For that is all there is. This present moment is all you have. There is no past. There is no future. You will find your emotions begin to fade away. Your mind will begin quieting. You will find yourself in a state of peace and comfort unlike any you may have felt before.

When you need to make a decision, please never make that decision without first reminding yourself you are pure infinite energy and then go into the Now and quiet your mind. You will find things become so much clearer. You will make an informed decision.

The more you practice becoming aware of your breath, observing your thoughts, and staying in the Now, the more amazing things will happen in your life. Guaranteed!

We are going to discuss more about the Now, but you need to learn more about Special Relativity and how it shows Now is all there is.

108

LESSON ELEVEN

THE SPECIAL THEORY OF RELATIVITY III

Two events that occur at the same time in one frame of reference may not occur at the same time in another frame of reference. Let's say I have two signs, one with the number one and one with the number two. If I hold up sign one and then sign two that is only in my frame of reference. Someone in another frame of reference could see me hold up sign two first and then sign one.

Who is correct?

You might be tempted to say it is me because I held up the signs. But no, we are all correct. Remember there is no special frame of reference. I cannot say I am right and you are wrong. That would be saying the laws of physics are correct in my reference frame and wrong in yours. Remember the laws of physics apply to everyone equally moving in uniform motion.

How can we see events in a different order?

It is because of length contraction. We have seen that the closer you get to moving at the speed of light the slower time moves for you. But not only is time affected, so is space. The closer you travel to the speed of light the shorter things become. This is not because objects are shrinking. All measures of space are changed. It's like time. You notice no shrinkage. Everything is normal for you.

Consider two spaceships moving towards each other at the same speed.

There is no contraction relative to each other so the front and back of the spaceships will meet each other at equal times.

Now let's say the top ship is speeding close to the speed of light. Its length will be contracted. The back of the top ship will meet the front of the bottom ship and later in time...

...the front of the top ship meets the back of the bottom ship. It is not simultaneous like when the ships are moving at the same speed.

Now let's make the bottom ship move at close to the speed of light so it's length contracts. Things change again. The front of the top ship will meet the back of the bottom ship and then later in time...

... the back of the top ship will meet the front of the bottom ship.

The order in which they happen in time is different. There were three different views.

1. Simultaneous
2. Back/front then front/back
3. Front/back then back/front

We have talked a lot about the speed of light now we need to discuss two more facts about light.

Light is information and nothing can move faster than the speed of light. These two facts create what is known as The Elsewhere. Let me give you an example of The Elsewhere.

It takes about 11 minutes for light to reach Mars from Earth. You can get no message (information) to Mars in less than 11 minutes because nothing can move faster than light. There is a time span in which we have no influence. It is the same for Mars to us. There are 22 minutes of no influence. Coming from Mars there are 11 minutes of nothing we can know about the past of Mars and if going from Earth to Mars there are 11 minutes of nothing, we can do to influence anything that might happen on Mars in the future.

These 22 minutes are in The Elsewhere. They are not in the past or future. They are not in the past because they cannot influence events on Earth, and they are not in the future because we can't influence them.

The past is those events that can influence the present moment.

The future is those events we can influence.

We have no influence because nothing can move faster than the speed of light.   To understand why nothing moves faster than the speed of light it will first be helpful to discuss Einstein's most famous equation -- $E=mc^2$.

What is $E=mc^2$?

Energy equals mass times the speed of light squared.

Mass is anything that has matter. Matter is everything you can see and touch. Energy is power derived from the utilization of physical or chemical resources, especially to provide light and heat or to work machines.

$E=mc^2$ says matter is equivalent to energy. Energy and matter are the same.

$E=mc^2$ shows matter and energy can be converted to each other. Notice that matter converts to energy multiplied by the speed of light squared. We already know the speed of light is a huge number. That means a huge amount of energy can be created from just a small amount of matter.

It is often mistakenly believed Einstein created the nuclear bomb with this equation. This is not true. The equation just shows why a nuclear bomb has such a big explosion. A nuclear bomb creates a lot of destructive energy from very little matter. Nuclear bombs get their explosive energy by splitting atoms and creating energy. Think about how small an atom is and how big a nuclear explosion is.

The equation $E=mc^2$ also shows us that nothing can move faster than the speed of light.

We have said energy and matter are the same. Therefore, just like mass, energy has inertia. The faster energy moves its energy increases its inertia which is a tendency to remain unchanged. It becomes harder to accelerate and it would take an infinite amount of energy to accelerate faster than the speed of light.

This lesson may have been a little more difficult. But if you grasped these two points you got it.

1. Two events that occur simultaneously in one frame of reference may not occur simultaneously in another frame of reference.

2. Nothing can move faster than the speed of light. This means the time information can reach you is limited by the speed of light.

Ready to take a break?

In the next lesson, we will be talking about sight but first, we need to talk more about the Now.

WHAT DO YOU REALLY NEED?

Right Now.

There is only Now. Past and future are an illusion created by our minds. Our mind keeps dwelling on the mistakes of the past and worrying about POSSIBLE problems in the future. Stay centered in the Now. The more centered in the Now we become the higher we vibrate and the harder it becomes for negative circumstances to enter.

Stay in the Now. Ask what we really need at this moment. Not a day from now. Not an hour from now. Not even a few minutes from now. And I must admit even with all my future worries, every time I ask that question, I really don't need anything.

So why keep worrying? Troublesome thoughts entered my mind a few days ago. But then I asked myself, "What do I really need now?" And I must be honest and say nothing. Troublesome thoughts entered my mind yesterday. But I again asked myself, "What do I need right now?" Again I needed nothing. Troublesome thoughts entered my mind today. But again I need nothing. Just a few minutes ago the troublesome thoughts arise again. But I concentrate on the Now and ask myself, "What do I really need at this moment?" Again the answer is NOTHING! So will there ever come a time when the answer will be something?

And it makes you wonder if we live in a constant Now with no past or present. Then everything we could ever need has to be with us right NOW, not on its way because that would imply a time frame. Everything has to be here now. It has to be that we just don't see how to get it. It must be there. It has to be.

Isn't it amazing how so many of the things we need arrive at just the opportune moment? Almost like magic or a miracle but it can't be a miracle if it is already there. It must be something in us that has let us see what we need.

We endure an unnecessary struggle. Fighting because we believe in scarcity when right in front of our eyes is a huge pot of gold. We have to come to a point where we say, "Enough is Enough! I'm sick of it and I'm not going to play this pointless, useless, unnecessary game anymore." And when the game ends the world is ours!

If the past and future are relative to everyone, as Einstein taught us in the last few lessons, then the only logical conclusion is there is no past and future, there is only Now. We saw examples of how individuals can experience different points in time. Points in time are infinite. Everyone can differ and no one has a privileged point.

This can only mean that all any of us ever really have is right Now.

Are you content with this moment or are you longing for something to happen in the future to make you the person you were truly meant to be?

The future does not exist. Have you ever done anything in the future? No. Everything you have done has taken place Now.

The more time you spend in the Now, the easier your life becomes. Your mind becomes more aware. You respond better to your environment. You do the things you need to do to make the changes in the Now.

The more time you spend in the Now the more you are connected to your higher self.

Practice staying in the Now. The more you do it the easier it will become. Accept the now as it is this very moment. Ask yourself. "What can I learn from what is happening right Now?"

Go for a walk. Notice each step. Notice all your surroundings. Keep your mind off "past" and "future" thoughts.

The more you do this the easier it will be for you to stay in the Now. The more you stay in the Now during relatively less stressful times, you are storing and building up calm and peace for when you need it. Then when life tries to trip you up you can access your stored-up peace and the situation will become so much easier, the path you need to follow so much clearer.

Here is a mind exercise that will help you stay in the now. Get ready I will teach you how to stop time. Not really, but the next best thing.

We all feel the flow of time but how we feel it depends on our situation. Think of a time when you were painstakingly bored and time seems to drag on at a snail's pace. Now imagine a time when you were having the time of your life and it seemed to be over as soon as it started. Our brains affect how we sense time. A child experiences time slower than an adult. Can you remember taking long drives in the car when you were a child and now they don't seem so long? As we get older time seems to pass faster. Have you ever wondered why?

One explanation is when we are 10 years old one year is 10% of our lives. When we are 50 years old one year is only 2% of our lives.

Another explanation is that because when we are younger our neural connections are not fully developed and fire at a slower rate. This slower firing rate also makes us feel the rate of time as slower.

Let's pretend like time is like a conveyer belt. Like being on a conveyer belt time keeps moving us forward and we need not do a thing. We can stand motionless on a conveyer belt and be moved forward in space. But let's pretend it's moving us forward in time.

But what happens if we step off to the side and are no longer on the conveyer belt of time? In this analogy let's say time stops. Everything and everyone are frozen in a single moment in time. But let's say we are not. We can still move around and see everyone as lifeless mannequins in a department store. But not just people, nothing would be moving. No clocks ticking. No wind blowing. No sound. Can you feel it? Can you feel the stoppage of time? Keep that feeling in mind when you are trying to stay in the NOW.

Imagine the jokes you could play. Can you think of some truly amazingly crazy things you could do if time stopped for everyone except you?

In the next lesson, we are going to discuss your reality. This lesson will forever change how you see things.

LESSON TWELVE

YOUR REALITY

What is this world we live in really like? You may be surprised. What you see and hear is the creation of your brain. Do you remember when we talked about electromagnetic waves and I said that was so important? That is because you create your entire world using electromagnetic waves. We will show you in this lesson.

Since our entire world is made with electromagnetic waves it might be important to come to a consensus on just what a wave is.

A wave is a disturbance and it transfers energy through matter or space. The most obvious example is the ocean. You can see the disturbance made in the water as the waves come crashing to the shore. The disturbance is made by the wind blowing over the surface of the water.

A sound wave is a disturbance caused by energy moving through the air. For example, when someone speaks it creates a wave of energy vibrating through the air from their mouth to your ear. This energy dies down and therefore it is harder to hear what someone is saying the farther away they are from you.

A light wave is energy but unlike sound waves that need air to travel, light can move on its own through space.

To better understand waves, get a piece of rope at least 6 feet long. Grab one end and have a friend grab the other. One of you shake the rope moving your wrist up and down. You will notice waves arching up and down across the rope. This is energy being sent through the rope.

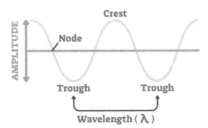

The high points on the rope are the wave crests and the bottom points are the wave troughs. The amplitude is the distance between a crest or trough and the node of the wave. Look at the line running through the middle of the wave. The farther the distance the crest or trough is from the node the larger the amplitude, which means more energy.

The wavelength is the distance from one crest or trough to another crest or trough.

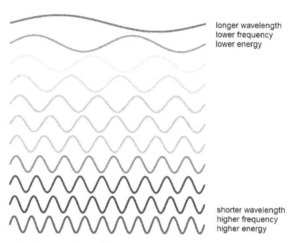

longer wavelength
lower frequency
lower energy

shorter wavelength
higher frequency
higher energy

A wave's frequency is the number of waves that pass a given point in a certain period of time.

The longer the wavelength the lower the frequency and energy. The shorter the wavelength the higher the frequency and energy. Try it with the rope. Shake the rope faster and you will see higher, thinner, faster-moving waves.

Now that we know more about waves, let's see how you hear something.

Anatomy of the ear

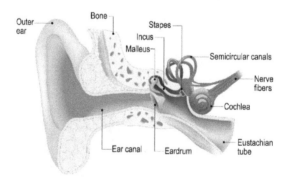

Look at the picture above.

Sound waves enter your ear and go through your ear canal to the eardrum. The waves make your eardrum vibrate and the vibrations are sent to three tiny bones. These bones are named the malleus, incus, and stapes. The bones amplify the sound and send vibrations to the cochlea, which looks like a snail. It is filled with fluid. The vibrations cause the fluid to ripple. This causes hair cells in the cochlea to move. Chemicals then rush into the cells, creating an electric signal. The signal is sent by the auditory nerve to the brain and the brain turns the signal into the sounds you hear.

The entire process is electrical and chemical. You "hear" with your brain.
Almost everyone has heard the question, "If a tree falls in the forest and no one is there to hear it does it make a sound?"

From what you just learned the answer should be obvious. Do you know what it is?

The answer is...

NO!

If a tree falls in the forest it produces sound waves but if there is no ear and brain to receive and interpret the waves there can be no sound.

If there is nothing conscious around, there can be no sound. (We may also say if there is no consciousness around, there is no tree, but we will save that for later lessons.)

Now let's discover how we see.

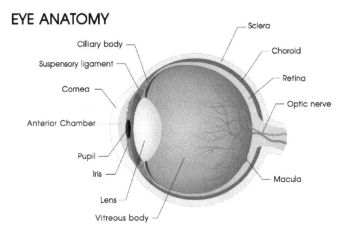

EYE ANATOMY

Sclera
Cilliary body
Choroid
Suspensory ligament
Retina
Cornea
Optic nerve
Anterior Chamber
Pupil
Iris
Macula
Lens
Vitreous body

Look at the image above.

This is so important. The only thing being taken in by the eye is light (an electromagnetic wave). The light comes in through the cornea which is the covering of the front of the eye. The cornea bends the light and the iris (the colored part of the eye) regulates how much light is taken in by changing the size of the pupil. This is why your pupil is smaller when you are in sunlight and larger in the dark, so you can see better.

Behind the pupil is the lens which focuses the light on the retina. The retina contains cells that convert the light to electrical signals. The electrical signals are sent to the brain by the optic nerve. What we then see is interpreted by our brain. We "see" with our brains.

Like with our hearing, what is out there is only electromagnetic waves. Our brain is translating these waves and creating sounds and images, inside us.

Kind of shocking the first time you are told this isn't it?

As we tend to do in this class let's get even more shocking.

What if we said you have never touched anything?

No way!

It has to do with atoms. We will talk about atoms in more detail in a later lesson.

Right now, you just need to know that atoms are the building blocks of the universe. Atoms are composed of particles called protons, neutrons, and electrons. It is the electrons we are concerned about. Remember in the lesson about electromagnetism we discussed how like charges repel each other. Electrons are negatively charged.

What happens is the electrons in your body are repelling the electrons in anything you try and touch. Touch something with your hand right now. You are not touching it. Your hand is hovering over the object at a negative 100,000,000 meters. The electrons in your hand are being repelled by the electrons in the object you think you are touching.

It is the nerve cells of your body signaling your brain giving you the sensation of touching something. That sensation depends on how your brain perceives the world.

All your ears are really "hearing" are electric waves.

All your eyes are really "seeing" are electric waves.

You touch nothing.

Welcome to your new world.

Now would probably be a good time to discuss the implications of living in this world. Don't you think?

The first thing to say is, how your brain interprets waves is not going to be the same way another person's brain interprets waves. Therefore, no two people will see the world the same.

This should lead us to tolerance. Two people can see the same thing from two different points of view and both can be right. Consider a person who is color blind. He may not see the colors of the world as most people do but you can't say he is not seeing correctly. His brain is just interpreting the world in a way that is different than you.

Even two individuals who are not color blind may see different shades of the same color. We may not even see objects in the same way.

I can remember one time when my brain was very vividly affecting how I saw my reality.

It was when I was going through my panic disorder. I am sure it was caused by the medication. They tried so many meds on me I can't even remember them all. Trust me when I tell you the answer is not always medication. But that doesn't mean they cannot be helpful. It's a very tricky situation.

One medication they put me on was Ativan. It is a very strong and addictive drug that is supposed to reduce anxiety and is also used to treat epilepsy. If that wasn't a warning here are the possible side effects.

Drowsiness, dizziness, loss of coordination, headache, nausea, blurred vision, change in sexual interest/ability, constipation, heartburn, change in appetite, mental/mood changes hallucinations, depression, thoughts of suicide slurred speech or difficulty talking, vision changes, unusual weakness, trouble walking, memory problems, signs of infection, fever, persistent sore throat, yellowing eyes or skin, seizures, slow/shallow breathing, serious allergic reaction, rash, itching, swelling of the face/tongue/throat, severe dizziness.

If that wasn't bad enough you are also told this is not a complete list of possible side effects. If you notice other effects not listed above, contact your doctor or pharmacist.

All it did was turn me into a zombie. I was freaking my family out. I would sit for hours, my eyes as wide as saucers, staring into oblivion. I had no desire. I had no hopes. I had no dreams. The anxiety it was supposed to cure did not fade. I sat in silent agony.

Now back to how my brain vividly changed my reality.

I woke up in the middle of the night. My cat was laying at the foot of my bed. I got up and walked around a little while. Nighttime was the only time I was relatively free from my panic attacks. It felt good to have a little break before the morning dawn. Of course, I always hoped the attacks would not come back as the day approached but for six months they always did.

I decided to go back to bed (even knowing that would make the morning arrive faster) but first I would get the cat a handful of treats and take them back to her.

As I was in the kitchen reaching in the treat bag I saw Sadie (my cat) walk in.

"Hey Sasie", I said. (I call her Sasie, long A, don't really know why.) "Do you want a treat?"

With that Sadie took off back to the bedroom. Don't ask how it got started but she always ate her treat at the foot of the bed. I followed Sadie down the hall to the bedroom. As always, I couldn't help but notice how overweight she was. She was and is a very big cat. Perhaps the late-night treats weren't such a good idea.

Sadie turned into the room before I did and as I entered the room, I saw her looking up at me from the floor beside the bed. You can imagine my surprise when I also saw her still asleep on the bed.

Right in front of my eyes, I saw two Sadies.

The hallucination was a result of my medication. Because of the medication and the numbness of my mind I wasn't too concerned about seeing two cats. I returned to bed and continued watching the second Sadie (the one not on my bed) in different places around the room until I fell asleep. When I awoke the second Sadie was gone and never returned.

I wish to this day I had tried to pet the second Sadie. Could I have felt her too?

The two Sadies were a side effect of my medication but even without medication what you think you see as things out in the world are not. They are pictures in your head created by you for you. You create your reality. Your beliefs and past experiences help form that reality. You see what you expect to see. You really do live in your own special universe.

Can you see how empowering this is? You and you alone create your universe. Sometimes we think we have trouble coming to grips with what we truly believe.

Do you want to know your beliefs? Look around you. You are seeing your beliefs. Look at your life. You are living your beliefs. What you believe becomes your reality. This is a scary thought for many people, but it shouldn't be.

Your brain creates the reality you see but as we have learned you have so much control over your brain. Your thoughts change your brain. Your thoughts grow dendrites and create neuron clusters. This changes what you think, know and feel.

Use your imagination. See and feel your future. Daydream as we discussed in lesson five. You will be amazed.

Was this lesson an "eye-opener" for you? Now go tell someone else what you just learned and open their eyes but first you might like to determine your wave frequency.

YOUR EMOTIONS DETERMINE YOUR FREQUENCY

Hopefully, by now you can see you are way more than just the physical body. You are waves of pure energy. Your brain is creating, turning waves into the physical reality you see and hear around you. Once we start the lessons in Quantum Physics you will understand this better and better.

As we have learned waves have a frequency. So that means you have a frequency.

What is your frequency? Is your frequency high or low?

Your frequency is determined by your emotions. So obviously your frequency varies from moment to moment. because we are constantly experiencing different emotions daily.

You want to keep your frequency vibrating as high as possible. In our reality, we are vibrating the highest when experiencing the emotion of love. On the opposite end of the scale, we are vibrating the lowest when experiencing the emotion of fear.

If we could constantly feel love nothing "bad" would ever happen to us in this life. But we know that will not happen. We will experience a range of emotions throughout our life and we will attract the situations that resonate with the frequency of the emotion we are feeling.

Our goal should be to constantly try and find ways to experience the higher frequency emotions.

Many have tried ranking the emotions to give you a guide.

Below is a list to help you determine what frequency level you are vibrating. We start with the highest and go to the lowest.

Love

Gratitude

Happiness

Optimism

Contentment

Boredom

Frustration

Overwhelmed

Anger

Guilt

Ungrateful

Fear

Always strive to get to the highest emotion you can. For example, if you are feeling fear it will be almost impossible for you to immediately jump to feeling love. But you may move to anger or disappointment which is a much better frequency than fear.

Everything is energy -- people, places, and things. Everything radiates a frequency and it is not a good idea not to stay along time with people and at places that vibrate negative, low energy (and yes places do give off harmful negative energy). Even the highest vibrating individuals may be brought down by prolonged exposure. There are times where you will have to be exposed but be sure to always take a break and take time for yourself to replenish your high frequency. This is a must.

Vibrations, good or bad, are easy to pick up on and change your state of mind, especially when they are being amplified by many feeling the same thing in the same location. I can remember being at Church during my hypocritical years after I no longer held most Christian beliefs. After one service there was a baptism. I still felt caught up in the euphoric emotion that warms Christian hearts during a baptism. Very interesting isn't it? Those vibrations are out there and you are going to feel them. Plus, if someone has found happiness in their truth at the moment, even if it contradicts yours, be happy for them.

You have learned that your eyes and ears take in waves of energy and this determines what you see and hear. Be assured that the universe will match your emotional frequency and send you waves of energy through your eyes and ears for your brain to process. You will see things in the world that match your emotional state. So do everything you can to stay away from negative emotions. Being ungrateful is just a little above fear. So if you are one of the many who like to go around complaining about everyone and everything you will keep a stream of events coming into your life you will not like.

Here is the cool thing. If you can keep yourself feeling positive emotions like optimism, happiness, gratitude, and love, know for sure the universe is sending good things your way. You can consider it a surprise gift. You may not have a clue until it arrives. But if you are thinking good thoughts and feeling good emotions the universe knows what you want and is good at giving gifts.

IS GRATITUDE MISSING FROM YOUR LIFE?

Our world comes from within. Our thoughts, our feelings, our emotions all shape how we perceive the world.

Some experience an incredible, amazing dream, some are experiencing a nightmare. Most are just there, not even experiencing much, just living out each day the same as the day before, not living, kind of just existing.

So what makes the difference? How do we perceive the dream world and avoid the nightmare?

One word -- Gratitude.

Gratitude is more than just being grateful when someone does something good for you or for the good things you have in your life. Gratitude is a way of life. It is to wake up each day and be happy with who you are and the life you are living. It is knowing that life will have its ups and downs, but life is good. You are unique. You are special. You are here to make a difference and you know it. You feel privileged to be you because you know something amazing will be revealed to you. You live each day in anticipation of the incredible gift.

"Gratitude unlocks the fullness of life. It turns what we have into enough and more. It turns denial into acceptance, chaos into order, confusion into clarity. It can turn a meal into a feast, a house into a home, a stranger into a friend." - Melodie Beattie

The more you are grateful the more you will have to be grateful. This life is full of amazing, simple, treasures undiscovered by most. Gratitude is seeing the beauty in this world that most cannot see. Gratitude is seeing each day as a new adventure where most see each day as something to struggle through, and survive, and then repeat endlessly over and over again, with no relief in sight, not knowing that relief is right beside them.

Most people do not know how to show gratitude for the life they have been given.

They prefer to complain.

Stop complaining and show gratitude and your world will change. Guaranteed!

Keep complaining, it may seem like a release at the moment, but you will only get more of the negative already coming to you. Guaranteed!

It all comes down to perspective. Where one only sees ugliness, another can see breathtaking beauty. Everything we see and hear is a perspective formed by our past experiences. The cool thing is we can change perspective whenever we want. You can be given new eyes. If you cannot see that which you desire, then that is a clear indication you need to change your perspective. Often just a little change in perspective can create a quantum leap in your life.

How do you change your perspective?

Question everything.

Evaluate your beliefs. Be willing to accept some of your beliefs are just not true. Your belief may be keeping you from attaining that which you have always wanted.

Now get ready we are going to start discussing Quantum Physics. Get ready to be shocked!

LESSON THIRTEEN

QUANTUM PHYSICS I

We are finally here. If you thought Special Relativity was strange you have seen nothing yet. It has been said no one understands Quantum Physics. That is because it is so unintuitive. So much so, many say it is hard to even visualize what Quantum Physics is trying to tell you. But I have pictures in my mind, and I will share those pictures with you. I know they helped me when I was coming to grips with Quantum reality and I know they will help you to.

Before we dive headfirst into Quantum Physics, we need to answer a question.

What is matter?

To answer that question, it is helpful to review a little history. Don't worry it will be brief.

Around 400 B.C.E., the Greek philosopher Democritus introduced the idea of the atom as the basic building block of matter. Democritus thought that atoms were tiny, uncuttable, solid particles surrounded by empty space and constantly moving at random.

In the late 1800s, Henri Becquerel discovered radiation. It was his work that made Marie Curie famous and eventually killed her. Through radioactivity, they discovered atoms were divisible because some atoms shoot out other particles.

Also, in the late 1800s, JJ Thompson was experimenting with cathode ray tubes which are high-vacuum tubes in which a beam of electrons produces a luminous image on a fluorescent screen. He discovered the electron, which he said was part of an atom. Again, the atom is shown to be divisible.

Thompson created the first model of the atom (above) which was called the plum pudding model. Picture pudding with a bunch of raisins in it except the raisins are electrons. The model had electrons embedded in Jello-like stuff. The Jello has a positive charge and cancels the negative charge of the electrons which makes the atom neutral.

Ernest Rutherford in the late 1800s shot radioactive particles at gold foil. Most went straight through the foil, but a few bounced back. He discovered the particles bouncing back were hitting the nucleus of the atom which contained most of the mass of the atom. He discovered the nucleus.

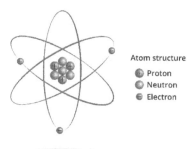

Atom structure
- Proton
- Neutron
- Electron

Rutherford developed the solar system model of the atom (above). He said the electrons were in orbit around the nucleus. He also showed electrons were very far away from the nucleus. If the nucleus was the size of a basketball the electrons would be 2 miles away. This shows, although we don't perceive it, our universe is mostly empty space.

There was a problem with the model. Using electromagnetic calculations (notice how everything always comes down to electromagnetism) electrons should run out of energy and crash into the nucleus of the atom. Atoms should not exist. We should not exist. Nothing should exist.

So, we answered the question we first asked. Matter is made of atoms. Every solid, liquid, gas and plasma is made of atoms. We also discovered that atoms are divisible. We learned a lot but were eventually led to the crazy conclusion that nothing should exist.

This was one of many problems that arose and it was Quantum Physics that came to the rescue. Unlike Special Relativity, developed by the genius of one man, Albert Einstein, over a short period of time, Quantum Physics was developed by many over decades, beginning in the early 1900s.

It took time and the contribution of many great scientists but it started with a man named Max Plank when he forever changed how the world viewed energy. He became known as the grandfather of Quantum Physics.

There was a huge problem for scientists in the early 1900s known as the Ultraviolet Catastrophe. According to the calculations of electromagnetism (It just doesn't go away does it? Important isn't it?) if you turned on your oven the temperature should get so hot that your oven and you with it should be burned to a crisp. Obviously, that's not what happens. There is a limit on the energy. But there shouldn't be. The energy should be limitless.

To see why let's go back to the wave/rope analogy we used in the last lesson.

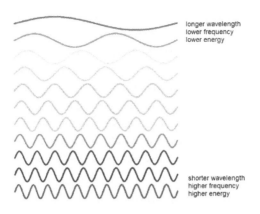

longer wavelength
lower frequency
lower energy

shorter wavelength
higher frequency
higher energy

If you and a friend each take the side of a piece of rope and you shake your end up and down, it will look like the picture above. Shake the rope slowly and it will look like the top waves. Shake it harder and it will look like the bottom waves.

When you shake harder there are more humps in the rope. Frequency is the word that describes how many humps there are in the rope. The more humps the HIGHER the frequency. The higher the frequency the higher the energy.

You can always imagine making the frequency higher. Let's say you shake the rope using all your strength you can find someone stronger to shake it harder and increase the frequency even more. Let's say we get the strongest man in the world to shake it. We still want more, so we hook it up to a machine to shake it harder and then another machine to shake it even harder. Finally, we get Superman to do it. Potentially there is no limit to how hard the rope can be shaken, so there is no limit to its frequency.

There is the problem. According to physics (electromagnetism) before the 1900s, these unlimited waves at super-high frequencies of energy should be in your oven and when you open the oven door all that energy should burn you to a crisp. Or if you wait long enough all that energy will blow your oven and your entire house to bits. Obviously, that is not what happens. Have you ever cooked using an oven? You didn't get burnt to a crisp, did you?

What was going on?

Here is where it gets strange. Max Plank proposed that energy was not continuous but came in chunks. What he said was the higher the frequency (the faster you move the rope) the bigger the chunk of energy.

But bigger is a relative term. Because even the biggest of these chunks are way too small for us to see even with the most powerful microscope. That is why the rope looks like it is moving smoothly.

128

Plank even came up with an easy equation to determine how much energy was in each chunk. Remember the higher the frequency of a wave the more energy so the bigger the chunk of energy.

The equation is E= hf. E stands for energy. The h is Plank's constant and f is the frequency of the wave. Planks constant is an incredibly small number 6.634×10^{-34} J. J stands for joule and represents energy.

All you do is multiply the wave frequency by the number 6.634×10^{-34} and you get the amount of energy. The more energy the bigger the chunk.

Another very important fact is these chunks are indivisible. You can have 1, 2, 3.... chunks. You cannot have half a chunk or a third of a chunk.

Now get ready here it comes. It is what you have been waiting for. When energy comes in indivisible chunks it is said to be quantized and there you have it...

QUANTUM PHYSICS WAS BORN!!!

So now you know what the word Quantum means. It is a discrete, indivisible quantity of energy proportional in magnitude to the frequency of its electromagnetic wave.

Now I will explain how this chunky energy of quantum physics keeps you from being incinerated by your oven in very simple terms. I am going to use something you probably had as a baby. You grasped the concept then so I'm sure you can grasp it now.

Remember the toy where you had kind of like a box with holes in it and all those shaped blocks and only certain blocks would fit in certain holes and you had to put the right blocks in the right holes. Well, we will make that even easier.

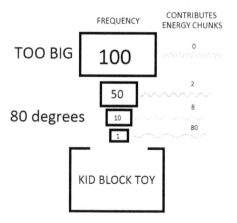

Look at the image above. Picture your kid block toy as having just one hole on top you can fit cubes into. The hole is only so big so if the cubes are too big they won't fit into the hole.

Let's pretend the size of the cubes is related to the size of a chunk of energy. Remember the higher the frequency the bigger the chunk of energy. So eventually you will get a chunk of energy that will not fit in the hole.

Now let's turn the toy into an oven. I know that's not a very smart thing to do with a kid's toy but it's the best way I could think of to do the analogy.

Let's set the oven to 80 degrees.

Each block/chunk of energy has to contribute the necessary multiple of its frequency to provide enough energy to heat the oven to 80 degrees. Frequency 1 has to contribute 80 blocks/chunks of energy (1 x 80 = 80). Frequency 10 has to contribute 8 blocks/chunks of energy (10 x 8 = 80). Frequency 50 is unique. It can fit into the box/oven so it has to contribute and reach the 80 but since you can't break up a chunk into smaller pieces it over contributes but gets no change. Frequency 50 has to contribute 2 blocks/chunks of energy (2 x 50 = 100). Frequency 100 is larger than 80 so it is too big to fit into the box and does not contribute.

That high-frequency big chunk of dangerous energy that will incinerate you can't get in. It is just too chunky. When you open your oven that high frequency isn't there. It is just too big.

Another way of looking at it is that more energy than is available is needed to produce the big 100 chunk of energy.

There you have it. The ultraviolet catastrophe was averted. The world won't burn.

Now think about what this chunky energy means for you.

Look at the lightning above. It may look like a continuous stream of energy but have no doubt it is chunky. It is just the chunks are so small you can't tell.

Now, this may freak you out a little. When you move, you use energy therefore you are moving in chunks. It is like you are constantly popping in and out of existence. It is for a crazy short time so you don't notice it. But you are.

Where are you going when you pop out of existence? I will show you in the next couple of lessons.

So now we have the first step that led to Quantum Physics as we see it today. And to help move it along to its next step was the genius of geniuses, Albert Einstein. His discovery led to him being given a Nobel Prize.

Have fun teaching this lesson. We know you can do it. We will discuss more Quantum Physics in the next lesson. Before we do, I would like to teach you how to play the card game Gin Rummy. Believe it or not Gin Rummy contains the secrets of life.

GIN RUMMY CONTAINS THE SECRETS OF LIFE

I have a very particular set of skills. Skills acquired from my family over the generations. Skills that can make me a nightmare for people like you.

That is if you want to play me in a game of cards.

The "card" gene runs in my family. Almost every member of my dad's side of the family is born with it. We are very good at card games. I once read a book on how to master Gin Rummy. The author invited his readers to play Gin with him online. I took him up on his offer and skunked him. He didn't score a single point. To be honest, I will admit I was dealt good cards.

Gin is one of my favorite card games to play. It is not only fun and exciting as you race to complete your hand before your opponent but it is also a microcosm of life. So many important lessons in life can be learned from the game of Gin.

Gin keeps you in the Now. Gin grounds you in the present moment. When concentrating on your cards your mind is not wandering back into the past or anticipating the future (except where the cards are concerned). Your concern is getting the cards you need to complete your hand. It is a great distraction from the worries of your life.

I will give you many more examples in a minute.

Right now I will do you an incredible favor. I will teach you how to play Gin. There are many versions. I will teach you my favorite way to play.

Gin is a two-player game. Each player is dealt 10 cards then the next card is turned face up and put beside the remaining deck of cards which are face down. This starts the face-up discard stack.

The basics of the game are easy. You take turns drawing cards trying to make matches with your cards. My nephew could play the game competitively when he was just five years old. I told you it is in our genes. It was funny, his hands were too small to hold all ten cards so he had to place a chair next to him with the seat hidden under the table to lay his cards on.

The object of the game is to complete your hand by making matches. There are two types of matches:

1. Runs with at least 3 consecutive cards of the same suit (4,5,6 of hearts, 9,10, Jack of diamonds). Aces are always low so you can only make a run with Ace,2,3, never Queen, King, Ace.

2. At least 3 of the same ranked cards (3 nines, 3 queens).

Play starts with the non-dealer deciding if they want the face-up card. If not, the dealer gets a chance to take the card. If a player takes the card, they must replace it by discarding a card from their hand onto the face-up discard stack. If neither player wants the first face-up card the non-dealer draws from the undealt, face down deck of cards and must decide whether to keep that card and discard a card already in his hand or discard the card he just drew.

Play now goes back and forth with each player deciding if they want to take the card just placed by their opponent in the discard stack of if they want to draw from the unused deck of cards.

Two very important facts to remember:

1. You must always have 10 cards (no more or no less) in your hand. Any time you keep a new card you discard one of your old ones. The cards in your hand are never shown until the end of the round.

2. Once a card is covered up in the discard stack it is gone forever. This isn't like regular rummy where you can go back through all the cards. I always like to make sure the discard pile is nice and tight so players can't look back and see what cards have been played. It is definitely to your advantage if you can remember cards which have been played.

When playing a hand you have two options, you can play to Gin or you can play to "go down."

When you play to Gin all 10 cards in your hand must be in some kind of match. You have 10 cards and it takes 3 cards to make a match. So that means one of your matches must contain at least 4 cards. For example (4,5,6 of hearts, 3 twos, and 9,10, Jack and Queen of diamonds would be Gin.) You show all your cards and say, "Gin."

You don't have to Gin every hand, you can also play to "go down." The card turned face up immediately after the deal is known as the down card. If the down card is an 8 you can go down with 8 points or less. What that means is if your unmatched cards total 8 or less you can "go down". You show all your cards and say, "I'm going down." This ends the hand.

Card values are as follows:

Aces = 1
Number cards = number value (2=2, 5=5, 7=7)
Face cards = 10

Unlike ginning which assures you win the hand, playing to go down can be a little dangerous. For example, if you go down with 6 points of unmatched cards and your opponent has just 4 points of unmatched cards, they have undercut you and they win the hand. Also if any of your opponent's unmatched cards can match your matches those

133

cards are now considered matched and will lesson your opponent's unmatched points and increase their chance to undercut you.

Scoring in Gin depends on whether you played to Gin or go down.

If you Gin you get 25 points for ginning plus the value of the unmatched cards in your opponent's hand.

If you go down you get the difference from the unmatched cards in your opponent's hand and your hand. For example, if you go down with 8 unmatched points in your hand and your opponent has 20 unmatched points you would score 12 points (20 - 8 = 12). However, if you get undercut as mentioned above your opponent gets 25 points as if they had ginned plus the difference of your unmatched cards.

Three more rules:

1. If the first card turned over after the deal is an Ace you must play to Gin, you cannot go down in that hand.

2. You can't use the last two cards in the deck. If you get down to the last two cards and no one has ginned or gone down the hand is a draw, no winner or loser.

3. The winner of the hand deals the next hand.

The game is played to a set score. We usually play to 150 or 200. We also play a game called Hollywood Gin where you play three games at one time but we will save that for later.

It is a fairly simple game but you can do many things to increase your chances of winning. You can learn techniques for drawing and keeping and discarding cards which increase your odds of making matches. If you can remember which cards have been discarded that is a huge advantage. You can keep track of what your opponent discards to learn what they are holding in their hand. For example, if you see your opponent pick up a 4 of hearts and later in the game discard a 4 of diamonds they are not trying to match 4s but have a run with like 3,4,5 of hearts. If you get lucky and draw the 6 of hearts you might not want to get rid of the card until you have to. You don't want to add more cards to their run. If you keep track of everything going on in the game often you can determine every card in your opponent's hand.

That is where skill comes into the game. It takes concentration and as I mentioned earlier, that concentration is great for keeping your mind in the present moment.

Gin teaches you many other life lessons.

You have probably heard the analogy to life, "It's not the cards you are dealt that matters but how you play them."

This is so true in Gin and life. In the game of Gin, if you know all the strategies and you keep track of the cards you can be dealt a terrible hand but still win, especially if you are playing someone who doesn't know what they are doing.

The same is true in life. It doesn't matter the circumstances you were born into. What matters is how you handle the circumstances. What matters is how you play the game of life. And just like in Gin there are so many strategies you can learn in life to ensure that you will "win." You have only to make sure you play the game of life, and discover its rules. Most people are not even close to understanding the rules. You can see it by the horrendously unproductive way they live their lives. Once you know the rules you have an incredible advantage over most of the world.

Do not think you will always come out on top every time you try something in life. In Gin, your opponent can be dealt a hand so good that no matter how good of a Gin player you are, you are probably not going to win that hand. In Gin, this is often called a "monkey hand". That means the hand was so easy a monkey could have played it and won.

Let me give you an example. I have played a lot of Gin so I have seen just about everything possible in a Gin game. Twice I have been dealt a hand so good I was able to pick up the first card and Gin. If you think that is amazing one time I was dealt a Gin hand. I didn't even need the first card. Right after the deal, to the shock of my cousin I was playing, I just threw my cards down and said, "Gin!" But it gets even more amazing. Just a week later my cousin did the same thing. He was dealt a Gin hand. I looked up the odds on the internet. The odds of being dealt Gin are 1 in 308,984. We saw it happen twice in one week.

In life, there will be times when the odds are so stacked against you that there is no way you are going to win. What do you do? Just like in Gin remember this is only one hand. There is another hand coming which has nothing to do with the previous hand. No matter how bad the previous hand, it will always end and you will always be given the opportunity to play a new hand. This applies both to Gin and life. Just never, never quit playing the game because of one bad hand, because sooner or later you will be dealt and be able to take advantage of the "monkey hand."

Life and cards are cyclical. Most of the time when you are playing Gin it will be an average paced game. You will go through at least one half to two thirds the deck of cards before someone wins the hand. But sometimes a player can get on a hot streak. They are dealt really good hands and the cards they need to Gin just happen to be at the top of the deck so they show up real fast. A hot streak doesn't just last one hand. It may last a whole game (which it usually seems to do). It may last for a whole evening of playing Gin. It may even last over many periods of getting together to play cards.

If someone is on a hot streak against you it can be very frustrating. There is nothing you can do but just sit there and take it. It can be unbearable if, as is often the case, there is money at stake. It is a great test for how much control you have over your ego. I have seen very mild-mannered people get so upset after being crushed by someone on a hot streak do everything from throw cards across the room to try and start a fight. But when you are the one on a hot streak it is a whole other story. It is a very enjoyable experience. It almost seems like magic when you just keep drawing card after card you need.

Just like in Gin, we also get on hot streaks in life. It will seem as if everything is going great and there is nothing we can do wrong. Life is incredible. Enjoy it. And you should.

But don't forget life and cards are cyclical. All hot streaks come to an end and the game returns to normal. Unfortunately, it doesn't stop there. There will be times when the cards, like life, turn bad. Now, no matter what you do you can't seem to win. You can't seem to get what you want and need. You may be dealt a good hand in Gin but never seem to draw the cards you need to make your matches. Your opponent may be dealt a terrible hand but draw every card he needs to win before you even draw one of yours Just like the hot streak a bad streak may last for a while. We all know this is true in life.

So what do you do when you are on a bad streak in Gin or life? You tell yourself that everything is cyclical and this too shall end. It may not end as fast as you want it to but it will end. Someday you will find yourself on another hot streak. But don't forget the hot streak will cycle out again. There lies the true mastery of your life. When you can accept life will bring you both the good and the bad and when you can be on a hot streak and everything going good in life and can say, "This too shall end", without becoming concerned, you are taking control of your life. You will still have the bad times but you will soon discover you will have a lot more good times. Your life will be amazing.

Now let's get back to the weirdness of Quantum Physics.

LESSON FOURTEEN

QUANTUM PHYSICS II

In the last lesson, we talked about how energy has been quantized. Energy is not smooth and continuous but comes in discreet, indivisible chunks. This explained the Ultraviolet Catastrophe and showed why the Earth wasn't just a big ball of flame.

Before we go any farther, we need to make sure you know the difference between a particle and a wave.

We talked about electrons in the last lesson. Electrons are particles. You can think of a particle as a very small object which has physical properties. Think of particles as super small billiard balls. If one particle hits another it will act the same way as the balls act when playing pool.

Consider how particles differ from waves. Waves have no substance. They cannot be felt. Waves can move through solid objects. Think about a sound wave. You can hear noises in another room because the sound waves are moving through the walls to get to your ears. A particle could not penetrate a wall.

Now that we know the difference between a particle and wave let's talk about the photoelectric effect.

You shine light on this metal sheet and electrons bounce off.

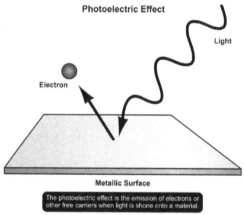

Photoelectric Effect

Light

Electron

Metallic Surface

The photoelectric effect is the emission of electrons or other free carriers when light is shone onto a material.

It was thought that if you shine a brighter light on the sheet such as going from a 50 watt to a 100-watt bulb you would see the electrons shooting off the sheet of metal faster with more energy like if you hit the pool ball harder. But all it did was shoot off more of electrons with the same energy.

Electromagnetic Spectrum

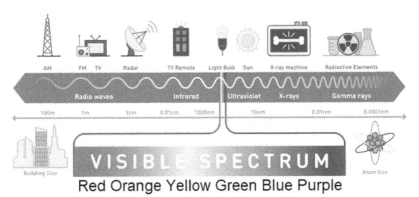

Red Orange Yellow Green Blue Purple

However, if you changed the frequency, the color of the light (see the chart above), the higher the frequency the faster the electrons were shot off the metal sheet. Purple light has a lot more energy than red light. Purple light shot off faster electrons.

Remember how Plank said the higher frequency the bigger the chunk. The higher the frequency the more energy so being hit by a bigger chunk of higher energy the faster the electron would fly off the sheet in the photoelectric effect.

Einstein took over from where Plank left off and said light was made of photons. Photons were particles of energy. Remember we said particles were like really small billiard balls. Light energy must come in chunks and the size he discovered could be determined by Plank's equation, E=hf. We talked about Plank's equation in the last lesson. The energy in the light chunks is their frequency times h known as Plank's constant which was a very small number.

Einstein explained the photoelectric effect.

Here is a simple way of looking at it. We used a kids' toy in the last lesson so let's get another kids toy, a nerf gun. If you shot at an object with a nerf bullet it might just bounce off the object and not do anything. This would be like a low-frequency photon. But now pull out a real gun and shoot the object with a bullet. The object might not only move but shatter. This would be like a high-frequency photon.

But wait, haven't we been saying throughout this course that light was an electromagnetic wave. How could an electromagnetic wave also be a particle? How can you shoot things with light? How can you play pool with light?

Think about this. Consider radio waves or waves sending information to your cell phone. We can't see or feel these waves, but we know they are all around us. So how can they also be physical particles? We don't feel ourselves being bombarded by little

138

pellets or something. How can something be a wave of energy and have physical properties simultaneously?

So, what is light? Is it a particle or a wave?

Are you ready for the answer?

It is both! It is both physical and non-physical.

What? That is not even possible.

Is it?

To discover the answer let's talk about the double-slit experiment. This is the heart of quantum physics. This is the experiment that changed the world. This is the experiment that is going to blow your mind and forever change how you perceive reality. Get excited. If you haven't heard of this before your world will never be the same.

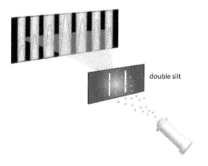

double slit

Look at the picture above. There is a board with two slits and behind the board is a photographic plate that will detect light. We will shine light through the slits.

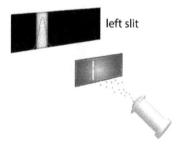

left slit

If we close the slit on the right and only let the light go through the left slit, we see that the light is detected by the photographic plate on the left directly behind the opening. Nothing unordinary yet. This would agree with Einstein. Just as if we had shot BBs through the slit at the board. The BBs would line up behind the open slit. Sounds like particles to me.

139

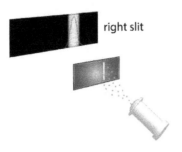

right slit

If we close the slit on the left and only let light go through the right side we see that the light is detected by the photographic plate only on the right. Again just as if the light was of made physical BBs.

both slits

What would you expect if you opened both slits simultaneously? You would expect most of the light to be photographed directly behind the slits as in the figure above.

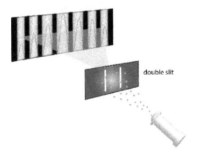

double slit

But that is not what happens. When you open both slits you get a pattern on the photographic plate like the one in the figure above. You get multiple alternating light and dark areas spreading across the entire plate. This is called an interference pattern. And this pattern is only made when two waves collide.

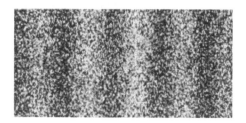

The image above is a picture of an actual wave interference pattern.

How can particles produce a wave pattern?

Let's do this. Let's keep both slits open and let's decrease the intensity of the light so only one photon goes through a slit every few seconds. Keep in mind just one photon every few seconds. If you wait long enough do you know what pattern you will see on the photographic plate? You will still see the wave interference pattern.

What? How can a single photon, which we know is a physical particle, go through a slit by itself and eventually produce a wave pattern like the one above?

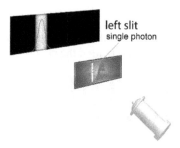

left slit
single photon

Now close the slit on the right so the single photon has to go through the left. Now the wave pattern disappears and we go back to what we would expect. The photons line up behind the slit on the left the same as if you were shooting BBs through the slit.

If you are confused about this don't worry. It makes no sense to the natural mind. How can something go from being a wave to being particle or from being a particle to being a wave? Waves can't be seen or felt. Particles are physical.

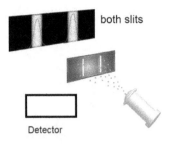

both slits

Detector

But it gets even worse. Scientists wanted to know what was going on. So they used a detector. They kept both slits opened and they fired individual photons through the slits and wanted to use the detector to see which slit it was going through. Something strange happened. When they used the detector to see which slit the particles went through you no longer got the wave interference pattern but the photons lined up behind the slit it went through. But when they took away the detector the interference pattern returned.

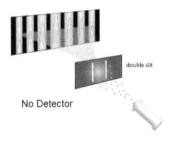

double slit

No Detector

What?

When we are looking the photons became real particles but when we aren't looking they are waves. Light is a wave and a particle.

We will be spending a lot of time in future lessons talking about what this means. But we must stop right now. This is something you just need to think about for a while. It is weird. It is strange. You can't make sense of it logically. Many things we will discuss in future lessons make no sense logically but they are true.

Don't forget to teach someone the crazy thing you just learned.

Are you starting to change the way you see the world? This is the perfect time to start making the changes in your life you have always wanted. This book will help.

GET PAST THE RESISTANCE

You are ready for a change. Just start. Do something to start the change. Don't worry about if you are making a correct decision. It need not be the correct decision. Once you take the initial step (right or wrong) you will be guided. The correct decisions will come to you. But not until you take that first step. Just start.

You know that feeling of resistance you have when you want to do something? You want to do it but something inside you doesn't seem to want you to do it. You have a very uncomfortable feeling and you tell yourself that you will do it when the uncomfortable feeling goes away.

Here is the thing. Until you do it the uncomfortable feeling will never go away. In fact, the more you want something the more resistance you will feel.

It is like you can see the door to your dream right in front of you but there is also a large, vicious, growling, snarling guard dog ready to attack you if you come near the door.

The secret is if you will just open the door the dog will not hurt you. In fact, it will turn into a cute little puppy.

We all have times where we fear the dog and sabotage our dreams. We need to decide to just do it.

Ignore the resistance and bring your dreams into reality.

HELP IS ALWAYS THERE WHEN YOU NEED IT

Most of the time we limit ourselves.

We limit ourselves to our five senses.

We have a higher self that can see infinitely beyond what we see with our five senses. Many like to call it our soul. Our higher self is not bound by the rules of this world we live in. Our higher self can work miracles. Constantly tell yourself the world may do it a certain way, but you have access to a higher self that can break all the rules.

Who cares about the likely chance of something happening? Who cares about odds and percentages? Your higher self doesn't recognize odds. Your higher self can make anything happen (or not happen).

The cool thing is your higher self is you. Your higher self wants everything you want just as much as you do. There is nothing more loving and caring than your higher self (soul).

But you have the choice. It is up to you.

You can limit yourself to just your five senses and not access the help from your higher self and you may still accomplish your goals. It will just be a lot harder and take a lot longer.

You also have the choice to communicate with your higher self. The closer you become with your higher self the more access you have to an infinite amount of possibilities that were not present before. You will open yourself to a whole new world that was not present before. You leave behind the world limited to your five senses.

Things will change. What was once a struggle will become an exciting adventure. You will see the world from a completely different view that most don't. You will want to show others. You will want to show them how they are limiting themselves and life need not be a hard struggle.

The help you want is here right now, the solutions to all your problems are here right this very second, just begging for you to see it.

Continue with the next lesson. You will soon see Quantum Physics is leading you to your higher self.

LESSON FIFTEEN

QUANTUM PHYSICS III

So, what have we learned so far?

We learned that Max Plank solved the Ultraviolet Catastrophe by showing energy from electromagnetic waves comes in discreet, indivisible, chunks of energy called Quanta, the plural of Quantum. We mentioned how a lightning bolt looks like a continuous stream of energy, but it is chunky. It's just that the chunks are too small for us to see so it looks continuous.

We saw Einstein introduce photons to the world. He said light was made of photons which were physical particles, not waves. He showed this with the photoelectric effect by shining light on metal plates and the photons knocked off electrons like they were playing a game of pool.

After that things only got weirder.

The double-slit experiment showed light could be both a wave and a particle even though that makes no sense. When you observe photons they are particles. When you aren't looking they are waves.

We now need to introduce the next major player in Quantum Physics, Niels Bohr. He was a Danish physicist and he helped to revolutionize how we see the atom today.

Let's go back for a minute and see where we left off with the atom.

If you remember we said JJ Thompson created the first model of the atom called the plum pudding model. Picture raisins in a pudding. Now think of the raisins as electrons. Now kind of think of an atom like electrons in Jello. The Jello has a positive charge and cancels the negative charge of the electrons making the atom neutral.

Rutherford developed the solar system model of the atom. He said electrons orbit around the nucleus. He also showed electrons were far away from the nucleus. This is how most of us picture an atom. It was what we are shown in our schoolbooks. It is wrong!

Remember we also said there was a problem with the model. Using electromagnetic calculations (notice how everything always comes down to electromagnetism) electrons should run out of energy and crash into the nucleus of the atom. Atoms should not exist. We should not exist. Nothing should exist.

Niels Bohr helped save the day. He moved from Denmark to England to work with JJ Thompson. Bohr and Thompson did not get along with each other. The problem probably stemmed from Bohr telling Thompson his model of the atom was wrong.

So, Bohr went to work as an assistant for Rutherford and helped to further develop the concept of the atom. He quantized the atom.

The first thing he did, unlike Thompson, was agree with Rutherford. He said electrons do orbit around the nucleus of the atom just like the moon orbits the earth. They too use angular momentum to stay in orbit and keep from crashing into the nucleus.

Second, Bohr said there are fixed orbits at specific distances from an atom's nucleus. Bohr said electrons don't give off energy when in an orbit but do give off energy when they "leap" from one orbit to the other. Hence the familiar term Quantum Leap. But do not picture the electron physically jumping from one orbit to the other. Picture it disappearing from one orbit and then suddenly reappearing in another. Where does the electron go when it disappears? It goes nowhere. It is just in one place then in another.

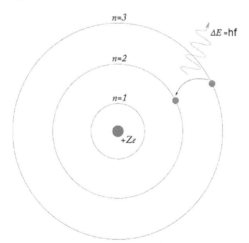

Bohr model

When the electron makes this leap it either absorbs or emits energy. It emits energy (a photon) when it drops to a lower orbital level and absorbs energy (a photon) when it jumps to a higher level. Guess what determines how much energy? It is the equation, E=hf. Look familiar. The electron gives or receives a quantum of energy and the amount of energy can be determined by Plank's formula.

Bohr's work also led him to develop the Principle of Complementarity. The principle states you can't define one thing without referring to its opposite. You can't have good without bad or up without down.

Just about 10 years after Bohr developed his model of the atom a French prince named Louis de Broglie came up with the crazy but correct conclusion that the electrons orbiting atoms were waves. He was influenced by Einstein's relativity and especially his great equation $E=mc^2$.

He was led to a conclusion that is the mother of all weirdness of Quantum Physics. Are you ready?

Not only does light behave as a particle and a wave but all matter behaves as a particle and a wave.

No. Just no. That can't be.

$E=mc^2$

Matter and energy are the same. Therefore, if light (which is energy) can be both a particle and wave then so can matter.

de Broglie even came up with an equation to calculate the wavelength of a particle of matter.

wavelength = h/mv

The wavelength of a particle is determined by Plank's Constant (h) divided by the mass (m) of the particle times its velocity (v). There is Plank's Constant once again. No wonder he was called the grandfather of Quantum Physics.

Think about this. Matter can be a particle and a wave. You are made of matter. Are you sometimes a particle and sometimes a wave?

The proof finally came by doing a different version of the double-slit experiment.

You will recall the first experiment involved sending photons of light through two slits, and depending on whether the experiment was observed, the photon was a wave (if not observed) or a particle (if observed). They could tell it was a wave because it displayed a wave interference pattern.

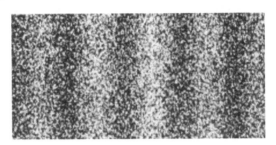

In the newer experiment they had the same setup but this time they sent electrons (matter) through the slit. Again they sent one electron at a time.

The results:

The same.

If the experiment was observed the electron was a particle. If the electron was not observed it was a wave. The wave interference pattern emerged.

How can you get a wave interference pattern from an electron? An electron is physical matter. You are made of electrons.

If you have not heard this before your life has just been forever changed.

Everything you see in the universe is made of electrons. So, does that mean if no one is looking the moon is not there or if no one is in your kitchen is it just a bunch of waves?

We have no problem saying there is no sound only waves if no one is there to listen. Should it not be the same with sight?

You have no problem with the fact that the sounds and images streaming on your smartphone are just waves until the phone converts the waves into what you see and hear. Should it not be the same with your brain? Is your brain not way more powerful than a phone?

You are made of electrons. You have about 100000000000000000000000 electrons in your body. You see your physical body but are you sometimes a wave?

Okay, we will stop here. You need to process this before we move on. And yes, there is more. Just wait and see. Right now you have a lot to think about. Seriously give this some consideration. What is your mind saying to you right now?

Tell others what you just learned. Draw that pic too!

In the next lesson, we are going to show that nothing in this universe is determined. But first, we want to tell you something about yourself that will help you with your choices in life. At first, it may not sound like good news but it is the secret to contentment and peace.

YOU ARE NEVER GOING TO BE SATISFIED

Do you still think you will find the one thing to give you full peace of mind and leave you satisfied with your life? Let me tell you right now you are not. Even if you do find what you think will bring you eternal happiness, perhaps a lot of money or a loving relationship, you will soon discover you were wrong. Until you realize you can only find contentment within you right now and not somewhere in the future, you will always be searching. You will be in a state of constant lack which you will never satisfy.

You are playing society's game. Go to elementary school, go to high school, go to college, get a job, get a promotion, buy that house, get another promotion, make more money, buy a bigger house, buy a fancy car...

Satisfaction always seems to lie in the future. You will never be satisfied.

I know someone is saying, "I don't care what you are saying. Give me a few million dollars and I am going to be pretty satisfied."

Coming from a family that has money, then starting my own business and not having money in the early years, then having money as it grew, then losing that business and not having money, and then starting another business and having money, I have lived both sides multiple times. I can say having money does make life easier. That is just common sense. It is nice to walk into a store and buy anything you want instead of worrying if you will be able to pay the bills.

Money cannot give you a sense of purpose. Money will not take away the longing feeling for something more. In fact, money can make things worse. Imagine the person who has enough money to buy anything they want and still finds himself or herself depressed. They thought once they got everything (physical) they wanted their world would be perfect. But now they still find themselves in a state of worry and anxiety. The situation looks bleak to them. They first thought to become rich would cure all the problems in their life, but now there seems to be no cure at all. They see no way to escape. Why do you think so many rich and famous people commit suicide? They feel as if they have reached the pinnacle of life and things still seem hopeless for them. They see no reason to go on.

Had they only learned that contentment, peace, and happiness were always there for the taking any moment they wanted it. It is not to be found in the physical world. It is to be found within ourselves.

We all want to live an abundant life. True abundance is always created from the inside out. Once you realize you are already abundant it will be natural for money to appear in your life but to chase after money for money's sake is the surest way to keep it away.

THE HEISENBERG UNCERTAINTY PRINCIPLE

Heisenberg's Uncertainty Principle shows we do not live in a deterministic universe. There will be things we can never know for sure. This is because, as we have discussed, the subatomic world comes in discreet units. It is quantized. There is a minimum size we can use when trying to figure out how the world works.

This led German physicist Werner Heisenberg to develop The Uncertainty Principle in 1927. Heisenberg's Principle says that at the microscopic level, position and velocity cannot both be measured simultaneously.

This seems very weird to us. Consider a car. We can tell where a car is and how fast it is going and where it is going. With subatomic particles such as electrons that is impossible. There is a trade-off. The more you know about the electron's position the less you know about its momentum and the more you know about its momentum the less you know about its position.

To understand this better let's quickly review waves.

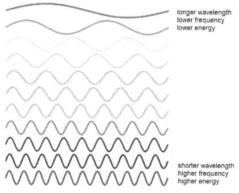

The waves at the top of the picture have longer wavelengths and therefore low frequency and low energy.

The waves at the bottom of the picture have shorter wavelengths than those at the top therefore they have a higher frequency and more energy.

We also know that just about everything we see in the world can be a particle and wave.

Particles are like BBs or billiard balls. Waves have no physical substance. Waves can move through walls.

We have learned when you look at something your eye is taking in light waves of the object.

To see something we need to have light.

Now let's say we want to find an electron. We have to hit it with a photon of light to determine where it is at. But the problem is a photon is a particle and a wave and we don't know where the photon is. So we don't know where the electron is and to find it we need to use a photon but we don't know where the photon is at either.

The best we can do is send out a wave of light, known as a wave packet, to detect the electron.

Look at the wave packet above. It is a narrow wave and therefore has a shorter wavelength and high frequency and energy.

Now, look at the second wave packet above. The wave is broader than the first therefore it has a longer wavelength and lower frequency and energy.

So we send out the wave packet in the direction we think the electron is. We are shooting a photon at the electron to determine where the electron is but the only thing we can say about the photon is that it is somewhere in the wave packet. Look at both wave packets. It is easy to see the first has a smaller area than the second. If we detect an electron using the first wave packet we are going to better know its location than if we detect it within the second wave packet which has a bigger area.

Think of it like you are trying to capture an invisible animal with a net. If you catch it in a smaller net you will know its location a lot better than if you catch it in a bigger net.

But getting back to waves there is a problem. The problem is the compact wave packet has a high frequency and high energy so when the photon hits the electron it will be like hitting a billiard ball very hard. The electron will shoot off in some direction at high speed so we can't know what the momentum of the electron was before we hit it.

Let's use a lower frequency photon with less energy so the electron doesn't shoot off away from us. But remember to use a lower frequency the wave is now broader taking up more area, now we can't determine the electron's location as well as we could before. Now we know its momentum better, but we are not quite as sure where its position is.

The more you know about the position the less you know about the momentum. The more you know about the momentum the less you know about the position.

Heisenberg's Uncertainty principle says you can never have complete certainty at the subatomic level. And guess what determines how small something must be for the uncertainty to kick in.? It is Planks constant (h). It all comes back to Plank's discovery. Remember Plank's number is very small. Therefore, we have uncertainty with very small subatomic particles and not with things like cars. We can easily see where a car is and how it is moving.

Now here is where it gets weird again. We have been saying the photon is somewhere in the wave but the photon is not really in the wave. It is and it isn't. I know it's so strange. No one can grasp it intuitively.

Remember Niels Bohr? He came up with The Copenhagen Interpretation to explain this uncertainty stuff. He said if you can't measure both position and momentum, there is no sense in which to say it has either. What you are trying to measure is not really there. The atom you see in schoolbooks is incorrect. The atom doesn't have electrons circling around it. The electron is only a fuzzy probability of what might be.

And what determines what might be?

Are you ready for this?

You do, by what you believe!

We will stop here. This is something you need to contemplate for a while.

In the next lesson, we will discuss Schrodinger's Equation and see if we can't make a little more sense of all of this. We will try to make sense of the senseless.

So go out there again and tell someone about this. Make your drawing.

Since you what you believe determines your reality do you think it would be a good idea to understand why you believe?

UNDERSTANDING WHY PEOPLE BELIEVE THE THINGS THEY DO

When you are convinced of something you become immune to logic. If we are confronted with something contrary to our beliefs we become uncomfortable. It produces a feeling inside us we try to avoid. Many will deny contradictory evidence which seems so obvious to others.

Two very common examples are...

1. A person in an abusive relationship.
2. So many contradictory religious beliefs.

This is called cognitive immunization. Our beliefs become immune to facts. Beliefs may even become stronger when challenged. We forget times in our lives when our beliefs have been challenged and remember the times when our beliefs have been strengthened. Once we accept a belief that belief becomes a part of us and often convincing us of the fallacy of that belief would be like convincing us to remove our arm or leg.

We are all guilty of confirmation bias. We avoid things that appear to contradict our beliefs and seek things that seem to support them. We like to associate with people who have beliefs similar to ours and we avoid spending time with those who have differing beliefs. We don't like to expose ourselves to ideas and beliefs that contradict ours.

We go even farther in our bias. If we think something is true, our brain will go out of its way to prove to us it is true. But what we believe our brain has proven true may not be true at all, it may be completely false. We are all guilty of confirmation bias. We all have many beliefs that are not true.

One of the biggest factors in deciding if we hold onto a belief is whether it is useful to us. If it is not it will probably not be a belief we hold very long.

If it is... It will be repeated over and over again in our lives. We will live that belief daily, monthly, yearly and it will grow stronger and stronger. We will connect powerful emotions to that belief. Eventually, that belief will become who we are. We and the belief are one. Changing a belief at that point is very rare but it does happen (I am proof of that).

Although hard we need to examine our beliefs and realize that in many ways we are all fooling ourselves.

Please examine your beliefs today.

Having spent over half of my life as a believing Christian I know that Christians see all the contradictions and crazy things in the Bible. The thing is Christians are very good at living with cognitive dissonance. Cognitive dissonance is the state of having inconsistent thoughts, beliefs, or attitudes. God is love but he kills people, kids, babies.

How do they reconcile that?

Here is how I did it when I was a Christian. You don't reconcile it. But you can put it out of your mind and not worry about it and feel okay doing that.

How is that possible?

Your main truth is the Christian God of The Bible exists and is all-powerful. If anything contradicts God it must be false. And you are secure in that belief even if you can't find a good reason to explain the contradiction.

As a faithful Christian, your reasoning then turns to God is all-powerful there is nothing He can't do. There are many things in this life we just cannot understand and will not be able to understand until we leave this life and are in Heaven with God.

And that allows Christians to keep the contradiction in the back of their mind and keep away the cognitive dissonance.

You don't know. You can't know. One glorious day it will all be revealed and you will know and it will all make perfect sense. So don't worry about it right now.

And most Christians don't worry about it until confronted with something that brings back the cognitive dissonance. When confronted with cognitive dissonance, circuits in the brain that deal with logic shut down and emotional circuits in the brain fire up. This is why quite often you see religious debates get heated and participants become quite angry or even enraged. At that point, they need to stop. Logic is useless, it has been thrown out the window.

The truth is cognitive dissonance plays a role in all our lives. Every day we find reasons to justify the decisions we have made in our lives. This is known as confirmation bias. We see things in the world that justify our beliefs even if they are wrong.. It is very easy to see cognitive dissonance in others but very hard to see it in ourselves. But be sure we are all fooling ourselves to one degree or another.

So how do we know if we are deceiving ourselves?

One of the best ways is our willingness to change what we believe. If you are convinced that you have found the absolute truth and there is nothing anyone will ever be able to say or do to change your mind then you are more than likely caught up in some major confirmation bias. You are not seeing things as clearly as you could.

One of the most dangerous effects of dogmatic beliefs is that you do not believe things that have been proven to be true beyond a shadow of any doubt or you agree or disagree with things merely on what you have been told to believe.

I grew up believing man and dinosaurs existed on earth at the same time. I was told all the dinosaurs were killed in the flood. Man and dinosaurs did not roam the earth at the same time. Dinosaurs were killed because an asteroid hit the earth.

You may argue against a scientifically proven fact and not even know the basic premise of what you are arguing against.

I remember sitting in church and listening to a man argue that the earth was only about 8,000 years old. He kept attacking carbon dating. Carbon dating can't prove how old things are. Carbon dating is wrong. Carbon dating doesn't prove a thing. But he had no clue what carbon dating was. He couldn't even begin to explain any of the processes.

So as not to follow in his footsteps here is a very brief explanation of carbon dating.

Carbon dating involves two carbon molecules, carbon-12 and carbon-14. Carbon-12 and carbon-14 make up carbon dioxide which plants breathe in. Animals eat plants. We eat plants and animals, so every living thing has carbon-12 and carbon-14 molecules.

A living organism has equal amounts of carbon-12 and carbon-14 until it dies and then the carbon-14 begins decaying. The carbon-12 is stable and does not decay. You can tell how long an organism has been dead by the ratio of carbon-12 to carbon-14.

Carbon-14 has a half-life of 5,730 years. This is the time it takes the amount of carbon-14 to decrease by half. Let's say you find a fossil and it has half the amount of carbon-14 as carbon-12, the fossil is 5,730 years old.

You can keep going. After 11,460 years (5,730 x 2 = 11,460) which is two half-lives, there will be just 1/4 the amount of carbon-14 compared to the carbon-12. After 17,190 years (5730 x 3 = 17,190) which is three half-lives, the ratio will decrease to 1/8.

Carbon dating is reliable for determining age up to about 50,000 years. For really old fossils you have to use other unstable molecules.

Do you really think biologists, archeologists, paleontologists, cosmologists, pathologists, immunologists, astrobiologists go to work every day all finding discoveries which not only further their work but also complement the work of each other are all mistaken? Is what appears to be factual evidence just a sham?

You hear the explanation, "Well God made things to appear that way. The age of the earth just appears to be billions of years old." That would mean God made things that appear to contradict the Bible. Great way to make believers. We are expected to believe the Earth appears to be billions of years old, but it is really only 8,000. We must take the word of a book written by an ancient race thousands of years ago over any type of modern technology.

Getting back to cognitive dissonance, when it sets in, you find things that agree with what you believe and ignore those things which don't match with your beliefs.

Even with over surmounting evidence against what you believe you just kind of withdrawal and tell yourself I don't care what anyone says, I don't care what all the evidence seems to say. I know I am right and that is good enough for me.

And soon you find yourself back with others who share your beliefs and all is well and good.

I know I used to do this all the time.

I spent the first half of my life as a fundamentalist Christian but after I started taking to heart all the many, many, many, many, many, many obvious logical contradictions, Christianity was no longer an option.

You will also notice by my writings neither was Atheism an option. So many in the world think religion and atheism are the only two choices. There are infinite options.

.

For one of the biggest logical fallacies, I must thank Ellen DeGeneres. I was just reminded of this the other day when she gave a deserving family on her show $1 Million.

Now we know according to most Christians, Ellen's lifestyle is a big NO, NO. So they want us to believe that even with all the incredible GOOD Ellen has done, and all the happiness she has brought to others over the years, there is a loving god who is still going to send her to burn in the fires of Hell for all eternity.

Are you kidding me? Seriously? Never going to happen.

We would also have to believe that since that god knows everything, he knew about Ellen before she was born and knew of her ultimate terrible fate but still allowed it to happen. That would be awful sadistic and cruel.

I feel very confident the energy which is at this moment Ellen DeGeneres will fair very well after this life.

Thank you, Ellen, for everything you do. You inspire my work at Paradigm Shift.

This was one of the major reasons I could no longer adhere to Christian belief. It is beyond all sense of morality to tell another they do not have the right to love. To try and stifle love is appalling, the consequences can never be good for the one who interferes with true love. Let the one who stands in the way of true love be warned.

It's now time to learn about the equation of equations.

THE SCHRODINGER EQUATION

Before we discuss Schrodinger's Equation you need to understand superposition.

To do that let's go back to the two-slit experiment. Remember when we sent one photon or electron at a time through the slits? You can't ask did the photon or electron go through the first or second opening. They are in a state of superposition. You have to say they went through both. But how can a physical particle go through two openings simultaneously? It would be like you walking through two doors at the same time.

The particle has a probability of showing up physically in one place or another (70/30, 60/40, 71.83/28.17).

When you observe the particle it ceases to be in a superposition state and comes into its physical state in one location. There is no more superposition. This is called collapsing the wave function.

To make more sense of this we need to introduce Erwin Schrodinger and the Schrodinger Equation. Born on August 12, 1887, in Vienna, Austria, Erwin Schrodinger became a noted theoretical physicist and scholar who came up with the groundbreaking wave equation. He was awarded the 1933 Nobel Prize in Physics.

Before we go into all the details of his equation let's talk about a thought experiment that Schrodinger came up with that became known as Schrodinger's Cat. It showed just how crazy superposition can be. This was just a thought experiment. It was never actually done. No cats were ever harmed.

Schrodinger wondered, what if a cat was placed in a box with a radioactive atom? The atom has a 50/50 chance of decaying in an hour. A radiation detector is set in the box and if it detects radiation from a decaying atom it is to release poison in the box and the cat dies.

But the atom is in a state of superposition until you observe it. It is in a state of being decayed and not being decayed simultaneously. Does that mean until you open the box the cat is also in a state of being both alive and dead? It is only when you open the box and collapse the wave function that the cat is either dead or alive.

There has been a lot of debate and discussion about Schrodinger's Cat. What do you think?

Now let's get to the Schrodinger Equation.

The Schrodinger Equation is a function. It gives you a wave function for finding a particle at a certain position. Remember back to when we were doing Calculus, you plug

159

numbers into a function and you get an output. Obviously, the Schrodinger Equation is a lot more complicated than the functions we did.

A wave function is a wave with varying amplitudes. The greater the amplitude the greater the chance of finding a particle in that position. The image above is a simplistic drawing of a wave function.

The Schrodinger Equation describes quantum behavior. It lets you know how a wave function evolves over space and time. It gives you the probability of finding a particle at a certain position.

Remember the weirdness of Quantum Physics, we are saying the probability of finding a particle at a certain position but don't be misled to think that when you find the particle that is where the particle always was. Remember superposition, the particle is considered in many places at one time. Only when we observe the wave does it collapse into a particle in one physical position. So weird isn't it?

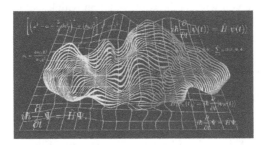

Look at the picture above, it is an example of a wave function. Where the wave is the highest there is a higher probability of seeing the particle when it collapses. But that does not mean it will be there. It may show up where the wave is the lowest. Kind of like when the weatherman says there is an 80% chance of sunny skies and only a 20% chance it will rain. It rains.

$$\frac{-h^2}{2m}\frac{\partial^2 \Psi(x)}{\partial x^2} + U(x)\Psi(x) = E\Psi(x)$$

And there it is! Look at the image above that is Schrodinger's Equation. Actually, that is one of its many forms. This one involves position in the x dimension. It does not involve time. This means the particle is not moving.

There are only a few new things you need to learn here.

160

The symbol ψ is the Greek letter psi. This represents the wave function of the particle.

The letter U is the potential energy of the wave. Potential energy is a type of energy an object has because of its position. A boulder on top of a hill has a lot of *potential energy* because it could roll down fast at any moment.

The letter E is the total energy of the wave.

We will not work out an example of Schrodinger's Equation. That is beyond the scope of these lessons but we will show you now understand everything in the equation.

The h as you know is Plank's constant. That very small number we keep seeing over and over again. You make it negative and then square it and divide it by 2 times the mass of the particle. You then take that result and multiply it by the 2nd derivative (which is taking the derivative of a derivative) of the wave function. Remember we said when we take a derivative we are finding the rate of change. You add that result to $U(x)\psi(x)$, which is the potential energy of the equation and that must all equal $E\psi(x)$, which is the total energy of the equation.

If you didn't get all that don't worry. We are not trying to learn to solve the equation. We are just seeing what needs to be inputted into the equation to solve it. And you know everything that needs to go in it.

Once you do all of that you will get the wave function which will tell you the probability of finding the particle at a specific location. Again, remember you are only getting the probability of where the particle might be when the wave function is collapsed. How do you collapse the wave function? You observe it. Until you observe it the particle is in many places at once. It is in a state of superposition.

But you are made of particles, aren't you? Can you be in a state of superposition?

Are the particles that makeup you once waves? Were you collapsed into reality? What does that even mean? This book will answer the question, "What does all of this mean for you?"

So go explain this to someone, if you can find them. They may be in a state of superposition.

Here is an interesting question. If you are a wave what does it mean to hurt a wave? What does it mean to offend a wave?

You need to understand something about your decisions. Let's use an example of buying a new house.

You are insecure about purchasing the house. You are not sure if you should go through with it. What if in the future you don't make the money you are making now? You could go into foreclosure or even worse have to file bankruptcy.

You decide not to buy the house it is just too risky.

A few years later your income does decline. Thank goodness you didn't buy the house. You just dodged a bullet.

Actually, you didn't.

You chose between thought patterns. If you had bought the house your thoughts would have been different. You would have collapsed a different quantum reality wave into your life.

After buying the house your mind would now be operating not only from a want position, to be able to make the house payment, but to a need and have to position. Your quantum probability waves would be completely different than if you had not bought the house. If you had bought the house it would be highly likely that you would make the money for the house payment.

What many don't realize is that you chose between realities Your decisions created your reality. The outcome in one reality is in no way related to the other.

Some people say there is a multiverse and when you make a choice you experience both realities. For now, just remember any decision you make sends your life off in one direction or the other. You can in no way assume that something that happens to you would have also happened if you had made another decision.

Consider an extreme example to show just how true that is. How different are your life experiences going to be if you choose to drop out of high school as opposed to becoming a doctor?

But here is what is so great. If you find yourself in a reality you don't like you can always bring yourself to EXACTLY where you want to be.

NO ONE CAN OFFEND YOU WITHOUT YOUR PERMISSION

I didn't hurt your feelings. I said something which caused you to make the decision that your feelings were hurt. You could have decided otherwise. What I said may have been bad but that is beside the point. I can't hurt your feelings unless you decide to let me.

Think about it. One individual says something to a person who just laughs at it like a joke and then the individual says the same thing to a second person who becomes depressed.

What was the difference?

Each person chose a different way to react to the comment. They decided for themselves how to feel about what the individual said.

Does that mean there is not some past conditioning or that it is easy to control our emotional responses? We all know those statements are not true. But when it is all said and done no one can offend you without your permission. If you don't like the way you react to certain situations you can work on obtaining your desired response.

Does that mean we shouldn't worry about saying things that hurt people?

Of course not.

But things are getting a little out of hand today. People are getting "offended" by just about anything you can think of and letting everyone know they have been made highly upset by what so and so said.

Seriously! Well, maybe I'm offended by you being offended. How is that?

When offended how are you hurt? Can you be hurt by a comment? Did it hurt you physically? Did you have to be rushed to the hospital? Did it hurt you financially? Is there anything you cannot do now that you could do before? Has your life even changed in one single way?

No!

So what's the big deal?

Don't be concerned with how others see you. We all create our own world. We all see each other through our unique interpretation of our world. No two people will see you the same.

I can remember in just two weeks I went from being carded to get in a casino to someone thinking I was the father of my 30-year-old friend. I can't be both.

This proves how others see us is a reflection of them not a reflection of us. We all have past experiences that make us see things differently. The more you realize what people say reflects them the more you close yourself from the hurt and pain you might otherwise have felt.

It all comes down to your attitude, the way you think or feel about something. Your attitude not only determines how you experience events in your life it also determines what events you experience in your life. Bad attitude, bad experiences. Good attitude, good experiences.

Your attitude attracts the energy of the universe, which is then interpreted by your brain and creates your physical reality. Your attitude creates the neural connections in your brain, which determines what you can and cannot do.

It all comes down to you. Take full responsibility for your life. Put the blame only on yourself for the world you have created.

LESSON EIGHTEEN

THE EPR EXPERIMENT

If you feel uneasy about the strangeness of Quantum Mechanics you are in good company. Einstein couldn't believe everything it was saying about the universe we live in either. He believed there had to be a hidden reality not yet discovered.

So, in 1935, Einstein and his buddies Podolsky and Rosen devised a thought experiment called The EPR Experiment (the first letter of their last names just in case you didn't figure it out). His goal was to prove there is a concrete reality out there, not one waiting on us to consciously view it before it exists. The moon is there even if no one is looking at it.

To understand The EPR Experiment we have to discuss more about particles. Particles have spin. For this experiment, we will say spin up and spin down. But remember until a particle is observed it is in a state of superposition so it has both spin up and spin down. How can something be spinning two ways simultaneously? Impossible. Einstein would agree.

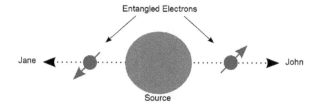

Look at the image above. We have a source that is going to decay. When it decays it sends out particles in two opposite directions. One goes towards Jane and one goes towards John. We give Jane a spin detector to observe the particle coming at her and determine if the spin is up or down. Remember the spin is undetermined until we make the measurement. Jane checks the detector and sees if the particle is spin up or spin down. Based on what she sees the particle sent to John is automatically the opposite. If Jane sees down, John sees up. If Jane sees up, John sees down. At first, that may not seem too weird but remember they were neither up nor down until detected. This means somehow the particle not detected knows its partner's spin has been detected and knows to take the opposite spin.

Einstein said it can't be that way. The spins had to be already determined before they shot off in opposite directions. Bohr disagreed with Einstein and said that they do not exist in any definite state until they are observed.

In 1964 John Bell developed an experiment that took incredible statistical mathematics (we will not get into) to show whether Einstein or Bohr was correct.

And the winner was Bohr. The particle's spin is not definite until it is determined by the spin detector.

Einstein called this, "Spooky action at a distance." This is also known as non-locality. Distance does not matter. There is a connection, an automatic communication, even if two particles are at opposite ends of the universe.

How could that be possible?

Could that mean everything in the universe is connected? Would that mean everything is one? If so, then connection at large distances is not a problem. You can always automatically communicate with yourself.

Everything is energy. Since everything is energy, there is no distinction where energy begins and ends -- therefore we are all one.

Everything and everyone are one. But that does not mean you are not unique. You are like a wave in the ocean. You are the individual wave but you are also the entire ocean. Everything you do affects everyone and everything.

There is a collective unconscious. If one person knows it be assured that information is available to you.

So, who are you?

You are whoever you want yourself to be.

You are here to create. You are here to create your world in any way you want.

To create, use your imagination. Picture anything you want in your mind and add emotion. Hold that for just a minute or two each day. It is that simple.

There is nothing you cannot do, be or have.

Even after this life, you are still creating. You are creating infinite creations for all eternity.

Get ready! We will show you amazing ways to create.

DON'T MAKE THE MISTAKE OF THINKING IT CAN'T HAPPEN RIGHT NOW

Change your life right now.

Change comes in a single moment.

We think change is not going to come right now so we reason what is one more day. But the change can come right now. Most don't see that and they let the days turn into years and the years turn into a lifetime and they never really live.

I will do it tomorrow, most will reason (incorrectly). What is one more day? They put off making the change. That is a HUGE mistake. They will not only put it off tomorrow but the next day and the next day and the next day and the next day...

Often we put off making the change we want because we think it will be a long and tedious process. We think it will be a struggle. We think it will be hard to do. That is just not true. Nothing could be farther from the truth.

Change comes in a single moment. And the only reason the moment won't be today is if you don't let it.

Today you can have that sudden realization. You can experience that moment when you discover something big that will change your life. You will feel excited because you know your world will never be the same.

You will see something you never saw before. It is amazing. What happens is the neurons in your brain will make a connection that was not there before. Once that connection is made, which takes only a millisecond, you will have a neuron pathway that is INSTANTLY going to let you see something you couldn't see.

I can't overemphasize this. The change you want can come right now. The only reason it won't is if you think it won't.

And here is where your mind tricks you. Change is often hard because *just the thought of change*, good or bad, causes your body to go into a state of chemical imbalance. You are going against the neural connections in your brain that you have grown accustomed to. This feels uncomfortable. Your body loses its ability to maintain homeostasis which is your body's ability to maintain a sense of internal balance and wellbeing. Your blood pressure may rise, your body temperature change, your breathing may shallow as your nervous system deals with the change or perceived change. Most prefer to avoid the thought and change and return the body to a state of balance and return to a comfortable feeling. This is why most push it off to tomorrow, it restores the comfort. But most won't do it tomorrow. They can't get past the discomfort to gain the benefits, even though they can see the benefits are right in front of them.

167

CREATE YOUR REALITY

We have now covered the majority of what you needed to learn about Special Relativity and Quantum Physics to create your reality any way you want. You will see you have always been the architect of your future.

So what have you learned?

You have learned the universe is nothing like most think it is. The material universe we see around us is a creation of our brain turning electromagnetic waves into the sights and sounds of our reality. A reality unique to each individual because not one of our brains is the same.

We have also learned about wave-particle duality. We know that all matter is both a wave and a particle and it takes consciousness to transfer the wave into a particle. Everything that we see and hear in our universe began as a wave. The true nature of the universe is more wave-like than matter like.

We know that waves are energy. The universe is pure energy. Your true nature is pure energy.

We know Einstein gave us the famous equation, $E=mc^2$, and from that equation, we know that energy and matter are the same. You can convert matter to energy and you can convert energy to matter.

We spend most of our time in our physical reality with all of its limitations and often forget we have another reality we can go to. We can enter the Quantum Field of Reality which is completely limitless.

The Quantum Field is pure energy. It is a field of infinite information. It is a field of Infinite Intelligence. It is consciousness. It cannot be perceived by any of our senses. It is outside of time and space. It governs all laws of nature.

This intelligence, this pure energy is organizing the universe. It is organizing energy into matter. The great thing is you have access to this Infinite Intelligence and have a say in what it does.

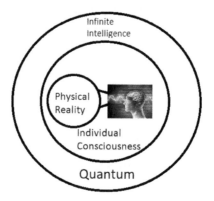

Your conscious mind can connect to this field and greater frequencies of information. Look at the image above. In previous lessons, we discussed how our brain converts a wave's energy into the sights and sounds of our reality. We know that we are not our brains nor our mind. We know we are the consciousness observing our brain and our mind. Just as we make our consciousness aware of our physical reality, we can also make our consciousness aware of the Quantum Reality. It's kind of like directing your consciousness in a different direction. Instead of looking forward look behind you. Don't take that literally. We know outside of reality there is no physical direction.

When we are in the Quantum Reality we can create our world any way we want.

How do we do that?

Do you remember we said waves have an infinite amount of frequencies? You will remember in the physical world these frequencies are limited by the quantum nature of physical reality which required energy to come in small, individual chunks. Well in the Quantum Reality frequencies are infinite.

Frequencies are carriers of information. You have access to an infinite amount of frequencies. Which means you have an infinite amount of energy and information with which to create your world. In the Quantum world all things, and I mean everything you could think of exists as a probability.

You are turning energy into the matter. Your consciousness is interacting with a greater consciousness, Infinite Intelligence and you are working together to turn probabilities into reality.

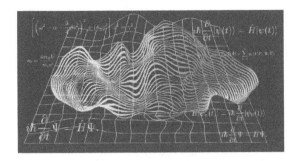

Hopefully, now you are thinking back to Schrodinger's Equation and how it lets us determine probability waves. You will remember the image above showing probability waves. The bigger the wave the bigger the chance of it collapsing into reality. Let's look at the waves a little differently now. The waves show the probability of events that may or may not happen in your life.

What determines what events the waves represent? Your imagination mixed with emotion. What you have running through your mind day after day and your emotional state create the probability waves.

So what determines the final result? Which wave collapses? Get ready for it. Here it comes. The biggest factor in determining which wave becomes your physical reality is your belief. If you truly believe it, you will see it.

So now I'm sure you want to know how to take your conscious awareness out of your physical reality and put it into the Quantum Realm. You need to bring yourself into and stay in the Now.

You need to take your mind off anything that concerns the material world. Easier said than done. Right?

The best way to do that is to sit in a dark room and close your eyes. Concentrate on slowing your breathing. You can learn to feel the energy all around you. You can learn to see the energy. This is a great way to stay in the Now which is your only entry point into the Quantum Realm. We will spend an entire lesson showing you how to feel the energy.

Concentrate on that energy. If a thought about the material world pops into your mind you have just been booted out of the Quantum Realm and the Now. Don't worry about it. Just start over and go back in. You will find the more you practice entering the Quantum Field the easier it will be to concentrate on just the energy and not have thoughts pop back into your head.

Most people get stuck in their lives. They collapse quantum waves into the same experience over and over again. You need to take your attention off everything you know in your life and center it on the Quantum Realm. The longer you can keep your attention in the Quantum Field, a field of pure, infinite, energy, the easier you create new experiences.

You are no longer affected by negative neural networks. Newer networks form. Your negative patterns of the past are changing.

Brainwaves get slower and move from beta to alpha and theta. This allows your subconscious to take over and connect with the Quantum Field and Infinite Intelligence.

You discover you can create new neural networks at an incredible rate. You might even say it is a Quantum Leap in intelligence. You suddenly know what you did not know. It is an incredible thing to experience.

Before you enter the Quantum Reality you need to have a clear intention and strong emotion. You need to decide what you want and feel the emotion of already having it. Don't see yourself getting what you want as happening in the future for that will make sure the future is where it stays. See yourself already having and living what you want. Involve every sense. What do you see, hear, touch, taste, smell?

Use your imagination to see what you want just as clearly as if you were watching it on a huge movie screen. Pay attention to every small detail you can think of.

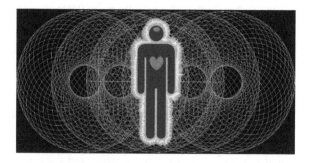

Do you remember in a previous lesson when we mentioned you have an electromagnetic field surrounding your body? Your intention is the electric charge created by your brain. Your emotion is the magnetic charge created by your heart. The two combine and make an electromagnetic field. Your brain creates the electric. Your heart creates the magnetic.

This attracts what you want to you. It connects with a vibrational frequency match between your energy and the energy of the Quantum Field.

You have only to focus on the intent and emotion. Do not worry about how you will get what you want. That is counterproductive. Infinite Intelligence will create the outcome.

Remember everything, absolutely everything exists as a probability frequency. The more you tune into the Quantum Realm the easier you can turn frequencies into physical reality.

Stop thinking somethings are just impossible for you to do, have or be. You are as much a part of Infinite Intelligence as any other person who has ever lived. Infinite intelligence does not play favorites. If it appears in one person's life be sure it can appear in yours too.

If you haven't collapsed the wave you want yet, you will. Remember the biggest determining factor for whether a wave collapses is belief. We know that it can be hard when everything around you seems to show the exact opposite of what you want.

The funny thing is people focus on the bad more often than the good and they wonder why their life is so hard.

If you practice this lesson you will become a master of collapsing wave functions into the reality of your choosing.

You know what to do next.

LET'S DO A THOUGHT EXPERIMENT

Like Einstein and Bohr and Schrodinger and many other quantum physicists, let's do a thought experiment. If you remember, a thought experiment is an experiment that takes place only in your mind. You use your thoughts and intuition to try and come up with a solution.

What we are about to talk about is purely hypothetical. We want to see if there is any way we can prove it to be true. That may turn out to be impossible, but we may also find we also can't prove it to be false.

Can you prove to me you even existed before you woke up this morning?

What if it is all in your mind?

The only thing you are experiencing is here right now.

What if all the thoughts you have in your head of the past are just thoughts?

Is there anything you can do to show that you existed yesterday?

Sure you can show something you did yesterday. Perhaps you can find leftover food that you know you ate yesterday. That proves that you existed yesterday, doesn't it? Somebody had to eat that food and you remember eating it.

But what if that food is nothing more than a creation in your mind?

What if your thought of eating it is only a thought in your mind?

What if everything you see around you is your mind creating your experience?

Like an actor, in a play, you are going to find props that draw you into the illusion of the reality of the play.

Albert Einstein once said, "Reality is merely an illusion, albeit a very persistent one."

What about others? What about those you met with or spoke with yesterday. Surely they will remember talking to you yesterday.

Of course, they will. But that doesn't prove there was a yesterday for either of you.

Perhaps they are no more than actors in your play.

Perhaps you are sharing a conscious reality or maybe they are just a creation in your reality. So, of course, they are going to agree with your creation, agree with your past.

Now that's just crazy, isn't it?

But let's not stop there.

When you sleep you may once again awaken to another day of the reality you have created or you may wake up to a completely new reality, with its ready-made past and experiences. You may find yourself in a new body, a new personality in ancient Egypt or Rome. You awaken again in a future land yet to be heard of by any alive today. Nothing about you resembles the person you are now but it is you and you know it; your consciousness is the same. You experience not only realities of this world but other planets, other universes, and other dimensions many indescribable by any of your five senses. You are experiencing many realities at a time and you chose the one to focus your consciousness on at the present moment. We know everything is infinite, limitless energy that our consciousness can collapse into reality.

Maybe it's like you are playing an advanced video game. When you play the game, you enter into it with its already made storyline and characters. If the character in the video was conscious, he would believe his world to be real, the story of the video game was the story of his past.

Just like playing a video game at any time we can choose to stop. We can choose to play a new game, or play the same game later, or choose to play nothing at all.

What is your backstory?

What if your backstory was just that and nothing more?

What if everything in your past was just a creation in your mind for you to experience Now?

How empowering would that be if your past is just setting up the backdrop for what you need to learn in this life's reality and you can leave this experience anytime you want and even come back to it later.

What if you have all eternity to create experiences? What if you could even re-experience this life and purposely make changes to see how it turns out differently? You could spend eternity experiencing different "story-lines" for the current life you are experiencing now.

If you knew that for a fact would that change how you live today? Would you accept the craziness that you are putting up with now or would you go with reckless abandon and make sure you got what you wanted out of this life?

Apply some of the things we have learned about Special Relativity and Quantum Mechanics and most importantly your higher self to the statements above. They may not be as "far out there" as they first sound.

174

THE HEIGHT OF ARROGANCE

You know enough Quantum Physics to see that something can be both true and false at the same time. Light is made of particles. TRUE. Light is a wave. TRUE. Light can't be both. FALSE.

Is Shrodinger's cat dead or alive? BOTH.

Can you see how truth and reality are unsubstantial, lack substance, and rely on individual interpretation to bring it into only a temporary, ephemeral, fleeting reality?

It is the height of arrogance to tell someone that what you believe is true and what they believe is false.

Never let anyone force you or cause you to live a life you don't want to live. If you are not hurting yourself or someone or something else then politely tell them you have the right to do what you want to do, not what they want you to do.

Find that feeling inside you that lets you know you are on the correct path. You will know it because when you think about what you are doing it will feel good to you. Let that feeling guide you. If the feeling changes and you feel uncomfortable you may need to analyze and adjust the path you are on. Know this, you will be guided.

Trust your feelings.

There are so many people who want others to live as they would have them live. Although they may have good intentions they live a life of misery. Everyone will not live as they want them to. Nobody is ever going to conform perfectly to their intentions. Wanting others to live as they desire is a road to unhappiness. It's funny they can't see it. Everyone is not doing what they want yet they are the ones who are not happy with their own life.

If you rely on others for your happiness you will be constantly disappointed. Happiness must come from within you, nowhere else.

Isn't it amazing how many people think they are entitled to something in life? Just by being alive, just by being who they are, they think the world owes them.

Hardly!

After you become an adult the world owes you nothing. If the world seems to send bad things your way it is your responsibility to fix it and no one else. It is your responsibility to give yourself the life you desire. That doesn't mean you can't ask for help. I'm sure you will find help coming from all around you and from many places you might not have expected. But in the end, it all comes down to you.

LESSON TWENTY

RELATIVITY REVISITED

In the previous lessons on Special Relativity, we learned the faster you move the slower time moves for you. We know this is called time dilation. We will now delve even deeper into that fact to show you just how amazingly crazy Special Relativity is and what that means for you. As we continue constantly remind yourself that as crazy as it sounds this stuff has been proven to be true over and over and over again. As we mentioned before, if not for the mathematics of Special Relativity we would not have GPS and many other advances we have today.

Don't make the mistake of thinking the effects of Special Relativity take effect only when you are moving super-fast. If your friend is sitting down and you just casually walk by, you are moving faster and time is moving slower for you. At a walking pace, time is moving about a billionth of one second slower. It is safe to say time dilation will not be very noticeable. You would have to take a billion steps for a difference in age of one second to occur. That's quite a bit different than the difference of years you would see when zooming off to other planets close to the speed of light and coming back to Earth to find everyone older than you or even long passed on, depending on how long your trip was.

Consider this. When you see someone standing next to you in a room, you are seeing light waves from that person. It took those light waves about a nanosecond to reach your eyes, so the best you can say is you know what that person was doing a billionth of a second ago. You are truly not seeing what that person is doing "now". Granted it is only a billionth of a second so for all intents and purposes you can say "now".

But what if that person was on a planet 5 light-years away from Earth. Let's say you could look at that person through a telescope, it would take the light waves 5 years to reach you. All you can ever know is what she was doing 5 years ago.

Here is where it gets super weird. Don't think that just because you can only see what she is doing 5 years ago that she is right "now" doing something on that planet which coincides with your "now" at this moment on Earth. Don't think you just can't see it yet. Don't think in the next five years you will able to see what she is doing right "now". Get ready for this next statement it may be a little shocking. According to Special Relativity, it is quite possible that she is already back on Earth and probably ten or more years in her future. You were just seeing that person on another planet who is already back on Earth. Freaky!!!

We could go over the math and I could show you how that is possible but to be honest, that would be long and tedious. Another way to show you is by using graphs which makes the concept a lot easier to see, plus it is pretty cool. I think you will like this.

First, let me remind you what an event is. In the earlier lessons on Special Relativity, we defined an event as something that happens in time and space. It must be described using both. For example, to just say her wedding, is not an event. To say her wedding at The Belle Church is not an event. To say her wedding at The Belle Church, July 15, 2020, is an event. You must have a time and a location in space for it to be an event.

Second, let's take another look at a cartesian coordinate system like we saw when we did the Calculus lesson.

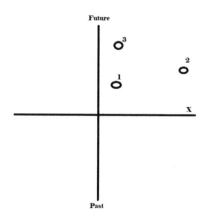

Looking at the image above you will notice we have a timeline running vertically and a spaceline running horizontally. The timeline runs from past to present. Our space line is represented by x. Technically we should also have a y and z line with the x because space has three dimensions. But we will only use x for simplicity. It all works out the same.

We put three circles in the coordinate system representing three events. Let's say event one is your graduation from school. Event two is meeting your true love. Event three is the two of you getting married. If you haven't done all these things let's just pretend you did.

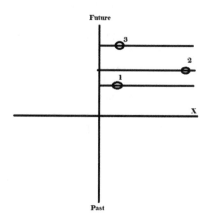

See yourself walking across the line in the image above from past to future looking to your right, what would you see?

You would see event one (your graduation) first. You would see event two (meeting your true love) second. You would see event three (your wedding) third.

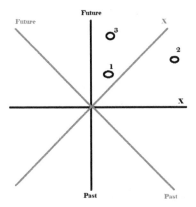

Looking at the image above, let's overlay another cartesian coordinate system on top of the first but let's tilt this one to the left 45 degrees. This is will represent another person in a different time frame relative to you.

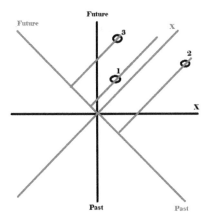

Now let's have this person walk the new line from past to future and look to their right. What will they see? They will see the events of your life in the order of event two, then one, then three. What?

They will see you meeting your true love (2) before you graduate (1). No way! That's not what happened. How can that be?

There is only now. Past and future are an illusion created by our brain.

That is so hard to grasp, isn't it? Everything around us seems to support time constantly marching forward. Clocks tick. We move from one place to another. Our heart beats. That all points to a real-time doesn't it?

Here is one way that might help you grasp the concept. Think about a book. The book has a beginning and an end. The narrative flows from past to present. But the entire book is also here at this moment right now. You don't have to read the book from front to back. You can automatically skip to and read any part of the book you want. You can read about their marriage before you read about them falling in love.

This brings up an interesting question. If, using the analogy of the book, the entire book is already written then does that mean your entire life is already written? If we live in the constant now does that mean everything we experience is already here? Does that mean that everything that can happen has already happened?

The answer to that is yes and no.

Does that mean we do not have free will?

The answer to that is a definite NO. We HAVE free will. You write the book of your life and that book is constantly changing.

We'll stop here now to give you some time to process what we just covered. I know it can make your brain feel a little weird.

Go tell somebody about what you just learned. Be sure to look at the expression on their face.

A NEW WAY OF LOOKING AT MONEY

Most need to change how they view money.

You have learned everything is energy, this includes money. It is easy to see now when most money is nothing more than digits you view on a computer screen. The energy of money can be positive or negative. For most, it is very negative. What type of energy is money for you?

This is easy for you to figure out. How does the thought of money make you feel? Are your emotions positive or negative? Does the thought of money make you feel insecure or even apprehensive or fearful? Or does the thought of money feel you with a sense of happiness, delight, and gratitude?

How you feel about money determines whether money is a source of negative or positive energy for you. Unfortunately for most, it is negative.

This is because they believe in scarcity. They believe if one person has more money there is less for them. This could not be farther from the truth. Money is energy and the universe has an infinite supply of energy. Therefore, there is an infinite supply of money.

Most just don't believe it. Do you?

The majority limit their supply of money by limiting the energy that flows to them. If you believe in scarcity, you will probably constantly struggle with money issues.

What can you do?

I want to show you a new way of looking at money.

Money is energy. Money can be both negative or positive. I want you to keep a positive supply of "money" energy flowing towards you.

Stop chasing after money.

What? How do you keep money flowing towards you when you stop chasing after it? That makes no sense, does it?

Yes, stop chasing after money and let money come to you. Money is the natural byproduct of your natural abundance and your natural abundance is a byproduct of you finding your purpose. When you find that which excites you, which gives you a reason for being, that which you care about more than money, the money will flow to you in ways you never could have imagined.

Then once you get money, let go of it.

What?

Let go of your money and feel good about letting go of your money. Let's repeat. Feel good about letting go of your money.

When you use your money in a positive manner and don't feel apprehensive about letting it go, it will come back to you multiplied.

Are you familiar with the phrase, "Nature abhors a vacuum"?

When you release money in a positive manner it creates an emptiness that the universe MUST refill and will not only refill but will overflow.

So how do you release your money in a positive manner?

Release it with a sense of gratitude. Take care of your needs and wants (yes be good to yourself) knowing there will always be more than enough. Give! Share your money with others. Help them with their wants and needs. Let go of your money with gratitude in your heart and you will be amazed at how fast it comes back.

There are givers and takers in this world, and though many times it may not seem like it, never doubt when all is said and done, the universe is the great equalizer. If you are a giver the universe will give back to you many times over. If you are a taker the universe will take from you. Here we define "taker" not someone who is in need but someone whose actions are defined by laziness, dishonesty, or any number of negative reasons. A situation in which the taker can take care of themselves. You may think you have gained when you take from someone, but it is only short term and when the universe takes, you will not like where you find yourself.

It is very important any negative feelings of having money are eliminated. Not having money is not a sign of humbleness or increased spirituality. Just as having a lot of money is not a sign of greed.

Money is a personality magnifier. Money will take a person's personality and broadcast it to the world. A person who truly cares about people will be shown to be even more caring. A greedy, self-absorbed individual will become worse.

Let's talk about work. Many have been wired with the wrong definition of work. Once you change your definition of work you will realize how you were throwing your time away. You were selling your life to others and getting paid nowhere near what your time is worth. Society has most convinced this is the only alternative. Not only are there other alternatives but better alternatives and here is the paradigm shift... Many of the other alternatives are less risky. Society has just convinced you they are not.

The 40-hour workweek is becoming a thing of the past. Your brain has been wired by society to make you believe you must work all your life only to retire at an old age. Most see this as an inescapable truth. As hard as it may seem to see right now, it is sooooo false.

We all hate rejection, so why are you constantly rejecting yourself and money? You are rejecting an incredible relationship with money.

So how do you stop the rejection?

It is time for you to believe in yourself. Especially now, and time is of the essence. Our economy is changing and it is waiting on no one. Technology is making a huge impact on the job market. The need for human labor will continue to decrease. You can ask employers if they ever plan on refilling positions they have let go. Most will tell you flat out "No." As our economy continues to change the safer bet is to bet on yourself. You take control. You decide how to create your financial future.

I quit my nine to five job after waking up on a Monday morning and checking my online sales before I went to work and seeing I had made more money that night while I slept than I was going to make all week at my job.

I always say, "Why work, when you can have a computer work for you?"

But it took me a while to get to that point. The simple reason was I didn't believe it would work for me. But now I do, and it has brought me a much better life than I had when I did the nine to five thing and it is so much easier not to mention less stressful.

This is not a book about making money but let me take just one brief moment to explain how you can make really good money if that appeals to you. And it should.

This will take all of about a minute.

First, find, or even better yet, create something useful people want to buy. But please make sure your product is good. No not just good, but incredible, outstanding. Make sure it is a benefit to those who purchase. Make it something that will change their life. Let your product flow from your passion.

Put up a web page selling your product. (It's best to make your product digital like a book or a video so they can download it automatically, that way you don't have to worry about shipping or even the transaction.)

Pay for ads to have Google and Facebook find customers who are interested in what you offer. Have the ads send the customers to your web page. Both Google and Facebook know just about everything about everyone. It never ceases to amaze me how they can constantly put you in touch with others who are ready and willing to buy exactly what you are selling.

The web page will make the sale for you and collect your money from your customers and your customers' email.

Build an email database of customers.

Keep having Google and/or Facebook send more customers to your web page.

Keep making sales and building the email database.

The database, your email list, is the key. As that gets bigger so does your potential to sell and your income.

Your list will be constantly growing and you will keep offering new, highly useful, high demand products to your constantly growing customer base.

As a result, not only will your customer base keep growing but so will your income.

And there you have it.

I have now told you all the steps to selling online. As you can see it's not a complicated process. You just have to do it. If you don't know how to do some of the things like put up a web page, pay someone who can, or read a book.

But know this-- you can do it. You can make incredible money with very little work involved. Maybe some work in the beginning but once everything starts snowballing you will be amazed at the results.

You may be telling yourself that you won't be able to make money like I just described. It may have worked for me, but it isn't going to work for you. I used to say that when I heard of others doing what I now do.

What if I told you the key to my "financial" success was not putting up the right kind of web page or selling the right kind of product? Although that is part of it.

The key to my success is my mind. What I do externally doesn't nearly matter as much as what I do internally.

It's all a creation of your mind. Seriously look around this is all you. What you see out there is a projection of your mind.

Why do I have a computer work for me instead of me working a 9 to 5 job?

Because my mind decided and I accepted, quite gladly, that was the way it was going to be for me.

STOP THINKING YOU NEED A JOB TO MAKE MONEY

You may have heard the saying that JOB stands for Just Over Broke.

The belief that you need to be hired by someone to pay you money to survive in this world was programmed into you by society mainly through the school system.

Believe it or not, schooling was not required in our country when it was founded. Education was up to the family and more importantly the individual. Yes, there were schools they could attend, and many did but it was not a requirement. George Washington, Benjamin Franklin, and Thomas Jefferson never graduated from high school, but they were successful.

Consider an example from today. Richard Branson dropped out of high school at age 16 to start a mail-order record company which became Virgin Records. Today he has an empire of over 200 businesses, including airlines, record labels, and mobile phones, in 30 countries. His net worth is over $6.8 billion.

The mandatory school system came about because those in power saw it as a way to take away an individual's self-identity and creativity and keep them satisfied with low paying jobs. They were shown no other alternative. They did not want the development of independent minds.

Think about some of the craziness of the school system. You send your child into a system for at least 12 years to be schooled by strangers. You have no control or don't even know what is being programmed into their mind.

Classes on art and music are taught to a lesser degree and not considered as important as math and science. Why? Because the arts foster creativity and individuality and the powers that be do not want that.

Consider this amazing (and yes often hidden) fact. You can learn all the writing, reading, and math you need to be productive in society in about 100 hours per subject. If you spent 5 hours a day learning those core subjects you would obtain a substantial understanding in just ONE year.

What?!?

So why in the world do we spend a mandatory 12 years in school?

Because after those 12 years your mind has been primed for a life of servitude to those in power. Schools do not encourage free-thinking or creativity. Schools only provide a rote curriculum of learning which will ensure your submission to others. Ensuring you are a "good little loyal worker."

You now think the only way you can make money is by getting a job.

You need to undo the programming. It's time for you to learn that you are a true genius. It is time for you to find within yourself that which was purposely hidden. It is time for you to become the you, you were meant to be.

LESSON TWENTY-ONE

EVERYTHING IS ONE

There exists within all of us the potential to shape our world so far beyond what is comprehendible, to most it is unbelievable. This is why you needed to learn about Special Relativity and Quantum Physics, so you now know what our universe is really like. Our universe and everything in it is pure energy we have the power to turn into our physical reality; waves of probability that are there but not there; that exist but do not exist.

Can you think of anything else in this world like that? There is one.

Think of your thoughts. Are your thoughts real? They are.

Do your thoughts not also exist? They are real for you and they also have the potential of taking form in the physical world.

So what have we learned so far?

We know there is a field of infinite potential which shapes the entire universe. We have no direct experience of this field because our brain converts the field into the physical reality we live in every day. But our physical reality is only of secondary importance.

Everything that happens to us in this life is first a state in the field of infinite potential. Anything and everything that can happen is ALREADY in this state of infinite potential.

Unfortunately, most of the world believes in materialism. They believe that all there is in the world is what we can observe with our five senses. They might believe in a higher spiritual plane beyond this world but they think the physical world they are living in is concrete, completely unchangeable.

We know differently. We know matter is shifting in and out of wave-like states. We say when matter is in a wave state it is nowhere. We know it takes consciousness to bring matter out of the wave state and into its concrete form. We know the universe is made of waveforms and our consciousness collapses those waveforms into what becomes our reality and as we mentioned above the waveforms are very similar to thoughts created by our mind.

Does this mean the universe has a mind? Does this mean our mind is connected to the entire universe?

Yes, it does.

We talked about Carl Jung and the Collective Unconscious mind we are all a part

186

of. This means that while our thoughts are our own, we also have access to thoughts from Infinite Intelligence. That field is always acting through us to guide us. There is a constant connection between our mind and the mind of the universe.

Here is another way of looking at it. There is this infinite realm of potentiality throughout the entire universe. Everything is connected to everything. You are an indivisible part of the universe. You can never be separate from it. Therefore, there is a constant infinite potential within you that is always going to be there whenever you need it. Because it is you.

Woah!

Infinite Intelligence is here in the form of you for a reason. You have meaning.

Stop seeing everything as separate. See the wholeness. See everyone as one.

How amazing would be the change if everyone saw the entire world as one?

In a past lesson, we discussed when you see something it is light entering your eyes. When we talked about Special Relativity, we said to see what a person is doing on a planet 5 light years away from you, it would take light 5 years to reach you, so you are essentially seeing something that happened 5 years in the past. The reason is that nothing can move faster than the speed of light. You will always measure the speed of light moving at the same rate no matter how fast you are moving.

We also talked about the EPR experiment and how each particle instantly knew when the other particle had been measured and instantly took its appropriate spin. The crazy thing is it doesn't matter how far the particles are away from each other. If the particles were five light-years away we would expect the information to take 5 years for the particles to communicate but the transformation is instantaneous. But how can that be possible? Information cannot spread faster than the speed of light?

If everything is one then there is no problem. We as finite beings may not be able to perceive information faster than the speed of light, but being one, Infinite Intelligence can know and control what is going on everywhere, instantly.

Never forget. Like a wave in the ocean, you are a part of the ocean of Infinite Intelligence. Infinite Intelligence is you.

Here is a fun experiment I want you to try. The next time you are at a mall or a place with many people just find a place to sit and observe. As people walk by tell yourself that person is me, that person is me, that person is me. See what happens. You will find the experience very interesting.

So go teach this lesson to someone and tell them you are me and I am you. See what they say.

WE THINK WE ARE BEING LOGICAL AND MAKING RATIONAL DECISIONS

What we need to understand is our subconscious mind (which we are mostly unaware of) is making most of our decisions. Our conscious mind is justifying a decision already made by the subconscious mind. We are fooling ourselves into believing our conscious mind has logically arrived at an answer. The subconscious mind does not respond to logic. It only responds to emotion. This does not mean we have no free will and are completely controlled by our subconscious. We can learn how to control our subconscious mind. We must learn how to control our subconscious mind.

We do many things automatically. That is because we have made neural connections that fire rapidly which means we give little conscious thought. This is why we are ALL blind to our imperfections, but they are all too apparent to others. We ALL have many things about ourselves we need to change. Fortunately, as you are well aware, we can change our neural connections just by thinking.

Most of our subconscious beliefs were formed when we were very young and we had little to no say in what we were told to believe. Most people carry those beliefs with them throughout their entire lives. They never question them. They are limiting themselves because they are shutting themselves off from amazing possibilities that do not fit their belief pattern. A little child has determined their fate.

We need to separate our beliefs from ourselves. Our beliefs can become so ingrained in us they become a part of who we are. Separating ourselves from our beliefs can become a very painful task, even though many of our beliefs are hurting us. They are keeping us from becoming what we want to be. The ironic thing is often we don't know what we believe. One moment we may think something is true the next we aren't sure. So we have a part us we are not even sure about that might be keeping us from everything we want in life. Confusing isn't it? I was confused too.

Change is often hard because it causes your body to go into a state of chemical imbalance. This feels uncomfortable. Most prefer to avoid the change and return the body to a state of balance and return to a comfortable feeling. They can't get past the short term discomfort to gain the long term benefits.

The cool thing is because you can think of something in a different way you have the power to make it different. No matter what situation you are in if you can picture a different situation you can change.

Start by questioning everything. The majority of the world live their lives with a need to be told what to think. And yes, question what you are reading right now. It is time for you to create your own belief patterns.

When you do you will discover a few things.

You will see this world is a magical place. Things you once thought were impossible will become a reality.

It will be very comforting when you discover this world is not ruled by random chance. You are not just a statistic. You are the creator. You are in control.

You will then realize you are here to help break the pattern this world is trapped in. You are here to show this is not a world of scarcity and fear but a world of unending abundance and love.

Begin questioning right now.

Here is an exercise to help you bring your subconscious thoughts out into the light.

Become aware of your thoughts. Concentrate on your breathing, eliminate all thoughts. When a thought comes into your head write it down. Go back and just concentrate on your breathing. Another thought will distract you. Write it down. Go back to your breathing. Repeat this until you have written down at least 10 thoughts. Read the list. You may learn something.

LESSON TWENTY-TWO

THE LITTLE BRAIN IN THE HEART

I want to ask you a question.

What is the purpose of your heart?

If you are like most, your answer is something like, "It pumps blood through my body." That is true. The heart beats over 100,000 times a day and circulates about 2,000 gallons of blood through over 60,000 miles of blood vessels.

Did you know the heart has other functions?

If you have not heard this information before this will be another lesson that is going to freak you out. Get ready!

What if the heart like the brain can also store memories?

What if the heart is also responsible for intuition?

What if the heart is also a source of wisdom?

Your heart has about 40,000 special neurons called neurites.

What?

Yes, your heart has neurons. Neurons are the brain cells we talked about in chapter one. These 40,000 neurites are called the little brain in the heart.

Here is an interesting story about the little brain.

Soon after a heart transplant, a young girl got cravings for chicken nuggets and green peppers. Can you imagine her surprise when she discovered that chicken nuggets and green peppers were the favorite foods of her heart donor?

Here is an even stranger story. An eight-year-old girl received the heart of a ten-year-old girl who had been murdered. After receiving the heart, she had dreams which were details of the murder. The details led authorities to track down the killer of her heart donor.

These phenomena have been reported over and over again by heart transplant recipients. There is a connection between the brain and the heart and when we make that connection our potential skyrockets.

We have always thought of our emotions as emanating from the heart and it appears that is exactly what happens. The heart converts emotions into the electrical language used by the brain. The heart tells our brain what our body needs during any emotional state. There is two-way communication between the heart and the brain.

When we use our brains, we try to be logical and think things out and see if we can find the best course of action. We weigh the pros and cons and then try and come up with a plan, steps one, two, three...

This is often necessary but we forget to consult with our heart. You need to rely on the incredible wisdom of your heart. There is no better way to say it except somehow the heart just knows.

We have shown how the heart retains memories; many memories you have long forgotten. The heart uses these memories and learns from them even without you knowing. Your heart takes your past experiences and remembers outcomes you have totally forgotten. Then it combines everything, takes a little bit here and a little bit there and combines everything to gain insights of pure wisdom. It then passes this wisdom on to you in a gut feeling. A feeling we have that something is correct or there is something we need to do but we don't know why. We just feel a pulling telling us this is the way to go.

Your heart doesn't have the time to tell you how it took all those memories and cut them up and recombined them to make its decision it just gives you that guiding feeling.

So how do we take advantage of the wisdom of our hearts?

Be open to it. Trust that feeling. Develop a relationship with your heart. When you follow your heart and discover what it is telling you to be correct over and over again, your trust in your heart will grow. You will then find that your heart begins communicating with you even more.

So, you know your heart will guide you. You know Infinite Intelligence will guide you. Are you feeling pretty safe? But it gets even better.

Let me remind you again of the electromagnetic field surrounding your body? Your intention is the electric charge created by your brain. Your emotion is the magnetic charge created by your heart. The two combine and make an electromagnetic field. Your brain creates the electric. Your heart creates the magnetic.

Put your heart into sync with your brain and you create a coherence that produces an electromagnetic field around your body that will interact with the Quantum Field and drastically increase the probability of the waves of your greatest desires which you will soon be able to collapse with your consciousness.

So how do you put the brain and heart in sync?

Develop an intent so strong that nothing will stand in your way of seeing your dream unfold and back that intent with an unwavering belief; you just know you will get what you want. You can feel the experience already. Positive emotions are high. You are feeling good. Again, you just know things will work out. A slight feeling of doubt may enter your mind, but you can dismiss it just as fast as it shows up. You know the doubt is nothing more than your mind lying to you.

When you are in that determined state of belief the electromagnetic field surrounding your body becomes a supercharged magnet and it instantly pulls your wants and desires to you at an incredible rate. Just don't turn it off. Too many people do that way too often. Their dream is right in front of them and then just before they can see it they turn off the magnet and away goes the dream.

Determine your intent. Feel the emotion. Enter the Quantum Field by clearing all your physical thoughts. This will connect you with Infinite Intelligence. Don't worry about the how of your intent. That is a physical thought. Just know what you want is coming. Just relax and enjoy.

YOU HAVE TO DISAPPOINT SOME PEOPLE TO BE TRUE TO YOURSELF

You can't keep holding on to a life you were not meant to live because you are worried about how others will feel about your choices. That is crazy. You have a gift to give to this world. And you can only give that gift to the world by being true to who you are. Never be afraid to be yourself.

"To be nobody but yourself -- in a world which is doing its best, night and day, to make you everybody else – means to fight the hardest battle which any human being can fight; and never stop fighting." - E.E. Cummings

Stop following the crowd. Why in the world would you want to be a carbon copy of everyone else? Those who make a difference in this world are unique, different, maybe even weird.

Your life is waiting. Are you where you want to be?

Are you playing it safe because of what you think might be a bad or risky decision? The irony is if you continue to play it safe you will one day look back on "playing it safe" in regret.

We all have dreams. Yet the sad fact is most will never get to experience those dreams and there is absolutely no reason they shouldn't.

Many are paralyzed by their limitations. Limitations of their creation. They are locked in a prison and do not realize they hold the key. You are not limited. You did not come here to have the same dull experience over and over again, every day, year in and year out, until your trips around the sun come to an end. You are here to experience so many of the amazing things this world has to offer. It is time for you to see what you have been missing.

Many are paralyzed because they are afraid of what others will think of them. The truth is it doesn't matter what others think. This is your life. You are here to create your masterpiece. Do not let limited, selfish minds, who cannot see it from your point of view, dictate how you should live your life. It goes beyond arrogance for someone to believe they should tell you how to spend the limited time you have been given on this planet.

This is first and foremost your life. Everyone needs to keep in mind we all have the right to live our own life. If someone is doing something and they are not hurting themselves or someone or something, you have no right to tell them to stop

You may find those whose life you think needs correction end up teaching you a lesson and they may do things with their life many only dream of. If they are doing no harm then you may just need to butt out and mind your own business.

Many are paralyzed because they just don't know what to do.

Here is the cool thing. You don't have to know what to do. You just must know what you want and then take a step towards getting what you want.
Here is where it gets cool. It doesn't even matter if the step you take is correct or completely wrong. The universe will guide you. Like a GPS in your car, the universe will let you know if you

are making a wrong turn. But you have to be making the move before it can tell you. Just like the GPS can't tell you what to do if you are sitting still in your car. The universe can't tell you what to do if you are sitting still in your life.

In the end, we only regret the chances we didn't take.

What you want is there for you whenever you want it. What you are doing is resisting the change. Change causes your body to go into a chemical imbalance. It doesn't feel that good. Most prefer to avoid temporary discomfort and avoid the change and bring the body back to a state of balance. They feel better. They rationalize they will do it, whatever it is, later. Maybe tomorrow. But tomorrow they repeat the same process. They push it off again until tomorrow, and they truly believe they will do it tomorrow. But tomorrow comes. Again they push it off. They are in a trap. Many never get out of the tomorrow trap.

What do you want?

Get up and do something to get it right now.

Just do something. Stop making excuses. This is the hardest thing for most people to do -- get off their butts and get something done. We all procrastinate and we always will.

When writing this book many days I would find myself making excuses for not writing.

I wake up and decide after I shower and have breakfast I will start writing. While making breakfast I notice the cats are low on cat food and I am almost out of Coke Zero (my lifesaver once I found out I was diabetic). I can't let the cats starve and I have to have my Coke Zero. I have to go to Kroger's. I will start writing when I get home from Kroger's. After getting the two essentials, cat food and Coke Zero, and many other items I didn't plan on buying I see Gabe's beside Kroger's. Many times you get some incredible deals on some really good finds in Gabe's. It's been a long time since I've shopped there, I should take a quick look and see what they have. I'm sure I will find something I like. After about an hour of looking, I don't find anything. Now it's almost lunchtime. I am super hungry. I am diabetic. I can't put off eating. I think it would be a good idea to invite my mom out to lunch. I'm a good son. After lunch, I return home to begin cranking out more of my book. Entering the house I realize I left the TV on. As I stop by the TV I see a commercial for today's Dr. Phil Show. Wow, that looks interesting. I have to watch that. It comes on in about an hour. I can't start writing now that isn't enough time to get started and get in a flow. I sit down on the couch and flip channels until the Dr. Phil Show comes on. That was a good show. I'm glad I didn't miss it. This is a comfortable couch. Sitting on this couch has made me a little sleepy. Plus during the Dr. Phil show, one of my cats decided to go to sleep on my lap. I will just lay here for a few minutes and get a little rest. I mean I can't knock the cat off my lap and interrupt her sleep. I decide to rest for a few minutes. It turns into a lot more than a few minutes. How did that happen? I didn't realize I was that tired. What time is it? It is almost dinner time. Ok. I will make dinner and then after dinner I will work on the book. There are still plenty of hours left in the day and I am a night owl. After dinner, I can't help but notice the house is a mess. I can't stand messes. The dishes need washing. The floors need sweeping. How can I concentrate on writing a book in a mess like this? I can't. I wash the dishes. I sweep the floors. I look outside and the sky is getting dark. Wow, where does the time go? That's okay I can still put in some good writing hours. Walking back to the computer it all of a sudden hits me… Tonight, America's Got Talent comes on and it is the champion show. I have never missed a single America's Got Talent since the show premiered years ago. After watching the show, I have another thought. I have a credit on Audible for a free book. I will find a good book that will give me some good insights into my writing. I should get those insights before I write. I find an incredible audiobook. I sit back in my massage chair. (Which by the way I highly recommend getting one. I would probably trade in my car before I would trade in my chair.) I begin listening to my new book. Yes, I was right, what an incredible book. I fall asleep in my chair. I wake up and it is one o'clock in the morning. Oh well, tomorrow is a new day. I will definitely spend the day writing tomorrow.

I wake up and decide after I shower and have breakfast I will start writing. While making breakfast I glance at the newspaper and notice my favorite store in the entire world is having a one-day sale. I can't pass up on that can I?

So often we make excuses for not doing the things we do and we accept those excuses. Sometimes we don't even make excuses. We know we need to do something but we just can't make ourselves do it.

The funny thing is you want to do it but you won't, even though you want to. You know this is the best thing in the world for you to do. But even though you want to, you can't make yourself do it, Even though you know all the incredible things this will bring into your life, your mind is now giving reasons you can't do it right now. You are having uneasy feelings. You can feel it in your stomach. It kind of tingles. Deep down you know this will be incredibly beneficial for you and that makes you feel even more uneasy. You feel your heart beating just slightly faster and your breathing becomes shallow. You still want to do it. But you just can't right now. You might do it later you tell yourself. That makes you feel a little better. The uneasy feeling decreases. But you know you aren't going to do it later. You know you have plenty of time to do it. You want to. You really do. But you just can't.

Stop making excuses.

For every person who gives you an excuse for why they can't do something, you can find another person in the exact same situation who did it.

Stop playing the blame game. Decide it doesn't matter who is right or wrong. Decide you are going to be the one to fix things. You will be surprised how fast you fix things.

You are where you are in life because of the choices you have made. You may not have caused many of the things to happen to you but you chose how to react to them. When we are presented with life's situations, we ask ourselves, "How am I supposed to feel about this situation?" We FIRST decide and THEN our brain fires the necessary neurons and produces the chemicals which make us feel like we THINK we should.

You do have the time, even if you just spend one minute today. Just do something. Do it NOW!

You can and you will.

Get everything you want out of life.

You can change your life in a split second. If you really wanted to you could do it right now.

Once you truly make up your mind to do something the universe instantly sets things in motion to help you.

Instantly! Not a week from now. Not a day from now. Not even an hour from now. Instantly!

You know what you need to do. Don't let the fear of the unknown or the fear of change stop you.

People ask me how I went from a failed business to being financially free and I tell them it was because at first I thought I knew everything but I soon learned I knew nothing. This world is nothing like I thought it was. There are things that most are not aware of. There are ways of doing things that go against everything we are taught in society. Being blunt, the majority are doing it all wrong. You can see it every day as they labor away at jobs they can't stand, just to make enough money to get by. You don't have to. It is not supposed to be that way.

One of the biggest plagues in our society is that everyone believes in scarcity. They feel threatened by those who they think are unreasonably taking their rare possession. In reality, it is like they are sitting on a beach and getting upset because someone is asking them for a hand full of sand.

You are here to create your own life, to live life on your terms, to be and do anything you want.

What you want is here right now. You just can't see it.

Did you know when you intend to do something your subconscious becomes aware of your intention before you are consciously aware of your intention? A part of your brain knows what you are going to do before you do. So understand this, your subconscious knows your dreams before you do and you will never be given a dream, a desire without the ability to make it come true. It is right there waiting for you right now. You can rewire your brain and you will start to see things that have always been there you just couldn't see before.

I can't overemphasize this enough. It is what is going on inside you that matters, not what you see going on outside you. I know that it is hard to accept, especially when what you see physically is not going your way. You want to keep searching for the answer outside of you in the physical world. It can be hard, discouraging and frustrating. I know. Been there. Done that. But you can truly change your physical world by changing your mental world. And until you change inside the outside change may never come at all or arrive very slowly.

That doesn't mean you don't need to do what is necessary in the physical world. Consider painting a picture. The picture comes from within and it can be anything you want it to be, but until you pick up the paintbrush it will never exist.

You have a desire within you. "The desire is simply the capacity for larger life seeking fulfillment; every desire is the effort of an unexpressed possibility to come into action. It is power seeking to manifest which causes desire. That which makes you want is the same as that which makes the plant grow; it is life, seeking fuller expression." - Wallace Wattles

Your desires are given to you for a reason. Those desires come from a higher place and only one thing in this physical world can prevent you from obtaining those desires. That one thing is you. Nothing else stands in your way. What you want is right here for the taking, right now.

"You are not a victim. You are responsible for your life. Whether comedy or tragedy, YOU DID IT!" – Alan Watts

LESSON TWENTY-THREE

ERASE A CLOUD WITH YOUR MIND

Sometimes you pick up a book expecting great things and it lets you down. Sometimes you pick up a book and find it was not only what you expected but so much more. "So much more," is the perfect description of Masaru Emoto's, "The Hidden Messages in Water."

I vaguely knew about the book before I read it. I knew that a scientist in Japan was photographing water crystals. Water crystals emerge for only twenty to thirty seconds as temperature rises and ice melts. As Masaru states, "The truths of the cosmos take shape and become visible, if only for a few seconds."

These water crystals were exposed to a variety of stimuli, including music and the spoken word. The stimuli had a dramatic effect on the crystals. Negative stimuli produced distorted, malformed crystals, while positive stimuli produced stunningly, beautiful crystals. For example, crystals exposed to the words, "Thank You" were beautiful and complete while crystals exposed to the words, "You Fool!" didn't even form.

Masaru draws our attention to the fact that our bodies are 70 percent water, we exist mostly as water. This is imperative when we consider that water is a transporter of energy throughout our entire body. Masaru also shows us how water can copy and memorize information. When you put these characteristics of water together you discover that you can change your life and create your world however you want it.

"Understanding the fact that we are essentially water is the key to uncovering the mysteries of the universe." - Masaru Emoto

Everything in the universe is vibrating and everything in the universe has its own frequency. The science of Quantum Physics has shown us that as we go deep into the level of the subatomic all matter disappears replaced by waves of energy. And since everything in the universe is vibrating, everything in the universe is also producing sound. And guess what is the "master listener" to receive this sound? Water!

"Water - so sensitive to the unique frequencies being emitted by the world - essentially and efficiently mirrors the outside world. The written words themselves emit a unique vibration that water is capable of sensing. Water faithfully mirrors all the vibrations created in the world and changes these vibrations into a form that can be seen with the human eye. When water is shown a written word, it receives it as vibration and expresses the message in a specific form." - Masaru Emoto

When we realize that everything is vibration the term resonance becomes very important. A simple way to define resonance is "like energies attract." Therefore, whatever frequency we are sending out we will attract frequencies of a like nature. What are you attracting? Love and gratitude or hate and fear.

One of Masaru's interesting theories is that gratitude is a more powerful vibration than love. As he uniquely puts it...

"A water molecule consists of two hydrogen atoms and one oxygen atom. If love and gratitude were linked together in a ratio of 1 to 2, gratitude would be twice as large as love. When you become the embodiment of gratitude think about how pure the water that fills your body will be."

"Everything exists in this one moment. You no longer need to be troubled by your past and can know that the future can be anything you will it to be. You, as you are, in this very moment hold the key to everything."

Masaru shows you how to prove to yourself that your consciousness has an incredible impact on the physical world. He teaches you how to erase a cloud with just your thoughts. You can make a cloud disappear. Everyone can do this and the first time you do, it is paradigm-shattering. When you see the cloud fade away because of your thoughts your life will change forever.

On a partially, clear day, look up in the sky and target just one cloud, maybe one not too large. You must believe the cloud will disappear, but you shouldn't try too hard. Imagine an invisible beam of energy being sent from your consciousness towards the cloud, breaking it into pieces. Say in the past tense, "The cloud has disappeared," say to the energy, "Thank you for doing that." If you follow these steps the cloud will start to thin out and disappear in a matter of minutes. Clouds are especially susceptible to our will because they are water in a gaseous form.

Here are tips that help me whenever I erase a cloud...

1. As Masaru mentions above, start small. It will take more time and perhaps hinder your confidence if you start with a large cloud.

2. On your first attempts, you will experience doubt. Keep telling yourself you can do this. Let the doubt run its course. It will fade away. Especially as you see the cloud start to fade away.

3. Having a feeling of gratitude is the key to erasing the cloud. If you do not hold a feeling of gratitude in your heart it is very difficult to erase the cloud. As Masaru mentions, thank the cloud for disappearing.

4. Relax your mind. As we spoke in earlier lessons try and put your mind in an alpha-theta state. Look at the cloud. Now picture it in your mind. Begin to see the cloud breaking up and disappearing in your mind. Bring your imagination outward. Overlay the cloud in your mind onto the cloud in "the real" world. See the cloud slowly disappearing right before your very eyes.

Now go out and make a cloud disappear. Then sit back and reflect on what you have just done and how powerful you are. You just changed the physical world with your thoughts. There is nothing you cannot do.

Another experiment Masaru has you perform is to put rice into two containers. On the first container write "Thank You" on the second write "You Fool." You will find the rice in the container with the words, "You Fool" will decay and rot a lot faster than the rice with the words, "Thank You." You can also speak the words to the rice instead of writing the words. Words are vibrations influence our world.

This got me thinking. If words are vibrations and we resonate, attract to us, what we are vibrating, then words play a very important role in attracting towards us the circumstances that make up our lives. Now add this to the fact that water can copy and memorize information. Write what you want to attract on a bottle of water. The vibrations enter the water. The water remembers the vibrations. You drink the water. You take on the vibration. You are after all 70% water. You are now resonating with what you want to attract.

Don't take my word for any of this. Try all these experiments yourself. They are easy to perform and the results will change your life forever.

"We all have an important mission. To make water clean again and to create a world that is easy and healthy to live in. To accomplish our mission, we must first make sure our hearts are clear and unpolluted." - Masaru Emoto

You are going to change physical reality with your mind. What other aspects of reality do you think you can change with just your mind?

AFTER THIS LIFE

We fear death, don't we? Why?

Very few of us want to die. Although most of us believe death will lead to bigger and better things; maybe even a paradise, where we will be free from the tortures that plague us in this life.

It is because of the unknown. We fear the unknown. We fear change.

No one can say for sure what death is like. To the best of our knowledge, no one has ever come back to give us a definitive answer, acceptable to all, telling us what happens when we die.

This concerns us. We reason in our minds there is more. We know in our hearts that a special part of us will continue. But every so often something in us asks, "What if death is the end?" And that part of us wants to cling to this life for all eternity. We cannot bear the thought of that which is us, forever ceasing to exist. To close our eyes forever and have all that we have struggled and fought for in our lives suddenly end, perhaps not even matter anymore and soon to be forgotten completely like we were never alive.

No one may have come back to tell us what death is like. But I believe we have advanced far enough where we can prove that we do not cease to exist after we die. We may not be able to describe exactly what is going to happen or what the experience will be like, but I think we are at a point where we can paint a pretty good picture of death and believe it or not it is a very beautiful picture.

You have learned at the very core of our existence we are this incredible vibrating energy. Everything is vibrating energy. It is this vibrational energy that our conscious mind transforms into the physical reality of our existence. This is very good news for us.

Energy cannot be destroyed. It can only change forms.

There is no such thing as death. That which is truly us will never die. Our brain may not be eternal, but our conscious mind is.

If we are energy we cannot cease to exist. We can only change forms. That which is truly us must continue for all eternity.

But what is eternity? Is it a place? Is it a state of existence?

We can define eternity as never-ending. Would that be a place where time continues forever? Or how about a place where there is no time only Now? Even Einstein tells us time is a tricky thing. Time is relative to everyone. We are in an eternal Now and our mind creates the illusion of moving time.

It's a hard concept for our minds to grasp. It's like a library. All the books exist but they still have a beginning and an end. It is a library where you wrote the books. You determined the beginning and end of each book. They are the books of your lives. You can pick out any book you want and read it. You may even want to read a different version of the life you are living now. Maybe make a different choice than you did before.

The books are created by our thoughts and feelings and the books we can create are unlimited. We can experience the same life again or start a new one. A lot will depend on what we have learned.

If our thoughts and feelings create our lives while we are alive, then why should anything be different after we die?

Dying is nothing more than moving our consciousness to a new reality.

Our "death" should be a continuation of our life and a continuation of our creation. If that is true, then everyone may be correct about what they will experience after they die. Christians may find themselves in heaven with the God they have envisioned. Or god-forbid in Hell with the devil they envisioned. All those who adhere to a particular religion may find themselves exactly where they expect

We create our afterlife. And that may be anything we want it to be. You will experience what you expect to experience when you "die". I think it would be great to reunite with past family and friends and even pets.

I don't think we "die" in this life until we are ready to move on. And the same will be true in all of our creations. We will continue with our creation for all eternity. And always remember it is our creation. We have nothing to fear.

Think of death as finally doing something you could not do in this life. What do you want to do in your next creation? Where do you want to go? Who do you want to see?

Your consciousness continues for all eternity.

Think about this. Not one cell in your body now, was there when you were a child. All the cells that made up you as a child have since died. Nothing physical of your body as a child now exists. You can say the child is dead and gone physically but you remember your child self. Depending on how old you are you may also say the same for your teen self, your young adult self, and so on. It will be the same when your body permanently dies from this physical existence, your consciousness will still exist and remember.

Look at a picture of you at 5 years old. You can say that was you but not you today.

You outgrew your childhood and your childhood body. You would not want to stay as a child your entire physical life. You will eventually outgrow this world and any physical body. Just as you would not want to stay as a child you would not want to keep the body and life you have now. It is a growth process. Twenty years from now, you may still be alive in this world but the you now, like the child before you, will no longer exist.

You will eventually outgrow this body and this world. When you "die" your consciousness will still exist and look upon you now as you look upon you as a child. It is just a continuation of a process you have already experienced. And so, it will be for all the transformations you make throughout all eternity. Your consciousness will never forget who you have been. You will always be you. You will always exist.

Many believe we are eventually going to create a body that can live forever or at least a very long time. That is never going to happen. Your higher self would never allow you to stunt your growth.

Saying you want to live forever would be like saying you want to stay a baby or a toddler your entire life. You would never want to limit yourself that way. Saying you want to live in this material world and never leave would be infinitely stifling. You would be denying yourself of the transformation into entities and seeing infinite realities that our minds cannot even grasp. Would you want to deprive yourself of infinite growth?

Many believe they will be able to transfer their brain into a computer to achieve immortality; even if every single nuance of your brain was successfully transferred to a computer; even if that computer could talk and sound like you; even if that computer seemed to have your personality; even if that computer could recall every single one of your memories, it would still be nothing more than a very good replica of what once was.

You are not your brain. You are not your mind. You are the conscious observer. The consciousness which is the real you would have moved on to continue its growth into far better things.

You are infinite.

LESSON TWENTY-FOUR

DIMENSIONS

This lesson is very cool.

We will take you on a journey through dimensions of time and space. We will show you how to picture things in your mind impossible for most. For example, we live in a three-dimensional world. Everything in our 3D world has a length, width, and height. We move up, down, left, right, diagonally. But are there other dimensions? Is there some other way we can move we don't know about? What would that even be like?

Can you picture something in your mind with four dimensions? How about a five-dimensional world? Is that even possible?

It is! And we will show you how to take your three-dimensional mind and visualize and make sense of multi-dimensional worlds.

To do that we must start with some basic geometry and work our way into the other dimensions.

●

In geometry, the dot above is known as a point. It has no length, width, or height. It has zero dimensions.

If you connect two points you now have a line. A line has one dimension. Let's call it length. It is easy to see nothing in our 3D world could exist in one dimension.

The familiar shapes pictured above are also known as planes and they take us into a two-dimensional world. Planes have length and height. When we draw, we make two-dimensional representations of things in our 3D world.

To enter the 3D world we must add width. Now we have length, height, and width and that brings us into the universe we are all familiar with. The picture above is a 2D picture but your mind is interpreting it as 3D. Remember that, that will be very important as we progress in this lesson.

Now here is where things get a little different. Are you ready to move into the fourth dimension? Well, it's not quite that simple. The first three dimensions involve a direction in space. The fourth dimension involves time. To make sense of this we need to go back to Albert Einstein and discuss what he called space-time.

Albert Einstein showed that space and time are inseparable. You cannot have one without the other. We are living in a four-dimensional universe. We have three dimensions of space and one dimension of time. Do you remember in past lessons when we talked about events? Consider a birthday party. To get to that birthday party you not only have to know only where it is in the three dimensions of space but you also have to know when in time, the fourth dimension, the party will be. If any information is missing, you are probably not going to make it to the party. We function daily using four dimensions.

Let's now look at a cool way of seeing the fourth dimension of time.

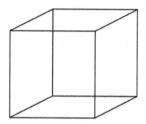

Consider the cube above. Although it is really a 2D image it looks 3D to you. Think of the cube as the entire 3D universe. But you can also picture yourself outside the cube looking into the universe. This is the first step to getting to 4D.

Now let's think of the cube as some event. Let's use the birthday party example again and let's say it starts at 1:00 PM, October 18, 2050. Picture yourself outside the cube looking in and watching the birthday party event. It is easy to see the 4D event going on in space but what about time. To picture that let's stack some cubes.

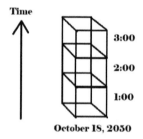

The stacking of the cubes represents a progression in time. View the bottom cube you can witness the party around one o'clock. View the middle cube you can witness the party around two o'clock. View the top cube and you can witness the party around three o'clock.

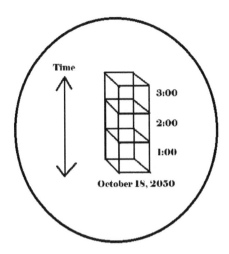

Picture yourself in the circle outside the boxes. You can move around in that circle any way you want. You can move back and forth between the boxes and see what is going on. You can see 1:00 then 3:00 then back to 1:00 then 2:00. You are moving through time.

Now here is where it gets a little tricky. We need to discuss space-time more. Space-time combines space and time. They are inseparable. The cubes you are looking at are both space and time. We live in a 4D world -- 3 space and 1 time. This means the next dimension up for us is the 5th dimension. Which is the 4th spatial dimension but we said time was the 4th dimension. So now we could say time is the 5th dimension – 4 space and 1 time. So how do we picture that?

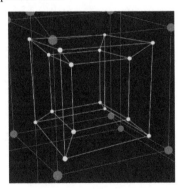

Introducing the Tesseract also known as a Hypercube.

Look at the image above. Picture the smaller cube in the center to be our entire 4D universe from the beginning of time till the end. Remember our time is not separable

208

from our space. Picture yourself stepping out of the smaller cube and finding yourself inside the larger cube. You can move anywhere you want in the larger cube to observe any point on the smaller cube. This means you can see any event in space and time in our universe from the beginning until the end of our universe.

Think about that. You can view the end of the universe. So the end of the universe does not mean the end of everything. Which means it does not mean the end of YOU.

Our universe is now all ONE for you. There is only NOW. Everything and every time are right there for you NOW to observe and experience however you wish. You are coming closer to the realm of your Higher Self and Infinite Intelligence.

Give this lesson some time to take hold in your mind and then go tell people.

BELIEF IS PERSONAL

Your belief is your personal belief. You cannot expect everyone to have the same belief you have because you have not had the same experiences.

No matter what authority you claim for your belief it was still your personal decision to make that your belief.

If you do not have firsthand evidence, you cannot know anything for sure. If you did not see it for yourself, you cannot truly know if it is true. Anything that you didn't experience for yourself is hearsay. That does not mean it isn't true. The source may be very reliable and very likely true but unless you saw it for yourself you can never be 100% sure of its validity.

We have seen how brains are wired and that determines how we see the world. No two brains are wired the same therefore no two people are seeing the world in the same way.

Look at the image above. Some see it as a candle. Some see it as two faces. Look long enough and you will see both. Can you see them both at the same time?

Imagine the faces to be one belief and the candle another belief. They are both correct depending on what the individual is seeing with his or her brain. You need to understand getting someone to accept your belief will often be an impossible task. Their brain is just not wired to see it the way you are seeing it.

I can remember sitting in a church service and would cringe when somebody would use the words, "The Truth!"

An all-knowing, all-powerful god, would know that the entire world would never be capable of coming to one "truth." There would just be too many experiences that would lead to seeing contradictions.

I want to tell you about a big contradiction I found in the Bible. I went so many years believing the Bible to be the inerrant word of God even though I could clearly see this contradiction. My position, still held by so many today, was that my human mind just could not comprehend it right now. That it was something I could only understand once I was with God in Heaven.

Here is the problem.

Okay, bear with me. I am going to revert by to my teaching days in church but this time I will say what I wish I had the courage to say those many years ago. This is very cathartic.

Being all-knowing, why did God create a world in which he knew billions and billions would be doomed to an eternity of punishment?

The Lord is not slack concerning his promise, as some men count slackness; but is longsuffering to us, not willing that ANY should perish, but that ALL should come to repentance. - 2 Peter 3:9

In 2 Peter 3:9, we are told that God wants EVERYONE to come to repentance.

But he made a world in which he knew so many wouldn't. Why did a loving god make a world in which he knew he would have to doom most of those whom he is supposed to love so dearly to an eternity of torment?

What God did and what he says contradict each other. You can't have an all-knowing god create a world in which he knew beforehand, that all would not come to repentance and then say after he made the world, he wants all to come to repentance.

Now, you may argue that God's first intention was to create a perfect world but man (specifically Adam and Eve) messed that up for everyone. Again, we are still confronted with the same issue at the heart of which is, God is all-knowing.

If God is all-knowing, then he had to know beforehand of Adam and Eve's sin. So, knowing they would sin by eating of the tree, why he did put the tree in the garden in the first place? To test them? There is no need to test them if you already know what will happen.

If I purposefully leave a poison cookie in a room with a five-year-old and tell him not to eat it, if the five-year-old eats the cookie and dies, who is to blame? I hope you would say I am.

We need dialogue. This world needs you to step out of your group to change our world for the better. No one expressed this better than Thich Nhat Hanh in his book, *Living Buddha, Living Christ.*

"In a true dialogue, both sides are willing to change. We have to appreciate that truth can be received from outside of—not only within—our own group. If we do not believe that, entering into dialogue would be a waste of time. If we think we monopolize the truth and we still organize a dialogue, it is not authentic. We have to believe that by engaging in dialogue with the other person, we have the possibility of making a change within ourselves, that we can become deeper. Dialogue is not a means for assimilation in the sense that one side expands and incorporates the other into its "self." Dialogue must be practiced on the basis of "non-self." We have to allow what is good, beautiful, and

meaningful in the other's tradition to transform us."
- Thich Nhat Hanh

It is so crazy so many would rather kill than sit and talk about possible solutions. You may not be out killing people, you may be doing amazing good works, but if you think your belief is the one and only "truth" you are still a huge part of the problem. Until we understand we are all part of one whole, the senseless fighting and killing will not end.

We need to learn to listen to each other. We need to understand that to some degree or another everyone is suffering. When we listen, we discover that we are not all that different. We all have the same desires and fears. When we listen to another, we need to cultivate compassion for that person, a longing to help them ease their suffering. In doing so we then find we also ease our own suffering. And never forget the opposite, to make a person suffer is to make yourself suffer.

I also like the words of The Dalai Lama.

"Although Buddhism has come to evolve as a religion with a characteristic body of scriptures and rituals, strictly speaking, in Buddhism scriptural authority cannot outweigh an understanding based on reason and experience. In fact, the Buddha himself, in a famous statement, undermines the scriptural authority of his own words when he exhorts his followers not to accept the validity of his teachings simply on the basis of reverence to him. Just as a seasoned goldsmith would test the purity of his gold through a meticulous process of examination, the Buddha advises that people should test the truth of what he has said through reasoned examination and personal experiment. Therefore, when it comes to validating the truth of a claim, Buddhism accords greatest authority to experience, with reason second and scripture last."
- The Dalai Lama

First comes experience.

Second comes reason.

Last comes scripture.

We need dialogue.

LESSON TWENTY-FIVE

FEEL THE ENERGY OF THE UNIVERSE

Everything is energy.

Your brain converts energy into the sights and sounds of your universe.

As we have learned this is the quantum energy probability waves that your conscious mind collapses into your reality.

This is the infinite energy you have available to you to create your world any way you want.

You need to understand what resonance is. In physics, resonance is a phenomenon in which a vibrating system drives another system to oscillate with greater amplitude at specific frequencies. That means energy waves vibrating at the same frequency will attract each other, combine and increase in amplitude. As you now know the bigger the amplitude the higher the probability the wave will collapse into its physical counterpart.

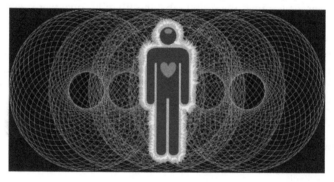

You have learned that your heart and brain create an electromagnetic field that is sent out into the universe. Now think about this, your heart and brain are a creation of energy. You are a creation of this energy. This electromagnetic field is YOU. Let that sink in.

You know you create your electromagnetic field with your emotions. Your field will pull towards you other fields that are a match to your emotional state.

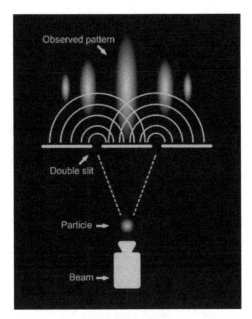

Now let's go back to the double-slit experiment. When the experiment was observed the electrons became physical matter. When the experiment was not observed the electrons became waves and interfered with each other as noted by the interference pattern on the screen. When the peaks and the troughs of the waves aligned it increased the amplitude of the wave but when they were not aligned it canceled the wave.

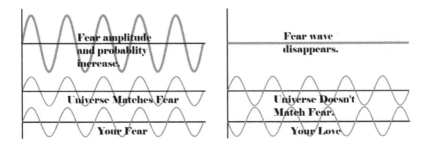

Look at the waves above. If you are sending out an emotional wave of fear and the universe matches your fear then your waves combine into one wave with a larger amplitude. We know this means a bigger probability of bringing about circumstances related to your fear.

But what if you are sending out the emotion of love? The universe can't match your wave of love with a wave of fear. The troughs and crests interfere with each other and cancel out the wave. The fear wave disappears. You kept the fear wave from manifesting. You might notice that your love wave got canceled too. But if you keep sending out the emotion of love you will find a match. It must happen. It is a law of the universe, just like the law of gravity.

214

Now I want to show you how to feel the energy of the universe. It is everywhere and constantly moving through you and everything in the universe. This is a very simple thing to do. You are energy. You are becoming aware of what you are. It's just like noticing a part of you, like your hand.

Don't look at your hand. But feel its presence. You can tell where it is in the space around you. Still not looking at your hand move it in a circular motion, like you are waving at someone by making a circle. See your hand in your mind. Now close your eyes and put your hand a few inches from your face. Can you feel the energy moving back and forth from your hand and face? Make an intention to feel the energy of the universe. Slow your breathing. Relax every muscle in your body. I find this experience to be more effective if you are lying flat on your back. A great time to do this is when you go to bed.

Slow your breathing and relax your body even more. Hold the intention of feeling universal energy. Keep your eyes closed. Picture waves of energy flowing through your hand. You will soon feel your hand start to tingle. The tingle will get stronger. You are feeling the energy, a little prickly sensation. Now picture that energy flowing through your entire body. You will feel your entire body start tingling a part at a time.

Once you feel the energy flowing through your entire body you can concentrate even more on the energy. You can increase the energy flow. Your body will tingle even more. Your whole body will begin vibrating. It will take some practice, but you can increase the vibration to a point where you no longer feel your body. All you experience is energy. You no longer have any distinction between your body and the outside world. You have merged with the entire universe. You are in the Now.

It is important to keep your eyes shut. Any identification with the physical world will lower your vibration. It is also important you only keep your mind on the vibration. Concentrating on physical thoughts will pull you out of the vibration.

This takes time to master. After I did it the first time I found it very hard to do again. I loved the experience so much. I so wanted to experience it again but every time I would get my vibration to a high level and know I was about to lose all distinction between the world and my body, I would get very excited. My breathing would become shallow. I wanted to experience it again so bad but the excited feeling would pull me back down to a lower vibration. Just keep practicing. You will experience something amazing.

Here is another even simpler way to experience the energy. This one is a little more subtle. You can do this one with your eyes open.

Relax your arms and hands. Feel the energy in your hands. Place your hands in front of you like you are holding a basketball. Feel the energy getting stronger. Slowly bring your hands closer together. Feel yourself pushing the energy between your hands. Keep moving your hands closer slowly and gently. Soon you will feel the energy ever so slightly pushing back. It will be as if your hands are two magnets repelling each other. This is a very subtle effect. But you will feel it.

215

Whether feeling the energy throughout your body like in the first example or just the subtle effect in the second example try and keep your mind off anything physical. Enjoy the experience for as long as you like. Stay in the Now. When you come back to experiencing the physical you will have the assurance of knowing that energy is always there and that energy is there for you. You will always have the energy available to shape and form your physical reality. You are an artist painting the canvas of your life. No matter your past, you are always free to start with a blank canvas and create a work of exquisite beauty. Nothing in the physical world can take that away from you. Absolutely nothing.

This energy is YOU. The energy is the true you. You in your true nature. It is not an interpretation of your finite brain. It is infinite. Learn to see past the limitation of your 3D brain and the limitations of this physical reality. Learn to translate the events in your life. See from the perspective of the energy which you really are. What has pure energy to fear? NOTHING!

The next time you are in a moment of distress, close your eyes and feel the energy. Remember what you truly are.

THE THEORY OF EVOLUTION

Many scientists criticize religion for producing fundamentalists when most scientists are huge fundamentalists adhering to a strict dogma themselves. That dogma is Darwin's Theory of Evolution. To many scientists, Darwin's book *On The Origin of Species* is their Bible. It is infallible and unquestionable.

But let's keep in mind *On The Origin of Species* was published in 1859. Cells were thought to be little gooey things, so important things like DNA were yet to be discovered. Even Darwin mentions in his book that his theory could have some problems.

It does have problems. That is not to say the theory is completely in error. We see examples of evolution and natural selection every day. The main problem is when we try to use evolution and natural selection as the single explanation of how everything developed from a single cell to complex organisms (you and me). We will show you 3 roadblocks to Darwin's Theory of Evolution, especially Darwin's Theory of Natural Selection, that show there had to be an intelligence involved, not just random chance. Intelligence and Natural Selection work together and the result is evolution.

Let's take a moment to make sure we are familiar with the terms, "evolution" and "natural selection."

When most people think of evolution, they think of a process by which monkeys and apes eventually developed into humans. Different species of animals come from common ancestors. Evolution can also refer to growth, advancement, progress. Consider how our technology has evolved over the years. A child evolves as he or she matures into adulthood. Our species is maturing.

Natural Selection was the theory that stated as each generation gives birth to the next generation slight changes occur. There is a variation of traits passed on to offspring and those whose changes best adapt to their environment live on to reproduce the changes. This was done naturally with no intelligent intervention.

These small changes may not be noticeable within the first few generations but given the estimated age of the earth at 4.5 billion years that was enough time for Darwin to postulate that everything evolved from a single ancestor, single-celled organisms called Prokaryotes to the Homo Sapiens we are today.

Over many years, after Darwin proposed his theory of Natural Selection, scientists have made many discoveries that cause many problems for Darwin's theory.

1. The Cambrian Explosion
2. DNA is coding
3. Consciousness

The Cambrian Explosion was the first roadblock to Darwin's theory of Natural Selection being the single source of our evolution. This was even known to Darwin and he mentions it in his book.

To understand the Cambrian Explosion you must first know about strata. Strata are layers of rock. As you go deeper and deeper into the layers it is like going back in time. The deeper the fossil the older it is.

The Cambrian Explosion refers to a time about 541 million years ago when most of the major plant and animal life suddenly appear in the fossil record with no previous record.

Do you see how Darwin has a problem with that? There is the Precambrian period in which you would expect to find fossils that represent earlier stages of those found in the Cambrian explosion. According to Darwin, you would see a record of stages of Natural Selection that led up to the fossils in the Cambrian Explosion. But we don't. They are just there, fully formed.

Darwin believed his theory would be justified, the strata with the earlier stages would eventually be found. However, as of today, many new discoveries have been made of strata showing fully formed fossils of the Cambrian period and absolutely nothing which would record an earlier stage of development.

Now, this does not mean we don't find records of species changing throughout the millions of years after the Precambrian period in the fossil record. Evolution and Natural Selection are all too apparent. All those fossils on display in museums had to come from somewhere. The fossils of the Cambrian period show that we all didn't come from one single cell.

So, where did we come from?

If all the species just suddenly appeared that is a quantum leap and a quantum leap shows design. There must be an intelligence.

Nowhere is intelligent creation more apparent than in our DNA.

DNA is short for Deoxyribonucleic acid. DNA contains the blueprint for all your genes. Your genes determine your traits and are how genetic information is passed from parents to their children.

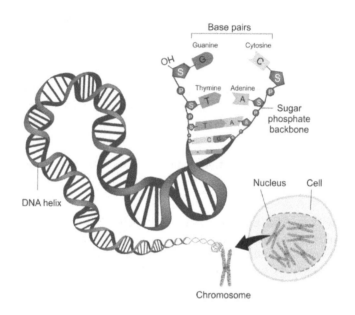

DNA has a backbone made of a sugar, a phosphate, and a base. Together the group is known as a nucleotide. There are four bases, Adenine, Cytosine, Guanine, and Thymine, which pair together to make the DNA ladder. The key thing to remember is like pieces in a puzzle, only Adenine and Thymine can pair together, and only Cytosine and Guanine can pair. The bases pair and the phosphate from the nucleotide attaches to the sugar of another nucleotide forming the DNA ladder. The ladder then curls into the shape of the DNA helix. An entire copy of your DNA is stored as chromosomes in the nucleus of every single cell in your body.

A gene is a certain section of the DNA. It may contain a few hundred base pairs or thousands. Now just think if one of those thousands of base pairs of just one gene is paired wrong then more than likely the gene will not function as it should and it's probably not going to function at all.

Consider a gene that has 100 base pairs. There are 10000000000000000000000000000000000000000000000000000000000000 ways of organizing those pairs. And that is just with 100 base pairs. Imagine how many options we have many when we get into the thousands and if one pair is wrong the DNA will probably not perform its intended task.

Now, are you going to tell me that just by trial and error against impossible odds your DNA formed by pure chance?

No way! I could go back to believing a man put two of every living creature in the world on one boat to save them from a god who wanted to wipe out mankind before I could believe that.

What I just described is coding. It involves inputting information to code the DNA to create the correct genes. Coding and information need a mind.

As a person who knows a little about computer programming. I programmed my first computer game when I was twelve years old, trust me when I tell you your DNA has been coded. There is a mind, not like ours, but a guiding intelligence needed to produce the incredible code behind our DNA. To say DNA evolved on its own is like saying computer programs create themselves. That is impossible.

I can remember writing programs and getting the dreaded SYNTAX ERROR. When that occurred your program came to a complete stop and would not run anymore. A SYNTAX ERROR usually was a spelling mistake. For example, I may have typed, "IMPUT" instead of "INPUT". The result was a computer crash. The same is true with DNA coding. One slight mistake like a misplaced base may cause one of your genes to crash.

DNA is also involved in another process requiring creation. Intelligence had to decide the steps in this process also.

Our DNA determines how proteins are made in our bodies. We usually think of protein as nutrition we get from the food we eat, but it is way more. Proteins made by our body use DNA as a blueprint to determine most of our physical traits.

It is known as protein synthesis. The first step is transcription and the second is translation. Two processes that require a mind. Here is what happens.

In transcription, the DNA unravels and unzips then an enzyme called RNA polymerase matches bases to the Adenine, Cytosine, Guanine, and Thymine of the DNA. This creates a strand of messenger RNA (mRNA). It is not like the bases just pair up and are ready to go, there are many more steps involved. There is a lot of editing that takes place. When this is finished the mRNA detaches from the DNA. It is a single strand that leaves the nucleus in search of a Ribosome. Ribosome's build proteins.

The building of Proteins is translation. The ribosome reads the mRNA three bases at a time. These three bases are known as a codon. The codon attaches to tRNA which has the exact bases need to pair with the codon. They are the anticodons. Attached to the tRNA are amino acids. This pairing of the codon and anticodon makes a chain of amino acids. And the order of the amino acids determines which protein will be made.

And this all happens randomly? Are you kidding me?

This is way beyond a slight change here and there over billions of years. Remember Darwin had no clue about DNA. He thought a cell was just some gooey stuff.

Think about it. The constant pairing of bases must be in a certain order to work correctly. Then the pairing switches to triplets that must be matched. All these different parts of the cell must move around and find each other. If this wasn't a process set in order by an intelligence how did they know how to find each other, or an even better question is why did they know they needed to find each other?

This is a process and a process requires intelligence.

Probably the biggest reason scientists hold so strongly to evolution is because it's hard to see why a creator would take the billions of years and have us evolve from a single cell to the Homosapien species we are today. Why wouldn't he just create us as fully grown as the Bible suggests?

The thing is for our creative source it didn't take billions of years. It all just happened. Evolution is part of the story of our reality. Notice I said part. For our higher self, there is no past nor future. There is just Now. At first it may seem hard to grasp but think of it as a book. When reading a book, you are going through a timeline. As you read a book the events are happening as any life event. As you read, the pages you have read become the past and the pages you still have to read are the future. But you are in the Now. The entire book for you is in the Now. You could easily skip to the end if you wanted.

Does that mean your life is just a book and the ending is already written? No. The book of your life is constantly changing, past and future.

But now we ask the most important question. As we have seen everything is just pure energy. It takes consciousness to turn this energy into our reality. What does it mean for energy to evolve?

Is all this evolution stuff real? Yes and no. It is the backstory of the reality you are experiencing at this moment. But how real can this reality be when your true essence is pure energy? As Einstein said we are living in a very persistent illusion.

Most things in life can be taken to two extremes, like fundamental Christianity on one end and fundamental Darwinism on the other. Usually, when you have your extremes a closer proximation of the truth is found somewhere in between.

LESSON TWENTY-SIX

CONSCIOUSNESS

What is consciousness?

Here are some dictionary definitions.

The state of being awake and aware of one's surroundings.
The awareness or perception of something by a person.
The fact of awareness by the mind of itself and the world.

We are constantly aware of two worlds - an inner world and an outer world. The outer world we believe we share with everyone. Our inner world is private. The outer world we believe to be created by matter. The inner world is created by thoughts. Almost everyone gives physical reality priority over the conscious mind. There is absolutely no logical reason that needs to be the case.

Our consciousness makes us aware of both the inner and outer worlds. As we have discussed in past lessons our consciousness creates our outer world when it collapses quantum probability waves into physical reality. But what about your inner world. Your world of thought and emotion. Where does that come from? Many believe that consciousness is just a creation of the brain. Is that correct? Before we get into that discussion let's tackle a few more questions?

Can you determine for sure that someone is conscious? You can't see or experience the consciousness of anyone else. You might conclude that a person seems to act and behave as you do so they are conscious. But you can't know for sure.

What about a pet dog or cat? Are animals conscious? Surely they are conscious. You see them showing their emotions. You can see a fearful cat as she hunches her back and her hair stands on end as she hisses and bears her claws. You can see the love of a dog as he greets you and jumps all over you trying to lick your face when you come home and he hasn't seen you for hours. Is this a result of consciousness or is this just a programmed reaction by their brain which our consciousness interprets as feelings?

How about those pesky flies that sometimes get into your house and you smash with a fly swatter? Or that unlucky, yucky bug that just crossed your path and gets its guts squished out when you stomp it? Are bugs conscious?

Let's go back to the question, "Is consciousness created by the brain?"

We have discussed a lot about the brain. We know the brain makes neuron clusters as it learns. We know the brain is constantly processing electrical and chemical signals so we can function in life. Do those signals also make us conscious?

We know the brain comprises four chemicals -- carbon, oxygen, hydrogen, and nitrogen.

Do those chemicals allow us to be conscious? Could we mix all those chemicals in the same percentages as in our brain and then send electricity running through it and somehow make that mixture aware of the universe? Not very likely. Isn't that kind of like what Dr. Frankenstein did?

How about our emotions? How could we ever think a mixture of four basic elements could ever produce love, hate, bliss, fear, gratitude, anger? They cannot.

I truly believe consciousness is not created by the brain. The brain is created by consciousness.

Why do I feel so confident in my belief? It goes back to Quantum Physics and the reasoning behind my belief is very simple.

We know from Quantum Physics that EVERY physical thing we experience in our world was once a wave of energy collapsed into physical reality by consciousness. Our brain is a physical thing. Therefore, it had to take consciousness to collapse the quantum wave which is our brain into physical reality. Consciousness came first. There was consciousness before the brain. If it were not for consciousness there could be no brain. Consciousness creates the brain. The brain does not create consciousness.

Where does your consciousness come from?

It comes from your Soul, your Higher Self, the Collective Unconscious, Infinite Intelligence.

We asked earlier, "Can you tell if someone else is conscious? Are animals conscious?" We have constantly stated in this course that everything is one. Everything in this universe (cats, dogs, bugs, plants, rocks) can be considered conscious.

I want to go back to Quantum Physics and discuss another area where consciousness has a huge effect on current beliefs about the universe.

We know the creation of our universe is often attributed to the Big Bang. The Big Bang was believed to be a big explosion that rapidly expanded matter from a state of extremely high density and temperature and according to current cosmological theories marked the origin of the universe.

The most important word in the sentence above is "matter." Again, we know from Quantum Physics all matter is first a quantum wave of energy collapsed into reality. Like our brain had to first have a consciousness so did the Big Bang. No physical matter can come into reality without consciousness being the cause. What is the consciousness responsible for the Big Bang?

Infinite intelligence.

We will stop here.

Next, we are going to discuss more things that show the universe had to be created by an intelligent consciousness and that consciousness could not have been created by the universe.

What if decisions your grandparents made when they were young could be affecting you today?

This is epigenetics. Epigenetics shows us that our genes are not set in stone. We are not destined to get a life-threatening disease because it is in our genes. We can change our genes by our diet, our habits, even our thoughts.

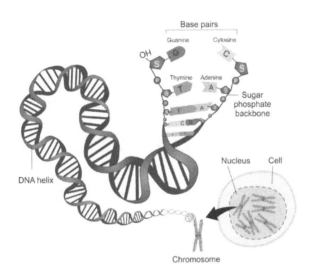

You will remember from our earlier discussion that DNA has four bases that pair with each other (Adenine, Guanine, Thymine, Cytosine). These pairings are the code that tells our body how to make proteins and proteins make just about everything in our body.

Epigenetics does not change our genes but changes how our genes are expressed and this can affect just about any trait you can think of.

We have for a long time known that exposure to harmful chemicals can mutate our DNA. For example, we have a gene that keeps us from getting tumors but smoking can mutate that gene and then it no longer aids our body in stopping tumor formation. Therefore, smoking can lead to cancer.

But this can also be done epigenetically. Instead of mutating the gene, the gene is just turned off. The gene stays the same but unfortunately since it is off it can no longer prevent tumors. But unlike a mutated gene that is permanently changed the gene that is turned off epigenetically can be turned back on and once again prevent tumors.

How is this done?

There are many ways this can be done but we will discuss the two main methods –
Methylation and Histone Acetylation.

Methylation is a process in which the gene is turned off. You will remember we
discussed transcription. The DNA unravels and unzips then an enzyme called RNA
polymerase matches bases to the Adenine, Cytosine, Guanine, and Thymine of the DNA.
This creates a strand of messenger RNA (mRNA).

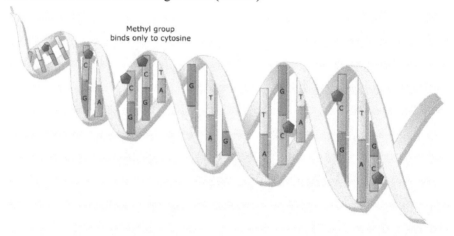

Methyl group
binds only to cytosine

Methylation occurs when a molecule called a methyl group is added to the DNA. It
attaches to areas in the DNA where Cytosine is paired with Guanine. These are known as
CpG islands. When attached it blocks the messenger RNA from being created. Therefore
eliminating the protein the DNA was responsible for making. It turns the gene off.

There is also a process called Demethylation which takes off the methyl groups and turns
the gene back on. This allows transcription and the gene can once again make its protein.

The other process is Histone Acetylation. To understand that process you need to know
what a histone is.

Histones

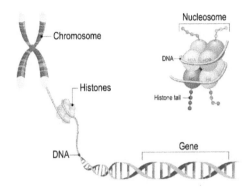

Histones are balls of protein the DNA wraps around. The histones have tails. There are four types of histones and two of each are wrapped by DNA to make a Nucleosome composed of eight histones.

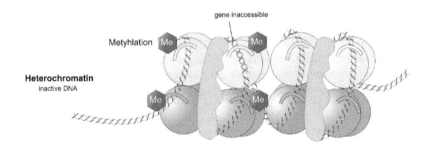

When Nucleosomes are bound tight tighter it makes the gene inaccessible and cannot be transcribed.

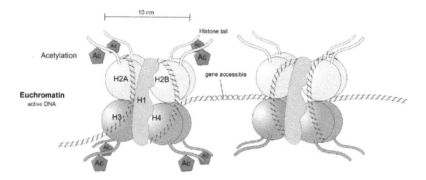

Histone Acetylation causes acetyl groups to be added to the histone tails which loosens up the DNA making it easier to be transcribed. If acetyl groups are removed it tightens the DNA making it harder to be transcribed.

Unlike Methylation, this is not an on or off process. There is a range of gene expression depending on how tight or loose the DNA is. The tighter the DNA the fewer proteins produced. The looser the DNA the more proteins produced.

So how does this let us control our genes and even pass the changes we have made onto future generations?

A good way to see how this happens is by looking at identical twins. At birth identical twins are born with the same genes but we have all seen as identical twins get older, they seem to look less and less alike. This is due to epigenetics.

Let's say both twins are born with a gene that predisposes them to obesity. One twin spends his life sitting on the couch, watching tv and eating everything he wants. Not surprisingly, the obesity gene is expressed in him and he puts on a lot of weight. Now the other twin lives a more active lifestyle, exercises and eats a healthy diet. This twin develops a slim, healthy body. The obesity gene was not expressed in him.

But now with epigenetics, we can see it goes much farther than just expressing or not expressing the obesity gene. By exercising and living a healthy lifestyle the active twin may have turned off the obesity gene in his body by methylation, or he may have lessened the effect of the obesity gene by histone acetylation.

Now here is where it gets interesting. If both twins have children, the unhealthy twin will still pass on the obese gene to his offspring while the healthy twin will pass on the epigenetically altered gene that shuts off obesity. The healthy twin's offspring will benefit from the decisions he made to be healthier. Unfortunately, the opposite is also true. Because of his decision to stay on the couch and eat whatever he wants the unhealthy twin's offspring will still be exposed to the obesity gene.

It looks like the decisions we make today not only affect us but can affect our children and grandchildren.

Mice are often used in genetic studies because they reach sexual maturity in about 4-5 weeks. You can easily have 10 generations or more within a year. You don't have to wait too long to see the genetic effects on the next generation.

In a study, rats were exposed to the smell of the chemical acetophenone and then given an electrical shock. As was to be expected the rats soon became very stressed and fearful when they smelled the acetophenone even when no electrical shock was given.

Remember this was not a fear the rats were born with. It was a fear given to them because of the experiment.

Now here is where Epigenetics can get amazing. Not only was fear of the smell of acetophenone instilled in the rats but it was also inherited by many generations to come. The children and grandchildren of the mice also had a fear of acetophenone.

Our thoughts and emotions can affect our descendants.

This goes back to what we were talking about with Darwin and evolution. Our genes are coded. They are not a process of billions of years of evolution. Epigenetics takes this even a step farther and shows not only have are genes been coded but WE can reprogram the code based on our diet, habits, and thoughts. Your thoughts can change your genes. How powerful is that? That needs repeating. Your thoughts can change your genes.

Share this lesson with someone you know.

LESSON TWENTY-SEVEN

THE GENERAL THEORY OF RELATIVITY

We have discussed a lot about Einstein's Theory of Special Relativity. Einstein not only developed The Special Theory of Relativity but also The General Theory of Relativity. Einstein published his work on General Relativity on November 25, 1915. The General Theory of Relativity concerns gravity. We often hear people say when talking about gravity, "What goes up must come down." There is more to it than that.

You will see there is a close relationship between gravity and acceleration.

Newton said gravity was a force. All objects attract each other. The more mass an object has the more attractive it is. The closer an object is the more attractive it is. According to Newton, this is why when we jump we are pulled back down to the earth. According to Einstein, there is more to it than that.

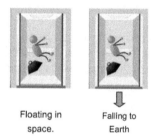

Floating in
space.

Falling to
Earth

To explain, let's say you enter an elevator and head to the top of a tall building. Suddenly the cable snaps and the elevator falls. Look at the image above. For you, it will seem as if everything is floating in the elevator. You can pull some change out of your pocket and you will see the change floating in front of you as if you were in outer space with no gravity. You are taking away gravity when you fall. It is exactly as if you are in outer space. Unfortunately, you are not in outer space and the elevator will hit the ground and the consequences will not be good for you, so we will stop talking about this before you hit the ground. You are safe.

At Rest On Earth   Accelerating In Rocket

Now pretend you are in another elevator. Look at the image above. This time you are safe on Earth, flat on the ground. If you pull out a weight and drop it what happens? It falls to the floor of the elevator. Because of gravity right?

Now let's say you are in the same looking elevator in a spaceship in space with no gravity. What happens when you release the weight? It floats.

But now let's have the spaceship accelerate upwards. If you drop the weight with the spaceship accelerating up, the floor of the elevator will rise to meet the weight. It will appear the same as if you dropped the weight on Earth and gravity pulled it down. If you are in an elevator, unless you are told, you have no way of knowing whether you are on Earth or accelerating in space. Assuming no windows, there is absolutely nothing you can do to tell the difference. This shows that acceleration and gravity can be considered the same thing.

This led Einstein to conclude that gravity is not real.

What?

It goes back to relativity. Remember we said it doesn't matter where you are there is no special place or state of motion. It doesn't matter how you are moving. If you are in a rocket ship zooming to the moon the physics is the same for you as it is for me. Relativity says no place in the entire universe is special. If we can put ourselves in a state of motion, as in the free-falling elevator, where we don't experience gravity then like Einstein said gravity cannot be real.

But it must be real right? If I jump, I get pulled back down to the earth. That is gravity, right?

Einstein said gravity is not a force but concerns geometry and the curvature of space. I know what you are saying. What in the world is the curvature of space?

Wave your hand back and forth in front of you. That "empty" space that your hand is moving through can actually be curved. Very, very hard to picture, right? Can you picture it at all? We will try and help you do that and see what that means for gravity.

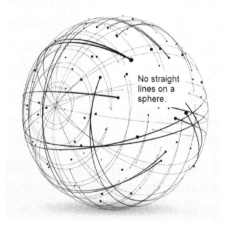

No straight lines on a sphere.

Look at the image above. Picture yourself standing on top of a big round ball. If you could walk around the ball without falling off you would not be walking in a straight line you would be walking in a curved line.

So what causes space to be curved?

Matter and energy cause space to be curved. Matter moves along this curved space and we experience this as gravity. The more massive the matter the more the space is curved. This is why the earth seems to have a gravitational attraction. Stick with me I will help you picture this a lot clearer.

First, let's make this interesting. Do you remember the lesson where we said we live in three dimensions of space and one of time? We live in a four-dimensional universe where time and space are inseparable. Einstein called this space-time. When we say matter and energy cause space to be curved, and we know space and time are inseparable, it then must cause time to be curved as well. It curves space-time. What in the world does it mean to curve time? We will discuss that later.

Look at the image above. It will help you grasp what it is like for space-time to be curved by the earth. I know it's hard because we think of space as empty nothingness.

Look at the image above. Picture a trampoline. Let's say the stretchy part of the trampoline is space-time. Now if we put a large heavy ball in the middle of the trampoline it will look like the picture above. It causes the trampoline to sink in and curve the space around it. If we took a smaller ball and roll it onto the trampoline and the ball enters the area where the trampoline curves in, the little ball will find itself moving towards the big ball. Now if we couldn't see the sunken curved trampoline-like we can't see space-time it will look to us as if the large heavy ball is pulling the little ball towards it. There is no attraction, all the little ball is doing is moving through curved space the only way it can.

This is Einstein's General Theory of Relativity.

Think about the genius of Einstein. Einstein discovered General Relativity by just using his mind. During his time there was no experiment he could perform to prove his theory. But today we know beyond a shadow of a doubt he was correct. That is because of the invention of The Global Positioning System (GPS). We all know GPS can pinpoint our exact location. The thing is when making calculations GPS must take into account the curvature of space-time or it will not put us in the right location. And where do the calculations come from? The math equations Einstein developed in General Relativity. How connected was Einstein with Infinite Intelligence?

Next time we will talk about what it means for time to curve and black holes. I know you will enjoy the next lesson.

CRISPR

If you haven't yet heard of CRISPR this will either get you very excited or make you very uncomfortable.

We are on the verge of editing our genes just as easily as you would edit words on a word processor. Just like you can take a word out of a sentence you can remove a gene from your body or replace it with another gene or re-write the gene to do something different.

How does it make you feel to be able to choose your baby's height or hair color?

How does it make you feel to know we could engineer humans to be smarter, stronger, faster?

How does it make you feel to know we could dramatically increase our life span?

How does it make you feel to know we could eliminate many diseases?

You may have different reactions to those questions? Some you may like such as eliminating diseases. But how about designing and enhancing humans? That many are not sure about.

To grasp what CRISPR is you need to know what the human genome is.

Your genome is your complete set of DNA. It contains all the genes that build and make you. It is estimated you have between 20 to 25 thousand genes. Your genes range in size from a few hundred base pairs to over 2 million. You will remember that your DNA consists of base pairs, cytosine always pairs with guanine, and adenine with thymine. They combine to form the DNA double helix.

CRISPR is a cutting protein we can use to do everything from completely cut a gene out of our genome, insert a new gene or even get precise enough to change a single base pair out of millions.

Gene editing is here. This is not something that is going to happen in the future. This is something we can and are doing right now.

The problem right now is we don't know the effects of editing the genes. We do not know what to do with the genes to get our desired result. We don't know if changing a gene might cause an unintended disastrous result. It is like having a computer and not knowing how to use it.

What is CRISPR?

CRISPR stands for Clustered Regularly Interspaced Short Palindromic Repeats.

It was discovered by studying how bacteria defended itself from viruses.

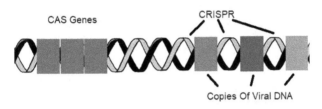

BACTERIAL DNA

Above is a representation of bacterial DNA. As implied by CRISPR you can see the DNA is clustered in an area and regularly interspaced between copies of viral DNA. The DNA is short and the DNA repeats. You can't tell from this diagram but palindromic refers to the DNA bases (adenine, thymine, cytosine, guanine). A palindrome is a word or a phrase that can be read the same frontwards and backward such as "Was it a car or a cat I saw?"

As you can see in the bases above, each side is a reverse (palindromic) of the other.

The CAS Genes make a protein called Cas9. We will discuss more about CAS9 later but for right now just think of Cas9 as a pair of scissors that holds copies of RNA.

The next thing you need to know is where the copies of the viral DNA came from. When a virus attacks a bacterium the CAS Genes make a protein to cut out some of the DNA from the Virus and then cut the CRISPR DNA of the bacterium and insert the Viral DNA into the CRISPR.

See the images below.

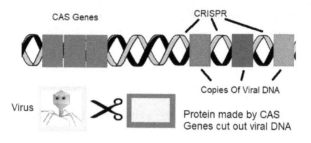

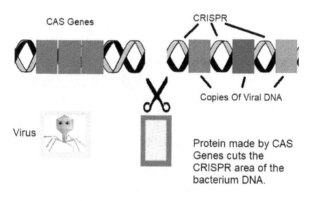

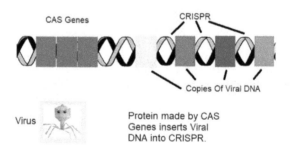

RNA copies of the Viral DNA are made and bind to a specific CAS protein known as CAS9. See the image below.

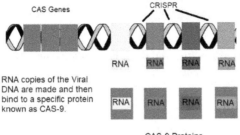

CAS Genes

CRISPR

RNA RNA RNA RNA

RNA copies of the Viral
DNA are made and then
bind to a specific protein
known as CAS-9.

RNA RNA RNA RNA

CAS-9 Proteins

The CAS9 proteins with the RNA then go on the look-out for Viruses whose DNA matches their RNA. When they find a matching virus they destroy the virus by cutting it. See the image below.

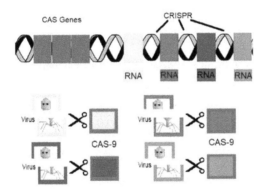

CAS Genes

CRISPR

RNA RNA RNA RNA

Virus — CAS-9

Virus — CAS-9

Virus

Virus

This process has been hijacked and altered and now we can edit genes. The process is called CRISPR. Here is how it is done.

Let's break it down.

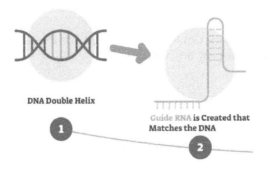

DNA Double Helix

Guide RNA is Created that
Matches the DNA

1

2

1. The gene responsible for the desired change is determined. Perhaps the gene controls eye color, or height, or causes disease.

2. Guide RNA is created in which the RNA bases match the DNA bases. Yes, this RNA is created synthetically by scientists in a laboratory.

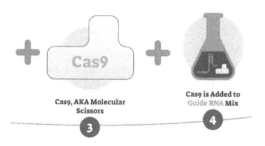

Cas9, AKA Molecular Scissors

Cas9 is Added to Guide RNA Mix

3. The CAS9 protein we discussed earlier, that did all the cutting in the bacteria, is hijacked.

4. The CAS9 protein and Guide RNA created in step 2 are mixed in the lab.

Cells are Injected with Guide RNA + Cas9 Mix

5. Cells are injected with the Guide RNA and CAS9 mixture. Every single cell in your body contains a complete copy of your DNA.

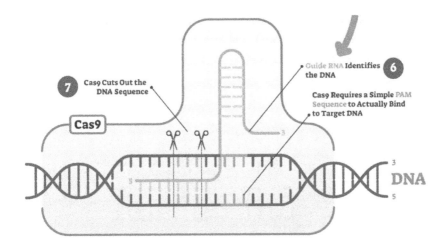

6. As we saw in the bacteria the CAS9 protein takes in the Guide DNA and then like it searched for viruses in the bacteria it now searches for DNA to match its RNA. The amazing thing is out of our 20 to 25 thousand genes CAS9 nine finds the gene that matches. How it does this we don't have a clue. But when it finds the gene it binds to it. There is a small DNA sequence known as PAM that the Guide RNA binds to and is necessary for the CAS9 protein to cut the target DNA.

7. The Cas9 then cuts out the targeted DNA sequence.

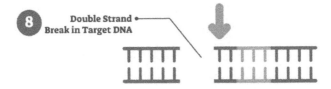

8. After the DNA is cut it leaves a double-strand break in the target DNA.

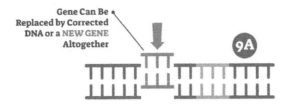

9a. Everything from a single base pair to an entirely new gene can be replaced. The gene has been changed to do what we want it to do, not what nature attended. To many that is a scary thought.

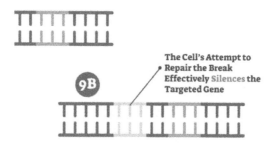

The Cell's Attempt to
Repair the Break
Effectively Silences the
Targeted Gene

9b. The cut DNA can also be left alone to let the cell attempt to repair the break. This will silence the targeted gene. This may be good when we determine a gene to cause disease.

CRISPR can allow us to do many things once thought impossible. Gene therapy can cure diseases. Gene drives can quickly pass a trait throughout an entire population. Would we want to design a "perfect" human? Will we be able to see pig's fly?

But two things to remember.

1. Does this all sound like it was a byproduct of mutations over billions of years just happening by chance? Or does it sound like the design of an intelligent mind with a purpose?

2. If we are all just energy then what does all this mean anyway?

TIME DILATION, BLACK HOLES, AND HOLOGRAMS

Time dilation tells us that where gravity is strong time slows down. But haven't we already said Einstein said there is no such a thing as gravity. Ok. Let's put it in General Relativity terms we learned in the last lesson. The bigger an object is, the more it curves space. Gravity is curved space. Stronger gravity means a larger curve in space. The more space is curved the slower time moves.

Another way to put this is the higher you are the faster time moves. We mentioned GPS last time. GPS calculations must consider time slowing where "gravity" is stronger or GPS could miscalculate your location as much as a mile. That would not be good for your next road trip.

We said before sometimes gravity is described as what goes up must come down. We know that is not always the case the farther away you get from gravity the weaker it becomes. This is why when we launch rockets into space it takes a lot of force to escape gravity and not come back down. An object needs to move about 7 miles a second to escape the earth's gravity. This is called escape speed. The sun's escape speed is 400 miles per second. It has a bigger mass than the earth.

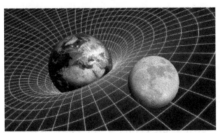

Look again at the picture above. Space-time is curved the most next to the earth. As you move away from the earth the curve gets smaller and smaller. Soon you find yourself out of the curve and space-time is flat. You are no longer feeling the "pull" of the earth's gravity.

Now picture taking the earth and squishing it smaller and smaller. You discover two very interesting things. First, this won't change the mass of the earth it will just be more compact. Second, it will increase the escape speed you need to escape the earth's gravity. If you squish the earth down to the size of a golf ball there is no escape speed. The speed required would be greater than the speed of light and there is nothing that can move faster than the speed of light.

The earth would become a black hole. Any object whose escape speed is greater than the speed of light is a black hole. Nothing can escape a black hole. Light cannot escape a black hole, therefore the term - Black Hole.

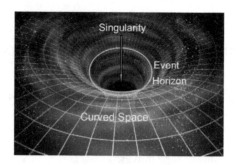

Look at the image above. The black hole has an event horizon. It is like a point of no return. Consider an imaginary border around the black hole and once you cross that borderline you are stuck. There is no speed at which you can move to turn around and go back where you came from.

As we discussed the stronger the gravity, the more space is curved, the slower time moves. The closer you get to a black hole the more space is curved; the slower time will move for you. This is like the twin paradox. Time will be moving slower for you than it is for people on Earth. If you are in a spaceship and near a black hole if you don't cross the event horizon, you can turn around and come back home. But when you get back, as with the twin paradox, you will find everyone has aged at a faster rate than you. If you were a twin, he or she will be older than you. This time it was caused by gravity and not speed.

Now, what happens if you do cross the horizon of a black hole? First, let's say you could be observed by somebody from Earth. They would see you moving slower and slower as you get closer to the horizon. Then at the horizon point, you would be obliterated.

The next question you hopefully are asking is what is happening from your viewpoint when you enter the black hole? Everything seems normal to you. Unfortunately, eventually, you will be drawn to the center of the black hole and crushed.

Physicist Stephen Hawking saw a paradox with black holes. Anything that falls into a black hole is lost. We can consider this losing information. Quantum Physics says information can't be lost.

Here is an example. If you pull a dollar out of your pocket and burn it, the dollar is lost but the particles that make the dollar are not lost. It is theoretically possible to put the atoms back together and reform the dollar, although that is way beyond our capabilities at this time. But if the dollar is put into a black hole the information is lost and we can never get it back. Hawking believed this to be true.

However, another physicist, Leonard Susskind, said that. you can't lose information. Losing information violates Quantum Physics.

Susskind said what was happening is the horizon of a black hole is like a two-dimensional holographic film and any information that crosses the horizon is preserved on that 2D holographic film. Now, this is just an analogy. It is not a holographic film.

Earlier we said If you cross the event horizon a viewer from Earth would see you obliterated but you would feel fine. How is that possible? Here is how...

You would be obliterated but your information would be stored on the 2D event horizon. Inside the black hole, this 2D horizon would reproduce you in all your 3D glory.

So, who turned out to be right, Hawking or Susskind?

Well, no one knows the answer for sure but the scientific community now agrees with Susskind.

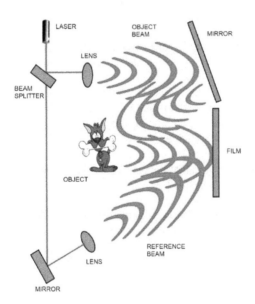

Consider the image above and we will see how a hologram is made. A laser is sent through a beam splitter. Half of the laser goes through a lens to a mirror where it is reflected off the mirror and onto the object which you want to make a 3D hologram. The image is then reflected to the 2D holographic film. The other half of the laser, known as the reference beam is reflected through another lens and sent directly to the film.

Here is where it gets interesting. A laser is an electromagnetic wave. When the two laser waves meet they interact as we discussed in the Quantum Physics double-slit experiment.

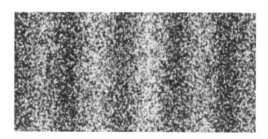

Look at the image above. The interference pattern, you are now familiar with, forms on 2D film by the combining of the laser beams. The film is then developed to make the 3D hologram.

Are you seeing the connection with this and what we discussed in Quantum Physics? We said the universe is nothing more than waves that show up as interference patterns until collapsed into our physical reality by consciousness. Just like a hologram is created from waves to form a 3D image, our universe is created from waves to form our 3D reality.

Scientists are now believing that the entire 3D universe could be a projection of a 2D horizon surrounding the universe. We are on the inside of the horizon. We are a 3D projection of this horizon.

What is real? Is the projection real, or that doing the projecting real? You could consider yourself to be both the projection and the projector. According to Susskind, it doesn't matter which one you choose. Both are correct.

We are projections of something that happens on the outside of our universe. You are here and there. How is that possible?

Here is one explanation. We can be considered as a holographic projection of our higher self. Now remember the hologram is just analogy so let's take that word away. We are a projection of our higher self.

YOUR HISTORY BOOKS ARE WRONG

History is written by the victor. History is often changed, written by those in power to promote their agenda. History written down is history seen through the eyes of the writer. It is influenced by his or her version of the world. It can be no other way.

I will give you two examples from history that may not be exactly what you were taught to believe.

Please do not just jump on the defensive and immediately dismiss what I am saying based on nothing more than your personal belief.

Neither do I want you to take my word for it.

I want you to do your own research. Get on the internet and look up the topics I am talking about and make your own decision. Try to approach it in an unbiased way. That will be hard because you will be tempted to see things through your viewpoint.

Woodrow Wilson

Thomas Woodrow Wilson (December 28, 1856 - February 3, 1924) was the 28th President of the United States from 1913 - 1921. He is best known for leading America during World War I (1914-1918). He is also known for many other accomplishments. The Federal Reserve Act was signed into law by Wilson establishing the Federal Reserve System. Wilson established many laws to protect consumers from businesses. He established an eight-hour workday with extra payment for overtime. Wilson also helped establish The League of Nations which was the forerunner of The United Nations. For this, he received The Nobel Peace Prize in 1919. Wilson also helped give women the right to vote.

All the information above can be found in every American History textbook in our school system but there is also a lot of information about Wilson you will find in very few history books. Here are a few examples of information kept from you.

Woodrow Wilson was the instigator of one of the darkest acts in American history, The Occupation of Haiti. In 1915 the U.S. Marines invaded Haiti and forced on them a new constitution and forced them to elect the president the U.S. wanted into office. The poor were put in chains and forced to do grueling manual labor.

In 1919 the Haitians revolted in a guerrilla war that cost over 3000 lives, mostly Haitian.

The killing of the Haitians by marines became indiscriminate. There were stories of the marines kicking around the head of a decapitated man and of nailing bodies to doors to let them rot in the sun. During the entire occupation, an estimated 15,000 Haitians were killed.

246

Please don't be naïve enough to believe that The United States always plays the good guy in all its confrontations and is always looking out for the best interests of others.

Another fact that many don't know about Wilson is he was an outspoken racist. He tried to pass numerous legislative laws to limit the rights of African Americans, which fortunately were not passed by Congress. Wilson segregated the Navy and The Federal Government. His goal was to eliminate all African Americans from representation in the Federal Government.

Grab any history textbook from any school and you will be hard-pressed to find the information above.

Constantine

We discussed how history books may not give correct information. Here is another example.

Constantine was the first Roman emperor to convert to Christianity. He played an influential role in the proclamation of the Edict of Milan in 313, which declared religious tolerance for Christianity in the Roman empire.

In the year 312, the Roman Empire was divided. It was at The Battle of the Milvian Bridge, in which Constantine defeated Emperor Maxentius, that Constantine took control of the entire Roman empire.

According to Christian tradition, Constantine said he saw of vision of Christ and he renounced his pagan gods and ordered his soldiers to paint the cross on their shields. This led to his victory and conversion to Christianity. Through Constantine, Christianity spread across the world.

But was his motive really to spread Christianity as the Christians of that day knew it or his version?

To commemorate his victory at The Battle of the Milvian Bridge, Constantine had the Arch of Constantine erected in 315. It sits right across from the Roman Colosseum where Christians were once killed for sport. The Arch is engraved with images of the battle but there are no traces of any crosses on the shields on the Arch. There is no trace of Christianity on the monument.

But there are images of pagan gods on the Arch.

There was a cult called Mithraism popular with many of the Roman elite. Mithras was originally a Persian sun god. There have been many Mithraic temples found across the Roman empire and most were found under the first Christian churches. These were secret rooms not known to the Christians but only the Roman elite. This was where they came to worship Mithras.

247

Could it be possible that Constantine was using both Christians and the Roman elite to further his ends and, in the process, create a religion that blended both Christianity and Mithraism?

An inscription on one wall of a Mithraic temple translates, "And thou hast saved us by shedding the eternal blood." Sound familiar?

Another similarity to today's Christianity was remembering the sacrifice by partaking in a meal of bread and wine to ensure eternal life.

The followers of Mithras also believed he died and was resurrected and they celebrated his birth on December 25th.

The Mithraic priesthood wore Phrygian caps and although there are no Christian symbols on The Arch of Constantine, eight figures are wearing Phrygian caps.

Did Constantine pretend to be Christian while slowly infusing Christianity with parts of Mithraism?

In 330 Constantine moved the Roman capital to the city of Byzantium and renamed it Constantinople, after himself.

Constantine had a huge column erected with a huge statue of Apollo the sun god, the son of the Greek god Zeus, placed at the top of the column and he had the face of the statue created in his image.

Does all this point to Constantine being a devout Christian following the teachings of Jesus?

Does it sound more like an egomaniac concerned with his own needs?

Consider this...

Are the teachings of Jesus that Christians follow today even the teachings of the original Jesus?

Constantine called the Council of Nicea in 325 to determine a uniform Christian doctrine. Constantine was present. It makes you wonder how much influence he had on determining the Christian doctrine.

Did Constantine convert to Christianity or is Christianity as we know it today a creation by Constantine?

Think about it.

Think about this too.

How did the New Testament Gospels Come About?

I am sure you know the gospels tell the story of the life and death of Jesus Christ.

Here are some things you may not know about the gospels (Matthew, Mark, Luke, and John).

1. None of the writers of the gospels were eyewitnesses to anything that Jesus said or did.

2. The writings are attributed to Matthew, Mark, Luke, and John but the books were written anonymously. It was decades before anyone attached an author to each book but no one knows for sure who wrote them.

3. The gospels were written anywhere from 50 to 100 years after the death of Jesus.

4. Not only were the writers not eyewitnesses but they didn't even live in the same area and didn't even speak the same language as Jesus.

5. Only about 10% of the population at that time could read so the gospel stories were transferred by word of mouth. There would have been no way to monitor what was being said and you know it would be impossible for details not to have been changed and exaggerated.

6. We don't know the exact order, but perhaps "Mark" first heard the story and wrote it down. Then "Matthew" read "Mark's" story and told his own version, and so on. Now we have the four gospels.

7. The gospels have a lot of contradictions and information which is not historical.

What if Jesus' message was changed and distorted?

What if Jesus was trying to show us we are not all doomed to an eternity of punishment if we briefly mess up in this world? What if Jesus was trying to show us we are all like God? What if Jesus was trying to show us we all have the potential to create miracles?

LESSON TWENTY-NINE

VIRTUAL REALITY

Are we living in a virtual reality? Are we living in a computer simulation?

Everyone has seen the amazing worlds created by computers. We see them in computer games and movies and they look "real." They are getting so realistic some movies have even created computer-generated actors to play in movies with real people and it is almost impossible to tell the computer generation was not a real person.

Think about how far we have come in such a short amount of time. I can remember when Atari first came out, games were nothing more than big blocks moving around on the screen and now just 35 to 40 years later we can simulate reality. At least its appearance.

Are we living in a computer simulation? Physics experiments may be suggesting this is true.

Let's look at some similarities and see what you think. I will then tell you what I think.

Most scientists agree that our universe began in the past known as the Big Bang. This was the beginning of all space and time. Before the Big Bang, there was nothing.

A Big Bang could be a computer game booting up. There is nothing for the computer to process about the game before the game boots up. It is as if the computer game comes from nothing.

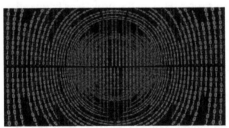

We know all every computer program can be broken down into bits of zeros and ones. The smallest piece of information possible in a computer is a bit. This is like the quantum world we have discussed. We know our world is quantized. Just like a computer is quantized as bits of information.

We have discussed the speed of light as the maximum speed of nature. Why should there be a set speed for light? Why couldn't it move like just one mile per hour faster? This is like the processor speed of a computer. Your computer will never be able to do anything faster than its processor will allow.

We have talked about curved space and time dilation. Perhaps that could be because of the demands put on the computer processor. Everyone has experienced their computer moving slow. When a computer is processing a lot of information it gets slower.

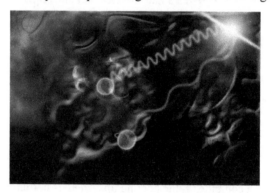

We talked about quantum entanglement and non-locality. Two particles being far apart and knowing what the other is doing. This supports virtual reality. If our reality is controlled by a computer processer then the processor knows everything at once. All bits that make up a program are in the same location as the processor.

You could be playing a computer game that takes place throughout an entire universe. But you know all the information is coming from the processor.

We have said matter doesn't exist until consciousness is aware of it. A computer only shows you what you need to see. Consider a video game where you are walking through a house. You can see the room you are in, but you know the other rooms aren't anywhere until you walk into them. The rooms are just information potential waiting to see how you interact with the game. Does that sound eerily familiar?

We mentioned the holographic principle and how our 3D universe is created by information. A computer simulation is a creation by a program of information.

So, is our world nothing more than a very advanced computer program? What do you think?

251

Here is what I think.

Let's keep in mind we are making comparisons. Any creation could be considered a simulation. Our simulations at best must be considered very primitive. We can create computer games and characters in those games. However, we can in no way create conscious life.

But consider Infinite Intelligence. Infinite Intelligence created the world we live in and it could be called a simulation. It's just a way of using words. It is semantics. If we are in a simulation, there must be something being simulated. That something simulated we only know a small infinitesimal part. Infinite Intelligence has ways of creating, our minds can't even begin to grasp, things that our brains just can't process.

From past lessons, we know we are here to create. We are here to create our world any way we want. You can change the "simulation."

Perhaps this is just the beginning stage for us. Perhaps we are learning to create on a small scale and as our creative powers grow that scale will get larger and larger. As our awareness grows, our ability to create will grow. We are learning how to shape the world we live in. Perhaps one day we will learn to create not only our world but other worlds. Perhaps we will create our own planet. Perhaps we will create our own universe.

OUR SCHOOL SYSTEM NEEDS FIXED AND HERE IS EXACTLY HOW TO DO IT

Do you remember what we told you in the introduction? Our school system came from Prussia. In the 1840s Horace Mann went to Prussia to study what was becoming a very popular way of teaching children. He brought the system back to the United States and industry giants like Rockefeller and Carnegie fell in love with it for its ability to consistently churn out supplies of "worker bees" year after year. Not surprisingly, the school system is also called the "factory model." What is unbelievable is that nothing has changed for almost 200 years.

Schooling creates a labor class. The most important goals are to teach reading, writing, and punctuality, to prepare students for working long hours, and to teach how to follow instructions.

This stifles creativity and prohibits students from pursuing their own interests.

This has led to the dreadful classification of students based on how "smart" they are and dividing them up into classes - the advanced, the average, and the below average. The school system decides how smart you will be and most blindly agree and submit to a self-fulfilling prophecy which has a huge impact (and for most, not a good one) on the rest of their lives.

This is not a reflection on the quality of teachers of today. We are not saying the teachers are not doing their job. They are. But their job involves working in an outdated system everyone is trapped in.

Fortunately, my father saved me from that fate. On my first day of high school, I showed my dad my class schedule. He noticed only one class listed was advanced.

"Are there other advanced classes?" he asked.

"Yes," I replied.

"Then why aren't you in them?"

"That's the ones they put me in," I told him consentingly.

"No," said my dad.

That next day I discovered my father had been at the school early that morning and told them to put me in every advanced class my schedule would allow.

If it were not for my father, it would have been impossible for me to have graduated third in my high school class and been voted "The Most Likely To Succeed". I would have succumbed to the fate the school had imposed on me of being an average student. No one should be an average student.

According to society, I did everything "right" in school. It was my "success" in the school system that allowed me to look back and see just how bad a shape it is in. However, my "success" did not prepare me to create the dream life I envisioned. I had to learn that for myself.

Can the school system be fixed?

Yes, it can and I will tell you how right now.

First, we must stop looking at classes like art and music as inferior to math and science. Art and music foster creativity. They set you apart from the crowd. They show you are unique. Students need to spend at least as much time, if not more, developing their creativity as they do learning math and science. Math and science are very important but should not be used to further the agenda of making you a person good at blindly following instructions. I can remember taking Calculus. I could follow the instructions I was given to make sure I gave the correct answer on a Calculus problem but back then I could not tell you for the life of me how doing that served any conceivable purpose.

Please don't make the mistake of thinking I am condemning teachers. I had many great teachers in school. They were just not given the correct tools and curriculum to follow.

As I mentioned earlier, we need to cut back on math and science and add more classes that help promote creativity and individuality. Below is a list of classes that should be required courses, not electives.

Art
Music
Creative Writing
Literature/Poetry
Philosophy
Foreign Languages
Cultural Studies
Comparative Religion

We also need to create classes where students choose their own topics and take it upon themselves to learn without an instructor. The internet makes this easy.

We need to outlaw homework. Students spend enough hours a day at school. They don't need important family time taken away. The family time which parents need to demand of their children.

Speaking of hours in school we need to cut the school day in half. Remember the long school day was designed to prepare for working long hours. From kindergarten through high school you spend between 12,000 and 13,000 hours in school. They estimate reading and basic math takes about 100 hours to learn. Do you really think you need 12,900 more hours after learning to read and do math?

No.

Even worse we spend all those years and hours in school and consciously forget over 90% of what we "learned." How can that in any sense be justified as anything but a waste of precious time that could be spent on more important and beneficial endeavors?

Because of the excessive hours, schooling after Middle School should not be required. If students want to take the higher math and science classes needed for certain jobs then that should be 100% their choice.

An apprenticeship would be a great alternative. Instead of taking more classes they will have no use for and not remember, they could apprentice a few hours a day in a field that interests them. Imagine if today's doctors had been working in a hospital since age 13 or 14. How skilled would they be at a much earlier age with all the on-hand experience? Think about it.

Until we change our school system we will keep seeing the same cycle in government and big business. The income gap will keep getting bigger and bigger. We need to start the change and we need to do it now.

LESSON THIRTY

THE BEGINNING

Congratulations!!! You have reached the end of the book but this is just the beginning for you.

You now understand topics considered the hardest concepts in the world to grasp. But do you see it now? They were not that hard to learn were they?

So have we convinced you now there is nothing you cannot learn?

Let this give you confidence that if you set your mind towards something there is nothing you cannot achieve. If someone else can do it so can you.

But here is our challenge. Try and do something no one has ever done before. You can.

Let's take a moment to review what we have covered in the class.

In lesson one, you learned that the main factor determining whether something is easy or hard for you is your belief. You learned your brain cells (neurons) make dendrite connections with other brain cells and this is how you learn. Neural clusters are formed and the bigger the cluster the better you understand and can do something. At first, you may see no way you can learn something but as the neural connections are made things become clearer and clearer.

In lesson two you learned how to use your amazing memory by creating crazy images and linking them. You also learned how to create mind maps to help you organize your thoughts.

In lesson three you discovered a very important lesson. You are not the voice in your head. You are not the voice of your mind. You are the one who is observing the voice. You learned that you are consciousness, you are awareness, you are unlimited.

In lesson four you learned your subconscious mind is in contact with Infinite Intelligence and you have access to Infinite Intelligence for all your needs.

In lesson five you were taught how to use daydreaming to communicate with your conscious mind and Infinite Intelligence.

In lesson six you started learning some of the basics of Calculus. You learned some of the math behind taking a derivative, which you now know, is finding the rate of change of anything.

In lesson seven we went over the history and the laws of motion. Most important you were introduced to the concept of relativity which says it doesn't matter where you are physics looks the same for you as it does for everyone else. It makes us all equal. There is no special place or state of motion.

In lesson eight we discussed electromagnetism. You saw how electromagnetic waves are waves of electricity changing to magnetism, then magnetism to electricity, and so on back and forth. You also discovered that light was an electromagnetic wave.

In lesson nine we began the journey into Special Relativity. You learned the speed of light is always measured the same (670,616,629 miles per hour) no matter your motion. We showed how this led Einstein to the correct conclusion time in two events can be different. Time depends on your point of view. The faster you move the slower time moves relative to another person. This is called time dilation.

In lesson ten you were presented with the twin paradox. You saw the amazing prediction of Special Relativity showing a person could travel very fast to a star light years away and come back to Earth and be many years younger than his or her twin. In a sense, it would be like traveling into the future.

In lesson eleven you learned another crazy prediction of Special Relativity. You were hit with the crazy fact that two events may occur in a different order depending on your frame of reference. If I hold up sign one and then sign two, someone else may see me hold up sign two and later sign one.

In lesson twelve we started the daunting task of talking about reality. You were made aware of the fact that you create your entire world using electromagnetic waves. Everything you see and hear is electromagnetic waves taken in by your eyes and ears and interpreted by your brain. Your brain interprets based on past experience.

In lesson thirteen we began the impossible mission of trying to make sense of Quantum Physics. You first had to be made aware that energy is quantized. It is not smooth but comes in discreet, indivisible chunks. The higher the frequency of the energy the bigger the chunk. But even the "big" chunks are super, super small.

In lesson fourteen it just kept getting weirder as you learned about The Photoelectric Effect and The Double Slit Experiment. You learned about the wave-particle duality of light. Photons of light could be both a wave and a particle.

In lesson fifteen we made the conclusion which is the mother of all weirdness of Quantum Physics. The Double Slit Experiment was repeated with electrons. Not only does light behave as a particle and a wave but all matter behaves as a particle and a wave. You are matter. You are energy.

In lesson sixteen you learned about The Heisenberg Uncertainty Principle which shows we do not live in a deterministic universe. There will be things we can never know for sure. There is a minimum size we can use when trying to figure out how the world works.

In lesson seventeen you finally got to the equation of all equations -- Schrodinger's Equation. The equation shows how everything exists as only a probability until it is collapsed into physical reality by consciousness.

In lesson eighteen we discussed The EPR Experiment where Einstein tried to prove that particles over great distances could not automatically communicate with each other. You saw this was one of the few times Einstein was wrong.

In lesson nineteen you learned how to create your reality. You saw you need to get thoughts of the material world out of your mind to enter the quantum realm. You create with your imagination and emotions. Belief determines the probabilities produced by Schrodinger's Equation. The more you believe the higher the probability.

In lesson twenty we revisited relativity and you saw a graphical way to see that two individuals could see events in a different order. What you may see as the past another person may see as the future.

In lesson twenty-one, we saw that everything that happens to us in this life is first a state in the field of infinite potential throughout the entire universe. Everything is connected to everything. There is a constant infinite potential within you that is always going to be there whenever you need it. Because it is you.

In lesson twenty-two, you were let in on some information that very few know. The heart has brain cells. The heart can store memories. The heart is responsible for intuition. The heart is responsible for wisdom.

In lesson twenty-three you were instructed how to do something life-changing. You were taught how to erase a cloud with your mind. You learned how to change physical reality right in front of your eyes with your mind. Hopefully, you have done that many times now.

In lesson twenty-four we stepped out of 3D reality into other dimensions. You saw we live in a 4D reality where space and time are inseparable. You were shown how to visualize walking around in a fifth dimension and viewing any time and place in our 4D reality.

In lesson twenty-five, you were shown how to feel the energy of the universe. You were shown how to feel the energy flowing through your body and if you get good at it you no longer have any distinction between your body and an outside world. You have merged with the entire universe.

In lesson twenty-six we brought up the age-old debate about consciousness. Is consciousness created by the brain or the brain by consciousness? I tried to show my viewpoint by showing our brain is a physical thing. Therefore, it must take consciousness to collapse the quantum wave which is our brain into reality. Consciousness must come first. If it were not for consciousness there can be no physical reality and that includes the brain.

In lesson twenty-seven we went back to Einstein to discuss The General Theory of Relativity. His theory showed that matter and energy cause space to curve. Matter moves along this curved space and this is what we perceive as gravity.

In lesson twenty-eight, we saw how The General Theory of Relativity predicted black holes, which turned out to be true. Once something passes the horizon of a black hole it is doomed never to escape from the hole again. We also saw how black holes led to what is now being considered by scientists the real possibility we are living in a holographic universe.

In lesson twenty-nine we discussed more what it might mean to live in a holographic universe, computer simulation, virtual reality.

Congratulations you have reached the end of the book. You now know more about the universe you live in than 95% of the rest of the world. You should feel very good about your accomplishment.

If some things we discussed are a little unclear go back and reread the lessons. In fact, if you read the entire book again you will find many things you may have missed the first time around.

Please share what you have learned with others. Everyone needs to know this stuff. Like I said it is beyond me why this isn't required reading in schools.

THIS IS A PLEA, A CALL TO BECOME ONE

I am often asked, "How can I be so sure there is an Infinite Intelligence? How can I be so sure we have a Higher Self?"

Are you familiar with the word "synchronicity"?

Synchronicity is often seen as a coincidence. Coincidence can be defined as an event that defies probability; it seems like it was planned but it was not. For example, a few years ago, I was flying home from Vegas and after a layover at O'hare Airport in Chicago, I discovered an old friend from high school was also on the flight back home.

Synchronicity, however, is much more than a coincidence. Synchronicity has a deeper meaning and speaks to something going on inside of you. Things just seem to show up to aid you in your journey through life. The right person shows up at the right time to assist you. You find a much-needed item in a store which is exactly what you have been looking for. You hear something said on television which answers a question you have been struggling with. You "randomly" stumble upon a link on the Internet which takes you to a webpage with information you had previously been unable to find.

The more you see synchronistic events happen in your life the more you know it is more than mere chance or luck. When events happen over and over and over to point you in the right direction and assist you in life, you know there is a higher power at work. The probability of that many coincidences happening that often is zero.

When synchronistic events happen, it is a sign you are on the right track. Your higher self is helping you get what you want.

To say we live in a fragmented world is a huge understatement. We are all divided in so many ways – religion, politics, race, and gender to name a few. The division is keeping us in a world filled with inequality, hunger, and disease which we could easily fix if we set aside our differences. We need to understand we are all one. The paradox is, once we do, the oneness allows the uniqueness of everyone to shine brighter than ever before.

We need to understand we are more than just our physical body and we "die" we do not cease to exist.

We need to get a grasp on God and religion. For the most part, if you were born in a North American, European culture your brain has been wired with Christian concepts. If you live in the east, China, India you are more wired for the concepts of Buddhism, Hinduism, and other eastern religions. If you live in the Middle East your brain has a lot of synapses firing with Muslim beliefs.

You may not want to admit it emotionally, but you must see there is a lot of truth to it.

But let's not single out religion. Even the diehard, atheist, scientist who won't believe it until they see it, has still had their brain wired. Just as Christians have their churches, scientists have their colleges and universities which have told them what to think and believe. We have all had our brains wired.

We live in a world where science has tried to replace magic and miracles but are now finding science is returning us to a place where imagination is supreme. We need to stop taking away the imagination of children and forcing them to believe in the "real world."

"There are more things in heaven and earth, Horatio, than are dreamt of in your philosophy." – Shakespeare, *Hamlet*

We are made aware by our five senses. That limits us from seeing so much of the universe we inhabit. What if we could change our perception of the laws of nature? Many often proclaim to possess a sixth sense. Can we not imagine more? How about a seventh or eighth sense? How far can we go? Infinity?

Infinity is a hard concept for us to grasp but its definition implies that nothing is impossible that anything can exist.

"I believe in everything until it's disproved. So I believe in fairies, the myths, dragons. It all exists, even if it's in your mind. Who's to say that dreams and nightmares aren't as real as the here and now?" - John Lennon

We are pure infinite energy, which cannot be defined. Energy which creates our reality and has no bounds. Impossible is only a limitation set by our minds.

"Why, sometimes I've believed as many as six impossible things before breakfast." — Lewis Carroll, Alice in Wonderland

We need to show there are many more alternatives than religion and atheism. There are more ways to accept the supernatural than by adhering to the impossible concepts presented in many religious books. When given the choice of the Bible and Atheism, it is no wonder many favor Atheism. They need to see the supernatural is believable and makes sense.

We need more scientists to start exploring areas once considered taboo. We need open minds. We need minds to accept infinite reality. This life is just a flicker of experience. Nothing, absolutely nothing, is an impossible reality. If you can picture it in your mind, somewhere it exists.

For the most part, your brain was wired when you were a child. You may think you have come to conclusions on your own, but your brain has been conditioned to see the world in such a way that supports conclusions you have been given. Your brain is bombarded with millions of bits of data every day. To keep you from going insane you take in the data

261

that coincides with your beliefs and discard most of the data that does not. You do this subconsciously. Most of the time you are unaware. Therefore, the world seems to conform to what you believe. Everyone thinks their way of seeing is correct.

Does it make you pause for a moment to know those with different beliefs from you have just as strong a faith their belief is correct and yours is not? They believe just as strongly that you are incorrect as you believe they are incorrect. They are seeing a world that shows their beliefs are correct just as you are seeing a world that shows your beliefs are correct.

You say "The Truth" but you can't know for sure. Deep down you understand.

The best you can say is I have faith, and faith is a feeling. Respect others' feelings just as much as your own. Their feelings are just as strong as yours.

Do not criticize others who do not believe as you. They feel as passionate about what they believe as you do.

Everyone has an infinite amount of experiences available. It would, therefore, be impossible for everybody to come to one incontrovertible truth.

Never try and force a person to live your point of view.

No matter what authority you claim, it is still your point of view that accepted the authority.

And that is fine because that is the reason you are in this life. You are a necessary part of existence. The world needs your point of view. The world needs you.